MAGIC IN THE NIGHT

*

Also by Rob Kirkpatrick

1969
Cecil Travis of the Washington Senators
The Quotable Sixties

THE WORDS
AND MUSIC OF
BRUCE SPRINGSTEEN

✳

MAGIC IN THE NIGHT

ROB KIRKPATRICK

ST. MARTIN'S GRIFFIN

NEW YORK

www.stmartins.com

Book design by Kathryn Parise

PHOTO CREDITS

1. Chuck Pulin/Star File Photo.
2. Jeff Albertson/Corbis.
3. Howard B. Leibowitz/B.L. Howard Productions.
4. Chuck Pulin/Star File Photo.
5. Felix Photography/ B.L. Howard Productions.
6. Corbis.
7. Bettmann/Corbis.
8. Chuck Pulin/Star File Photo.
9. Chuck Pulin/Star File Photo.
10. Mitchell Gerber/Corbis.
11. Brian Snyder/Reuters/Corbis.
12. David Rae Morris/epa/Corbis.
13. David Bergman/www.DavidBergman.net/Corbis.

LIBRARY OF CONGRESS CATALOGING-IN-PUBLICATION DATA

Kirkpatrick, Rob.
    Magic in the night : the words and music of Bruce Springsteen / Rob Kirkpatrick.—1st ed.
        p. cm.
    "Part of this book was originally published by Praeger Publishers under the title The words and music of Bruce Springsteen."
    Includes bibliographical references and index.
    ISBN-13: 978-0-312-53380-9
    ISBN-10: 0-312-53380-2
    1. Springsteen, Bruce—Criticism and interpretation.   I. Kirkpatrick, Rob. Words and Music of Bruce Springsteen.   II. Title.
    ML420.S77K57 2009
    782.42166092—dc22

2008048294

Part of this book was originally published
by Praeger Publishers under the title
The Words and Music of Bruce Springsteen

First Edition: March 2009

10 9 8 7 6 5 4 3 2 1

To Casey

✶ Contents ✶

∗ Acknowledgments ∗

I would like to thank Michelle Richter at St. Martin's Press for making this paperback edition possible. Thanks, also, to Kenneth J. Silver, Susan Joseph, Kathryn Parise, and Rich Klin for their fine work.

✳ Introduction ✳

Writing about music is like dancing about architecture—it's a really stupid thing to want to do.[1]

ELVIS COSTELLO

Elvis Costello's "dancing about architecture" line is one of my favorite quotes. (It's unclear whether he was the first person to ever say it, but it makes a better quote than that thing he once said about Ray Charles, so let's let him have this one.) The image of "dancing about architecture" is a brilliant abstraction, one that makes you ponder the possibilities: One could cook about painting, hum about photographs, jog about sculpture. Even though I think he was wrong, Costello's line is such a good one that I feel compelled to confront it before moving forward here. Why would one want to write a book about a singer-songwriter—especially one whose life and career has already proved to be a gold mine for so many writers?

In his introduction to *Runaway American Dreams: Listening to Bruce Springsteen,* Jimmy Guterman suggests that the authors of the many books already published on Springsteen have an agenda of "I think Bruce is great and maybe if I write a book about him I'll get to meet him or something," and that most of these works can be described as "'How Bruce's music changed my life' books."[2]

He's probably right. To this I would add that a good deal of writing on Springsteen has sought to show how he speaks for *us*—the American, the Everyman, the Average Joe—even, how he *is* us. Then there are the ever-growing studies that want to place Springsteen within the literary tradition of Emerson, Thoreau, Twain, and Steinbeck.

I didn't write this book hoping to meet Bruce Springsteen. I imagine he'd be good company, but I don't listen to his albums because I think he'd offer scintillating dinner conversation or make a good teammate at darts. I'm not writing this to tell people that the man changed my life—I doubt most people would care, and why should they? Nor do I claim that he speaks for *me*. About the only things that Springsteen and I have in common are that I lived in New Jersey for the better part of four years, and that both of us were once stuffed into a garbage can by a teacher in elementary school.

As far as Springsteen's place in the literary canon, I'll leave that to others to determine. My concern here is Springsteen's place in the American singer-songwriter tradition.

One of the reasons I've wanted to write about Springsteen is that I've found myself having discussions over the years about how he has been misunderstood. I grew up in the midst of *Born in the U.S.A.*, and in the mid-1980s this seemed to be the only album anyone had ever heard by him. *Born to Run* had been released only nine years earlier, but even then it was an album that your uncle or older sister had, maybe on eight-track. When I told people that Bruce Springsteen was my favorite artist, the picture they had was of a lip-synced MTV video ("Dancing in the Dark") with a then-unknown Courtney Cox, and of another song ("Born in the U.S.A.") that was more of a misunderstood rally cry than groundbreaking music. During my freshman year in college, my roommate told me that Frankie Goes to Hollywood's remake of "Born to Run" was better than the original.

People just didn't know.

I wrote film and record reviews for the *Daily Targum* at Rutgers. A 20-something undergraduate on the staff who (I must admit) had an amazing record collection told me Springsteen wasn't all that. For him, Lou Reed's view of New York was more gritty and, thus, more "real" than the one Springsteen offered on *Born to Run*. Funnily enough, critic Lester

Bangs had reported an identical sentiment back in 1975. A friend had told Bangs, "When I listen to Bruce Springsteen, I hear a romanticization of New York. When I listen to Lou Reed, I hear New York."[3] Similarly, an angry young Bob Geldof once said, "I don't believe Springsteen. He writes fiction. The Magic Rat did not drive his sleek machine over that Jersey state line."[4]

I suspect that my college newspaper colleague had gotten his opinion from Bangs's column, as he was the type of guy who would have spent his free hours between classes reading rock criticism. As for me, I didn't know Bangs from the Bangles at the time. "Gimme a break," I imagine myself telling him in hindsight. "I'm 20 years old and it's 1988. Be glad that I don't listen to Phil Collins."

For lily-white college students in the 1980s, perhaps songs of sado-masochism and smack offered a more "real" version of New York City. (I say this as someone who thinks the Velvet Underground didn't release a bad song until their fourth album.) But as Bangs himself argued back in 1975, that was precisely the point with Springsteen. When Springsteen wrote and recorded the songs for *Born to Run,* he wasn't striving for realism; he aimed to explore the romance and mythology of American cities, American car culture, and rock 'n' roll. He sought to portray larger-than-life characters and situations reminiscent of Sal Paradise's words in Jack Kerouac's *On the Road:*

> The only people for me are the mad ones, the ones who are mad to live, mad to talk, mad to be saved, desirous of everything at the same time, the ones who never yawn or say a commonplace thing, but burn burn burn, like fabulous yellow roman candles exploding like spiders across the stars and in the middle you see the blue center light pop and everybody goes "AWWW!"[5]

Ironically, Lou Reed recruited Springsteen to provide a street-tough rap interlude on the title track of Reed's 1978 album *Street Hassle.* I don't know anyone who ever bought that record—apparently, Reed's street opera was too "real" for most people.

"He can't sing," a drama student told me in the lounge of our dorm at Rutgers, just down the street from a tiny place called The Ledge, where in 1972 Springsteen had made his last known performance as an un-signed artist. I forget what kind of music this drama student liked, but I can't say she's the only person I've ever heard make this claim.

Many rock singers have better voices than Bruce Springsteen's. Springsteen would tell you this himself. He can't soar among high regis-ters like Roy Orbison. He will never melt butter with his voice like David Gray or Roxy Music's Bryan Ferry, nor will he make woofers vibrate like Johnny Cash or Crash Test Dummies front man Brad Roberts. He doesn't have the voice of extended puberty required to sing songs about dragons or black holes like Yes's Jon Anderson or Rush's Geddy Lee. And he won't be singing the theme song for very many high school proms.

But this isn't opera we're talking about, folks. The musical genres that Springsteen has explored throughout his career—whether rock 'n' roll, soul-inspired rock, or retro-folk—grew in large part out of the do-it-yourself traditions of garages, bars, roadhouses, honky-tonks, and Ap-palachian front porches. A good many artists have had stellar careers with less powerful voices—and with less range—and few singers have been able to succeed within the variety of musical genres Springsteen has. It's a rare singer who can sustain the force of "Jungleland" or "Back in Your Arms Again," the soulfulness of "Fade Away" or "Roll of the Dice," the rustic twang of "The River" or "Into the Fire," the melodic richness of "One Step Up" or "Loose Change," *and* the restrained falsetto of "Lift Me Up" or "All I'm Thinkin' 'Bout Is You."

Springsteen might not have a voice as resonant as Roger Daltry's or even as likeable as Ray Davies's. But when all is said and done, can we re-ally say that Mick Jagger's or John Lennon's voice was any better? Could Mick in his prime have attempted "Born to Run" without sounding like a wounded rooster? Could John have pulled off "Spirit in the Night" with-out sounding hopelessly sardonic and goofy?

One of the challenges in writing any biography—and on one level, this is a "musical biography" of Springsteen—is to determine the extent to which the author's voice should come through in the writing. After all, the writer is telling a character's story not neccessarily his own; the one who writes it, and no matter how objectively an author approaches his subject, the author's own perspective and voice inevitably shape the story.

It strikes me that while writing this book, the process of writing it mirrored various stages of Springsteen's career. I was still finding my way into the book as I wrote the first chapter, much like Springsteen himself was still finding his own way when he recorded his debut album, *Greetings from Asbury Park, N.J.* I started to hit a groove as I wrote the second chapter, much like Springsteen and the E Street Band found their studio groove while recording their second album, *The Wild, the Innocent & the E Street Shuffle.* As Springsteen struggled while recording the classic *Born to Run*—doing everything over and over again so that he would get it just right—so did I while writing the chapter on *Born to Run,* revising it several times over, hoping to do justice to one of the great albums of all time. And much like Springsteen threw out the initial masters of the *Born to Run* album in a fit of frustration with the release date looming, I found myself fighting the urge to rewrite every other sentence of my manuscript just a week before it was due to the publisher.

My aim with this book is to examine Springsteen's songwriting process. I consider not just his lyrics—for while any pop song might be considered a poem set to music, Springsteen wrote songs, not poems—but, just as importantly, his music (both with and without the E Street Band). I look at the cultural and social forces that have influenced his writing, as well as the role that Springsteen has played within the ever-changing landscape of American popular music.

In discussing his songs, I refer to the narrator of a given song as being distinct from the songwriter himself, for just as the narrator of a short story or speaker of a poem must be considered as an imagined identity distinct from the author, the voice of any song is almost always an identity visited temporarily within the finite space of the song. As Springsteen said back in 1974, "The mistake is when you start thinking that you are your songs. To me a song is a vision, a flash."[6] Three decades later, he told an audience in Red Bank, New Jersey, "Over 30 years you internalize your craft, and the mechanics of storytelling becomes like a second language that you speak without thinking, like a second skin that you feel with."[7]

In the end, maybe writing this book is about as constructive an act as doing a pirouette about the Parthenon. But in focusing on the craft of Springsteen's songwriting, I hope to add something to the ongoing dialogue between his music and those who listen to it. I didn't write this book to argue that Springsteen is the best singer-songwriter in American music. I don't know who the "best" one is or was. Nor am I here to say that he is the most influential. (That might be Bob Dylan.) But I have to think that Springsteen has become the most *significant* American singer-songwriter today.

As many Springsteen fans could tell you, there are a good many Springsteen books out there already, and in providing my own perspective on his work, I acknowledge most of the writers who've come before me and how they've shaped our understanding of the man and his music. My hope is that this book can be a "prequel" of sorts to Guterman's book about the "end user" experience, with mine examining Springsteen's creative processes—his writing, his inspirations and source material (be it musical, literary, cinematic, or biographical), as well as his performing and recording techniques—and I hope that my book will help readers become more familiar with his songs and how he came to create them.

MAGIC IN THE NIGHT

*

* 1 *

Jukebox Graduate

There was Jimmie Rodgers, the "Singing Brakeman" who started it all, singing blue yodels of trains and travelin' and TB. There was Roy Acuff, the Father of Country Music, riding the Wabash Cannonball out of Tennessee. And there was Hank Williams, the long-gone daddy from Alabama who howled at the moon while singing of her cheatin' heart.

Moon Mullican was there, too, dishing jambalaya on the bayou. There was Fats Domino forever finding his thrill on Blueberry Hill, and Jerry Lee Lewis pounding out breathless boogie-woogie with great balls of fire. There were the Pentecostal preachers—the original front men—and Bill Monroe's Blue Grass Boys. There were Roy Orbison's melancholy cries for the lonely, and there was the man in Reno shot down by the Man in Black. And there was a truck driver named Elvis Presley, who discovered rock 'n' roll by accident one day with Scotty Moore and Bill Black.

There was Robert Johnson and Son House, sending Muddy Waters on the way up the Mississippi, where Bob Dylan was waiting to meet Woody Guthrie.

There was Big Joe Turner, shouting the blues from Kansas City to New York to L.A. And there were shouts from Wynonie Harris, "Mr. Blues" to you, singing of sex and booze. There was Chuck Berry, who jumped across the Atlantic with Maybelline, where The Beatles and The Rolling Stones were waiting for them.

There were the power chords of Link Wray, raw and ready to rumble, giving fodder to Pete Townshend and The Who's mod-rock operas. There was the working-class pop of Eric Burdon and The Animals. And there was Jimi Hendrix, America's psychedelic prodigal son, who blew them all away at Monterey.

There was Otis Redding and the deep soul of the South, with all the grit and brass of the sweet Stax sound. There was Sam and Dave and Booker T and the MGs. There was Phil Spector from behind a wall of sound, and there was Detroit and Motown and the soundtrack of Young America. And there was Van Morrison sending Caledonia soul back over the ocean.

And there was all of this coming together on the shores of New Jersey, where water met sand, rich met poor, white met black, boardwalk life met New York bohemia, California surf met Philadelphia soul, and music's past gave birth to rock 'n' roll's future. . . .

Greetings from Asbury Park, N.J. (1973)

Bruce Frederick Springsteen was born in Long Branch, New Jersey on September 23, 1949. During much of Bruce's youth, the Springsteens lived in Freehold, a working-class town 17 miles inland in Monmouth County. Jim Cullen reminds us in *Born in the U.S.A.* that the term *freeholder* "typically referred to a person who owned a relatively small piece of land farmed for family use . . . in marked contrast to plantation owners who controlled vast estates."[1] Back during the Depression, the *WPA Guide to New Jersey* stated that Freehold "in an unobtrusive way . . . seems to embody America's growth from farm to factory."[2]

In an article from 2003, Kevin Coyne reports, "There have been Springsteens in New Jersey almost as long as there has been a New Jersey; it's an old Dutch name that goes back to the colony's early settlers. Springsteens from Monmouth County fought in the Revolution, the War of 1812, and the Civil War."[3] But the Springsteens of twentieth-century Freehold owned no vast estates; they lived in a particularly poor section of town known as "Texas," misnamed after the southern drawl spoken by Appalachian families who had migrated to the area. Bruce's first house was on Randolph Street, a stone's throw from the site of the Battle of Monmouth in 1778. The house was near a gas station, and on hot nights when Springsteen would drag his mattress outside and sleep on the roof, he would spend nights watching cars pull in and out of the station. "And I watched these different guys—the station closed at one and these guys, they'd be pullin' in and pullin' out all night long. They'd be meeting people there. They'd be rippin' off down the highway."[4]

During his formative years, Springsteen developed a fascination with the technology of transportation and mobility—a motif which would come to define his lyrics. Their second house was just blocks away on Institute Street. The railway ran close by their house, and for years Bruce would lie awake at night listening to the shuffle of freight trains and boxcars as they chugged in and headed south.[5]

Springsteen's first experiences with music seem to have come as a result of his family's poverty. Both of his parents held low-paying jobs. His father Douglas held a number of blue-collar jobs, including rug-mill worker and prison guard; his mother Adele was a secretary. During times when his family couldn't afford the rent, they lived with Adele's parents, the Zerellis, one of Freehold's many Italian families to arrive during the twentieth-century wave of immigration. In the Zerelli household, Bruce was exposed to country-western hits from Gene Autry, Roy Rogers, and Hank Williams.[6] On weekends, his mother would take him to Smithburg to barn dances on the Appel Farm (a name that would prove prophetic) where cowboy musicians served up fiddle- and yodel-laden tunes. He also developed a liking for Appalachian folk tunes and the work of populist balladeer Woody Guthrie.[7]

Springsteen's mother liked popular music. As her son would remember later, "Every morning in my house, you'd come down before you'd go to school, my mother's cookin' up the breakfast, got the radio on, on top of the refrigerator, tuned to the AM station."[8] She was a fan of Elvis Presley, and his first profound encounter with the music that would be known as rock 'n' roll came when he saw Presley on the *Ed Sullivan Show*. "Man, when I was nine, I couldn't imagine anyone *not* wanting to be Elvis Presley," he once said. Soon after, his mother bought him a guitar, but his hands were too small to play, and he was uninterested in the formality of guitar lessons. He lost interest until he caught the rock bug as a teenager. "I was dead until I was thirteen."[9] As with the rest of the country, The Beatles left an indelible impression on Springsteen, as did other prepsychedelic British invasion bands such as The Rolling Stones, The Who, and The Animals. Also, there were the Motown hits that served as the unofficial soundtrack for the Youth of America; the records of Roy Orbison, Sam Cooke, and Gary U.S. Bonds; Stax artists such as Sam and Dave and Eddie and Floyd; and white R&B from The Rascals and Mitch Ryder.[10]

When Springsteen turned 14, his mother bought him a Kent guitar; later, Springsteen bought a Fender guitar from a local pawnshop, and a cousin on his mother's side gave him some pointers on 12-bar songwriting. Bruce estimated that as a kid, from the time he first figured out Keith Richards's lead on "It's All Over Now" (the first song he learned to play), he practiced six to eight hours at a time, every night.[11]

To Douglas, Bruce's musical pursuits were a waste of time. The tensions between the adolescent Springsteen and his father have been recounted in Springsteen biographies many times over. In these accounts, one gets the picture of a man beaten down by a blue-collar life that yielded none of the prosperity enjoyed elsewhere in postwar America. The core image that Springsteen has portrayed of his father is one of Douglas sitting in the living room after a hard day's work, smoking a cigarette in the dark. Bruce would later say that he didn't remember his father having any friends or, in 20 years, ever having someone come visit him at their home.

As for Bruce, he seemed destined to follow in his father's footsteps as a loner. He was an unpopular student with both students and teachers alike. He hated school, especially the parochial education he received at St. Rose of Lima in Freehold from 1955 to 1963. Springsteen wasn't a serious student, nor did he care for religion. He has recounted various tales for biographers: of a nun stuffing him in a trash can in third grade to, literally, show where trash belonged; of another nun instructing a younger student to hit Bruce in the face for misbehaving; as an altar boy, getting knocked down by a priest after messing up the Mass ritual; of getting sent to the principal's office after drawing Jesus crucified on a guitar.

Springsteen transferred to Freehold Regional High School but remained an outsider—not even popular enough, he would later note, to attain the status of class clown. He did, however, find a sense of purpose through music. There is confusion as to the identity of Springsteen's first band. Most sources cite The Castiles as Springsteen's first rock group. In two mid-1970s interviews, though, Springsteen alluded to playing with a group called The Rogues as early as 1965, and according to Robert Santelli, Springsteen played guitar with The Rogues during his freshman year, performing (almost always for free) at local teen dances.[12] (It was after a teen dance that Springsteen had his first kiss, with a Puerto Rican girl from Freehold named Maria Espinoza—a bit of trivia that becomes more interesting considering the many references to *Marias* and *Marys* in his songs to date.)[13] Although Santelli implies The Rogues were based in Freehold, the *Brucebase* Web site says that The Rogues were a "Rumson-Fairhaven based group" that played "vocal surf-related music," and that in interviews with several members from the band's 1965 lineup, they were all "adamant that Springsteen was never an official, unofficial, apprentice or try-out member of their band"—though they couldn't rule out jamming with him during any of the two or three dates they played in Freehold in 1965.[14]

Members of The Rogues do remember jamming with Springsteen in 1966 when they played a gig at the Surf 'n' See Club with The Castiles, a band Springsteen was in at the time.[15] In 1965, Springsteen learned of a Freehold band called The Castiles, a "surf/grease hybrid" group whose lead singer and rhythm guitarist, George Theiss, had a thing for Springsteen's sister, Ginny.[16] The band was managed by Tex and Marion Vinyard, a sort of mom-and-pop tandem in what passed for the Freehold music scene. As the story goes, one day Springsteen showed up on the Vinyards' door looking for an audition. He demonstrated a few chords for Tex and asked if he could be in The Castiles. Vinyard suggested the would-be guitar slinger come back when he'd learned more songs. Springsteen went home, turned on the radio, taught himself five songs, and showed up at the Vinyards' the very next night. "Well, this damn kid sat down and knocked out five songs that would blow your *ears*," Vinyard later remembered. "Five. Leads. No amplifier but five leads." Then Springsteen added: " 'Oh, by the way, I learned a couple more.' "[17] Soon afterwards, Springsteen auditioned for the rest of the band and was promptly accepted as the group's lead guitarist.

With Springsteen on board, Vinyard booked the group's first performance, a gig at the Woodhaven Swim Club in 1965. The Castiles—who took their name from a popular shampoo—were largely a cover band that sampled hits from shaggy-haired UK bands including The Animals, The Rolling Stones, The Yardbirds, The Who, and the Dave Clark Five. Springsteen's first experience in songwriting might have come when he composed an arrangement of Glenn Miller's "In the Mood" (one of Vinyard's favorites) especially for the West Haven gig.[18] This experience seems to have planted a seed, as Springsteen would perform arrangements of jazz standards such as "Satin Doll" and "Sentimental Journey" in the early days of the E Street Band.

The Castiles played teen events in Freehold at places like The Left Foot or the Hullabaloo Scene Teen Dance Club, and in venues in nearby towns, including the Surf 'n' See Club in Sea Bright, the Matawan-Keyport Roller Dome in Matawan, Le Teendezvous in New Shrewsbury, and the Loew's 35 Drive-In in Hazlet. For the Hazlet drive-in performance, a newspaper article announced their gig by describing the band as "a local rock 'n' roll band, which will provide music with a beat very different from other rock bands. Their uniqueness has made them great favorites on the teen set."[19]

At first, the group performed strictly cover tunes, and Springsteen was kept from the mic—Vinyard did not think Springsteen's vocal talents matched his guitar skills—though eventually he was allowed to sing the lead on two songs: The Them's "Mystic Eye" and The Who's "My Generation." The band began to dabble with original material, including a song, "Sidewalk," which seems to have been a favorite among the group's local fan base.[20] (Even then, Springsteen's lyricism paralleled images of the road.)

In the spring of 1966, The Castiles went to Mr. Music, a low-low-budget recording studio in Bricktown, New Jersey, and recorded a demo single. As Springsteen later described: "It is a little, like, plastic demo record. Tex brought us to this place, this little studio on Highway 35. We went in and had a half hour or an hour and we did it . . . it was funny. It was just to say that you made a record, I guess."[21] The single consisted of two songs: "That's What You Get" and (on the flip side) "Baby I." Both tracks were cowritten by Springsteen and lead singer/rhythm guitarist George Theiss, and both were representative of the catchy yet uncomplicated songs of early 1960s British Invasion pop-rock. "Baby I" evoked the sound of Liverpool-era Beatles, but its kiss-off sentiment ("I got someone new/Somebody better than you/Somebody who'll be true") pointed more toward early Who or Rolling Stones.

The Castiles followed the popular music scene as it evolved in the late 1960s. Jimi Hendrix helped invent and popularize psychedelic rock, and The Castiles covered the Hendrix tunes "Purple Haze" and "Fire." In 2004, NPR premiered a recently discovered recording of the band playing The Left Foot in September 1967, and listeners were treated to Springsteen playing lead guitar on these Hendrix tunes. He also took the lead vocal on Leonard Cohen's "Suzanne" and an original song that he cowrote, "Mr. Jones," and he sang and played harmonica for a cover of Donovan's "Catch the Wind."

The Castiles reached the pinnacle of their modest success when they performed at the Café Wha?, a popular Greenwich Village venue, for a series of dates in December 1967 and January 1968. But the band lost momentum and called it quits in the summer of 1968. Springsteen then formed a power trio called Earth with two local musicians, bassist John Graham and drummer Michael Burke. No known recordings of Earth have yet surfaced, but biographer Dave Marsh says the group's sound echoed elements of The Doors, Tim Buckley, and the archetypal power trio, Cream (though it's doubtful that Springsteen/Graham/Burke came anywhere close as musicians to Clapton/Bruce/Baker).[22]

The following year, Springsteen's parents moved to California, but Springsteen chose to stay behind in New Jersey. After he was evicted from their former home, he moved to the shore town of Asbury Park and took an apartment above a surfboard factory.

Founded in the mid-nineteenth century, Asbury Park's history is steeped in contradictions. Though named after Bishop Frances Asbury, a pioneer of American Methodism, founder James Bradley's vision was that it would become a beachfront resort "aimed to draw, entertain, and milk distant urban populations."[23] By the early twentieth century, with its carousel house, Ferris wheel, and Crystal Maze hall of mirrors, the boardwalk had taken an atmosphere more akin to tourists seeking novelty thrills than vacationers seeking a placid view of the Atlantic. Though not Memphis or Nashville, Asbury Park also developed a tradition of music along the shore dating from turn-of-the-century "oompah" bands to East coast jazz to early rock 'n' roll.

The emergence of rock 'n' roll culture in Asbury Park highlighted the complex divisions that had been deepening in the community for years. Asbury had become increasingly divided along racial lines, with the Eastern shore the province of white, upper-class tourist trappings and the inland West Side home to (mostly lower-income) blacks. Along the boardwalk, merchants who looked nostalgically back on Asbury Park's more genteel days were given pause by the flourishing of tourist trappings that seemed aimed more at thrill-seeking (and potentially unruly) teenagers than at moneyed vacationers. In *4th of July, Asbury Park: A History of the Promised Land*, Daniel Wolff notes that when the boardwalk's Tunnel of Love was extended by more than 80 feet in 1956, it gave "teenagers that much longer to sneak a kiss, a touch."[24]

Rock 'n' roll was central to 1950s American teenage culture, and in the summer of 1956, both rock 'n' roll and teenagers were supposedly at the center of an episode dubbed the Convention Hall Riot. During a performance of Frankie Lymon and the Teenagers at the Convention Hall on June 30, a fistfight broke out and spilled out to the boardwalk, onto Ocean Avenue, then escalated into the business district and inland to the Springboard Avenue slums. By the following day, local officials were blaming teenagers and racial tensions at the concert. Asbury Park cancelled all other teen dances for the rest of the summer. One newspaper headline announced: "CITY TO BAN ROCK 'N' ROLL."[25]

Rock 'n' roll never was banned in Asbury Park, but a decade and a half later, it seemed on the wane. Along the boardwalk, bars had taken on a "honky-tonk" feel. Bands made their money playing Top 40 covers. For one alternative, there was a "folkie-stoner" cafe called The Green Mermaid, located up the stairs from a shoe store on Cookman Avenue. If you climbed another set of stairs you came to The Upstage, a glorified storage room with no windows, and walls painted in Day-Glo colors. This was what passed for Asbury Park's counterculture scene. As Wolff records:

> The Upstage was not only counter to the nine-to-five world . . . but also to the typical shore bar. At the Upstage, the audience came to hear what it didn't know. In April 1970, a local reporter described the crowd as members of "what's come to be known as the Woodstock Nation."[26]

But as future E Street guitarist Steve Van Zandt remembered, whereas the music of Woodstock Nation once had been revolutionary, it was already considered "anachronistic" and "retro." According to Van Zandt, the musicians of his generation had a vague sense that "everything good had been done." Wolff reminds us that Little Richard, Elvis, Chuck Berry, Bill Haley, even the British Invasion were things of the past by 1970. As Van Zandt says, the Upstage regulars felt as if they "had missed the boat."[27]

All this is not to set up the notion that Bruce Springsteen saved Asbury Park (he didn't) or even The Upstage (ditto) when he found his way to its doors soon after moving to the town. Rather, the 20-year-old Springsteen's establishing himself as, in the words of Wolff, "the acknowledged star of this scene,"[28] in a retro-stoner bar on the outskirts of a shore town long past its heyday, is merely the point at which Bruce Springsteen becomes Bruce Springsteen.

One musician told Wolff:

> [He would] do these blues songs where he'd make up these lyrics off the top of his head. He had this one called "Heavy Louise." He was famous for it 'cause it would go on and on and on. He'd make up like nine stanzas of improvised lyrics . . . and he'd intersperse these made-up lyrics with these burning guitar solos.[29]

During the course of jamming at The Upstage, Springsteen met organist Danny Federici and drummer Vini "Mad Dog" Lopez. Together with bassist Vini Roslin, who had played with future Castiles drummer Bart Haynes in a group called The Sierras, they formed a blues-rock band called Child that (as Roslin remembers) did "original songs in a style that was close to what Cream and Jimi Hendrix were doing." Child was the first band with which Springsteen developed a following outside of the New York/New Jersey area. When the band discovered that another progressive-rock band already went by the name Child, they renamed themselves Steel Mill. In the spring of 1970, Steel Mill toured down through Virginia, where Richmond served as a second home base for the band, and played venues that served as a sort of "alternative circuit that was neither the white Top Forty beach bars nor the black inland R&B clubs."[30] "We used to play from Jersey down to Carolina," Springsteen remembered. "For a lot of colleges . . . I don't know how many."[31] (Despite

Springsteen's memory, which is not always perfect on the record, no dates for Steel Mill are recorded farther south than Virginia.)

The band's manager, Tinker West (who also owned the surfboard factory over which Springsteen lived) was from California, and he convinced the band that they needed to play on the West Coast. So Steel Mill headed west—to San Francisco, specifically, where they were well received at a number of successful dates. Their 90-minute set at The Matrix in San Francisco—which has been preserved on bootleg recordings—was favorably reviewed by Philip Elwood in the *San Francisco Examiner.* Elwood raved: "I have never been so overwhelmed by an unknown band," and dubbed it "one of the most memorable evenings of rock in a long time," specifically praising Springsteen as an "impressive composer."[32]

One of the songs singled out by Elwood was "America Under Fire" (also known as "American Song"). Back in 1967, the first Freehold native to lose his life in Vietnam was Bart Haynes, who had been the first drummer for The Castiles.[33] Springsteen, unwilling to fight in an ideological war when the children of more privileged families could secure college deferments, had purposely failed his own draft physical. "America Under Fire" was one of a number of Steel Mill songs, including "Sunlight Soldiers" and "The War Is Over," that were clearly inspired by the nation's escalating military involvement in Vietnam.

"America Under Fire" offered a seething satire very much in keeping with American youth counterculture, summarized in its opening lines about "conquered freak soldiers" returning home to the stares of their fellow countrymen, and to their women, who have become "whores." After the singer concludes, "And I'm tired and I think I'll go to bed/For America's under fire and the sky's turning red," the song's coda is downright subversive: As half of the band sings a line from the patriotic hymn "America the Beautiful" ("America, America, God shed his grace on me . . .") the other half superimposes a line from the *Mickey Mouse Club*: "M-I-C-K-E-Y-M-O-U-S-E." It's a chilling ending—one that might shock a fan who came to Springsteen during the *Born in the U.S.A.* era. But as subversive a song as "America Under Fire" might seem, the returning veterans of the song are actually sympathetic heroes; they return unceremoniously, betrayed by the women they loved, left to face the indifferent stares of their fellow Americans. As would be true in many songs throughout Springsteen's career as a songwriter, the song's protagonists are portrayed as victims of a larger system that has betrayed them.

Steel Mill's West Coast gigs were so well received that the band was offered an audition at the Fillmore West, and they recorded a demo for Bill Graham at the Fillmore Recording Studios. The band recorded three songs: "Going Back to Georgia," "Guilty (Send That Boy to Jail)"—aka "The Judge Song"—and "The Train Song." "The Train Song" is a wistful reworking of a familiar folk-song scenario: a weary traveler longing for home and the girl he loves (or lusts), heading home on a train. It's a likeable if somewhat long song at nearly seven minutes. Toward the end, though, the listener is thrown a curve when the singer strangely anticipates "waltzing arm in arm/With my darling electric chair." It's unclear whether this is a latter-day musical version of Robert Frost's pondering the miles he has to go before he can sleep, but in its synthesis of enduring folk motifs and its anticipation of journey's end ("... when the morning come ...") the song has an endearing charm.

Graham liked what he heard and offered Steel Mill a recording contract, but they were not happy with the advance (reportedly $1,000) so they turned down the offer. They returned eastward as conquering heroes of a sort—a band who had been *out west*, big fish in the small but fecund pond of the Asbury Park music scene. Perhaps more importantly, as Springsteen would remember, "my first trip to California with the band opened me up to new musical ideas."[34]

By then, Springsteen had refined his guitar technique to become, in the words of Van Zandt, "the fastest guy on the scene." Springsteen conceded later: "The concept of taste had not yet entered my thinking. I just wanted to play as fast as possible."[35] Rock critic Lenny Kaye remembers meeting Springsteen during this time. "He took me upstairs, where we stood in a tiny room and jammed. Bruce played the shit out of a [Donovan] song called 'Season of the Witch,' just winged it.... He blew me away."[36]

Steel Mill had moved toward a heavier guitar sound, and the band even opened up for Ozzy Osbourne and Black Sabbath on November 27, 1970 at Asbury Park's Sunshine Inn—billed as "Monmouth County's Biggest Concert Ever."[37] But inwardly, Springsteen sought a new musical direction. In this, he was most likely influenced by a new crop of musicians that he had met in Asbury Park. Van Zandt (then known as "Miami

Steve" because of a tropical shirt he'd brought back from a trip to Florida) had replaced Roslin on bass, bringing a pop sensibility that harkened back to preprogressive rock R&B. Also big on the scene was "Southside" Johnny Lyon, a soulful singer and harmonica player.

Then there was a guitarist/keyboardist named David Sancious. Van Zandt and Lyon embodied the spirit of "blued-eyed soul," white guys influenced by the horn-rich Philadelphia soul sound pioneered by the songwriting/producing team of Kenneth Gamble and Leon Huff (who worked with bands such as The O'Jays, The Intruders, MFSB, Harold Melvin and the Blue Notes, and Archie Bell and the Drells). On the other hand, Sancious—one of the few black musicians who dared to cross over the tracks into the white part of town—was schooled in classical and jazz.

This cross-fertilization of genres that were traditionally considered "white" or "black" music stood in contrast to the racial dynamics that were taking shape in Central and North Jersey. Racial tensions in Asbury Park—and throughout the United States—had gotten increasingly worse. In 1964, it had happened in Jersey City and Paterson; in 1968, Newark. In May 1969, a racially charged shooting had taken place on the corner of South Street and Route 33. Asbury Park had not seen any race riots, but there was nevertheless what Wolff calls a "geography of segregation." Blacks such as Sancious did not cross from the West Side over the tracks into the white part of town. (Less than 50 years earlier, Asbury Park had been a northeastern stronghold for the Ku Klux Klan.) Even established R&B bands such as Tony Blair and His Soul Flames didn't play the boardwalk, though it's unclear whether this was due more to fear of violence from whites or to the fact that club owners were reluctant to hire him because they feared racial troubles if they attracted a black audience.[38]

Even setting aside racial concerns, it was unlikely that any black musician—let alone Sancious, who was raised on soul music and on the cool jazz acts who played the Orchid Lounge on the West Side's Springboard Avenue—would have wanted to visit The Upstage. Retro acid rock was almost exclusively the domain of white musicians and fans. Yet Sancious had been inspired by another black musician, Jimi Hendrix, who made his name playing—if not reinventing—what had traditionally been the white man's rock. Looking to follow in Hendrix's footsteps, Sancious braved the walk across the tracks and worked his way into rock jam sessions at The Upstage in those days.

Come the summer of 1970, Asbury Park was no longer able to stay behind the times. Things came to a head on July 4 when an isolated incident on the West Side turned into a mass riot that spread eastward to the beachfront and engulfed much of the city in flames. As the series of conflagrations took over his adopted hometown, Springsteen walked out of his apartment over the surfboard factory and climbed to the top of a water tower and, like most of the town's residents, watched helplessly as Asbury Park burned. That September, Steel Mill was at the center of a near-riot when the police raided their concert at the Clearwater Swim Club in Atlantic Highlands, New Jersey, and pulled the plug. According to legend, Danny Federici assaulted a police officer during the melee but escaped arrest and slipped away, earning a nickname that he would carry for years: "The Phantom."[39]

Given such a history of racial divisions in Asbury Park, Springsteen's next group project takes on added significance. Steel Mill and its acid-rock stylings played for the final time in January 1971 at The Upstage Club. By the spring, Springsteen had formed Dr. Zoom and the Sonic Boom, an R&B-influenced ensemble. In Dr. Zoom, Springsteen was joined by Federici, Lopez, Van Zandt (now playing lead guitar to Springsteen's rhythm guitar), Sancious on keyboard, Lyon on harmonica, bassist Gary Tallent, a second percussionist, Bobby Williams, and two female background singers, Delores Holmes and Barbara Dinkins, called the "Zoomettes."

Dr. Zoom was part musical revue—including a 10-piece horn section—and part performance art, with an emcee and even someone who would play Monopoly onstage. Musically, the project blended R&B, jazz, and rock. Their theme, "The Zoom Song," was essentially a reworking of "Alexander's Ragtime Band" with new lyrics to fit the band, accompanied by a saxophone and tuba. Perhaps their one song of note, "Jambalaya"—inspired in name by the title of Hank Williams's "Jambalaya (On the Bayou)"—is a bluesy boast of a Delta beauty: "She's strong like a lion, she growls like a tiger/And I call my woman Jambalaya."

If the group's concept seems somewhat unfocused, it was. Dr. Zoom lasted for only a handful of performances. In the summer of 1971, Springsteen moved even more in the direction of blue-eyed soul with a self-titled band (known alternately as the Bruce Springsteen Band and the Bruce Springsteen Blues Band) to which he added a horn section. In July, the group opened up for Humble Pie at The Sunshine Inn and received a positive review in the *Asbury Park Evening Press*.[40]

One night, a saxophone player showed up to see the Bruce Springsteen Band at The Student Prince, one of the Asbury Park music venues, and announced that he wanted to sit in with them. Clarence Clemons was a member of another local band, Norman Seldin and the Joyful Noise, and had previously played with James Brown and the Famous Flames.[41] Formerly a football player at the University of Maryland Eastern Shore, Clemons was an imposing sight with the chops to match, and he had no trouble talking his way onto the stage. He joined the band for an early version of a soon-to-be famous song, "Spirit in the Night," and there was instant chemistry. Springsteen, who would retell the story of their meeting with over-the-top mythic dimensions while entertaining concert audiences, would later remember, "I knew I'd found my sax player."[42]

Just as Van Morrison had developed his self-dubbed "Caledonia Soul" on the other side of the Atlantic with albums such as *Moondance* and *His Band and Street Choir,* Springsteen migrated toward soulful elements that seemed straight out of Stax. One song, "I Want You for My Girl" (later retitled "You Mean So Much to Me"), blended sweet soul melodies with bittersweet lyrics that seemed miles away from Steel Mill. Springsteen's music had evolved to run the gamut of all the influences that he treasured, and he found himself at a crossroads. He had outgrown the cover-band scene on the Shore and was dedicated to playing his own material.

One day in November 1971, Tinker West drove by Springsteen's house and shouted to the singer that he was headed to New York City to meet with a music publisher named Mike Appel, and he said that Springsteen should come along. Springsteen agreed, and soon after arriving in the city, West introduced him to Appel and Mike Cretecos. The two men were aspiring producers who, at that time, were working in a songwriting factory under Wes Farrell.

Springsteen auditioned for the two at the writer's room of the Wes Farrell Organization, the pop-tune and ad-jingle factory where Appel and Cretecos were employed. Wearing ripped jeans and a T-shirt, Springsteen sat in front of a piano and performed two songs. Appel told Marc Eliot:

The first was the most boring thing I'd ever heard in my entire life. But the second had something. It was a song about dancing with a girl who was deaf, dumb, and blind with a lyric that included, "They danced all night to a silent band." . . . he sang that song like his life depended on it. Still, I didn't feel the earth moving beneath me. . . . I told him these were the worst two songs I ever heard, utterly devoid of any pop potential. Instead of being incensed, he said, ". . . I'll write some more songs and come back."[43]

This second song, "Baby Doll"—Springsteen's apparent attempt at reworking the idea behind The Who's *Tommy*—is pretty boring indeed, as anyone who has heard it on the unsanctioned *Before the Fame* collection can attest to. But something about Springsteen's lyrics and singing style stuck with Appel. Springsteen moved to California briefly and lost touch with Appel and Cretecos.

Springsteen was unable to establish himself as a solo artist on the West Coast, however, and moved back to New Jersey weeks later. He reconnected with Appel, who didn't remember him at first, and this time played a new song, "It's Hard to Be a Saint in the City." Appel was stunned. He later recalled, "As he was singing that song with those lyrics, I said, 'Why me, Lord?' I'm a guy with all this candy-assed pop commercial kind of records that I've been involved in all my life, like the Partridge Family. Why would I get a guy like this?"[44]

Bob Spitz, an associate of Appel and Cretecos, remembered being struck that Springsteen "was nothing in a social situation. He was shy. Bruce was like a social misfit—he couldn't handle his own stuff. He had a mousy little girlfriend who did all his talking for him, and he had a different one every week." Yet Springsteen himself seemed to understand that he spoke better through his music. Spitz remembers, "In 'No Need' [another early song] he had a line 'You know I stumble when I talk, so she says, "Babe, don't talk at all, just sing."' I thought, 'This guy knows what he's all about.' I knew right away this was the most amazing stuff I'd ever heard."[45]

Danny Federici said, "Bruce was incredibly energetic. He was writing an unbelievable amount of songs—five or ten a day. And they were epics . . . The most amazing thing was that one night, say a Friday, we'd do a thirty-song set. The next night, Saturday, we'd do an entirely different thirty-song set—all written that week."[46] They weren't all great songs; much of Springsteen's early material was raw and unfocused. Sam McKeith, Springsteen's first agent, said, "I could tell that this guy was very talented, but I found the stuff he was playing to be very depressing."[47] But Appel was so convinced of Springsteen's talent that he quit his job with Wes Farrell to manage his new find full-time.

In a sequence of events now famous in music industry circles, one day in May 1972 Appel called the office of John Hammond at CBS Records and managed to get Hammond's assistant, Liz Gilbert, to put Springsteen on Hammond's agenda that morning. Hammond was the man who had discovered music legends including Benny Goodman, Bessie Smith, Billie Holiday, Aretha Franklin, and—of most interest to Springsteen—Bob Dylan. Coincidentally, Springsteen was reading Tony Scaduto's Dylan biography, and just the previous day, he had finished reading the part in Scaduto's book in which Dylan meets Hammond. Now, Springsteen found himself taking a bus from Asbury Park to New York City and, after meeting Appel in midtown, walking over to the Columbia Records offices for an eleven o'clock meeting with the man who had signed Dylan.

Hammond later recalled that Appel came on strong with an aggressive sales pitch in their initial meeting. "You're the man who's supposed to have discovered Bob Dylan, aren't you?" Appel said. "I want to see if you have any ears. I've got an artist better than Bob Dylan."[48]

Appel remembers it slightly differently:

We walked in and Bruce sits down with his guitar, and I feel it's incumbent upon me to say something. I say to him—and I'll always remember this—"I've grappled with lyrics myself. This guy makes it seem like it's nothing to write reams and reams of poetry." And [Hammond's] nodding, you know, Okay, okay. Then I said, "I can't believe he's written as many things as he has in such a short period of time at such a high degree of quality."

Appel sensed Hammond getting annoyed with his "hype" so he reeled himself back in and said, "In short, you're the guy who discovered Bob Dylan for the right reasons. You won't miss this."[49]

Hammond endured Appel's hard sell and heard Springsteen play an original song on his acoustic guitar called "It's Hard to Be a Saint in the

City," which Hammond liked because of its "inner rhyme." Springsteen then played an autobiographical song, "Growin' Up," and another one that impressed Hammond less, "Mary Queen of Arkansas." At that point, Hammond looked to push Springsteen and asked him if there was any song that he had written but would never perform live. Springsteen responded with "If I Were the Priest."[50]

"Priest" has never appeared on any officially sanctioned release, but it's one of the most striking songs in the early Springsteen oeuvre. Sung in a deliberate and emotive style, the song presents a hypothetical scenario combining elements of Catholicism with images of the West: Jesus is a sheriff, the singer is a priest, his lady an heiress, his mother a thief. The song tells of the Holy Grail Saloon where the Holy Ghost is "the host with the most" and where a nickel gets you a shot of whiskey and a "personally blessed balloon"—most likely a condom. The Virgin Mary is a prostitute who gives Mass on Sunday but then sells her body to bootleggers on Monday. In an echo of the Immaculate Conception doctrine that Springsteen would have learned at St. Rose, she has been "made once or twice/By some kind of magic."

Hammond was sold on the singer's potential. "I couldn't believe it," he reflected later. "I reacted with a force I've felt maybe three times in my life."[51] Hammond later remembered that as Springsteen sang his songs for him, the music-business legend wrote in his notebook: " 'The greatest talent of the decade' or some 'understatement' like that."[52]

Appel remembers that Hammond had kept his glasses down over his eyes to perhaps hide his anger with the outspoken manager:

> But then he put his glasses back up on his head, looked at me, and said, "You were right." Then he looked back at Bruce. "Got any more songs, son?"
>
> After we walked out of the building, Springsteen . . . just balanced himself on the curb, walking down the street with his arms up in the air, balancing himself. He literally danced on the curb. It was that joyous and that pure a situation. How often do you just walk into a record label cold, the most prestigious record label in the world, with the greatest A&R man in the world, and he says to you, "Yeah, I love him."[53]

In keeping with his practice of needing to see artists perform live before signing them, Hammond arranged for Springsteen to play an acoustic set later that night at The Gaslight, the Greenwich Village club where Bob Dylan had performed back in 1962. The comparatively square-looking Hammond watched as Springsteen, looking equal parts Beat poet, motorcycle punk, and Bohemian gypsy, performed for the downtown crowd. Duly impressed with Springsteen's stage presence, Hammond arranged for him to record a demo. The following day, Springsteen recorded 12 songs: "Mary Queen of Arkansas," "It's Hard to be a Saint in the City," "Jazz Musician," "If I Were the Priest," "Arabian Night," "Growin' Up," "Does This Bus Stop at 82nd Street?," "Two Hearts in True Waltz Time," "Street Queen," "The Angel," "Southern Son," and "Cowboys of the Sea."

According to Springsteen, he wrote most of the material for his demo *underneath* his apartment, in a closed beauty salon, where he kept an Aeolian spinet piano that his aunt had given him. "I'd write the verses, then pick up the guitar or sit at the piano and follow the inner rhythm of the words," he remembered. Not surprisingly for an emerging artist, most of Springsteen's early songs were inspired by his own life—"twisted autobiographies," he would call them.[54] "They were written in half-hour, fifteen-minute blasts," Springsteen told the *Los Angeles Times*. "A few of them I worked on for a week or so, but most of them were just jets, a real energy situation."[55]

The inspiration behind the Catholic imagery in Springsteen's early songs—and in his music throughout his career—is obvious; less so the imagery of the Western frontier in his early work. But notions of the West had played a part in Springsteen's lyrics ever since his Steel Mill days. Aside from Springsteen's own trips to California, one could say that he had been abandoned by his family during their westward move while Springsteen was still, technically, a teenager (though closer to the truth, he seems to have abandoned them). The separation undoubtedly influenced his creative themes; indeed, in an early number called, "Family Song," he writes of a familial move to California. Lest any psychoanalytic critics assign some deep meaning to this episode, let's also remember that growing up in the fifties and early sixties, Springsteen would have seen a number of Westerns at local movie theaters. Early songs such as

"California, You're a Woman," "The Ballad of Jesse James," "Hollywood Kids," "Evacuation of the West," and "Cowboys of the Sea" show not only a preoccupation with the West but also an attempt to formulate his own version of its legends and mythology.

A few days after recording the demo, Hammond had Springsteen audition once again, this time for label president Clive Davis. In truth, Davis was already on board. On May 8, Hammond had sent Davis a copy of the demo along with a letter saying, "I think we better act quickly." Davis had written back the next day: "I love Bruce Springsteen! He's an original in every respect. I'd like to meet him if you can arrange it."[56] Soon after playing for Davis, Springsteen signed with Columbia Records for an advance of $25,000.

Having been given keys to the kingdom, Springsteen and Appel turned their attentions to recording the debut record, which presented an interesting dilemma. Springsteen had auditioned alone, and he signed as a solo act. Springsteen would remember: "I knew two things; one, I wanted to sign to a record company as a solo artist—the music I'd been writing on my own was more individual than the material I'd been working up with my bands. The independence of being a solo performer was important to me. And two, I was going to need a good group of songs if I ever did get the chance to record."[57]

That said, Columbia Records' new artist was a solo act in name only, a fact that seems to have been unbeknownst to Hammond and company. Faced with his dream of a record deal, Springsteen enlisted the talents of his Bruce Springsteen Band mates. At first, Appel was against the idea of a band. Hammond had signed Springsteen as a solo artist, Appel reminded his client. Having finally accomplished his dream of being a signed recording artist, Springsteen was determined to call the shots and held out for the band. Federici, Lopez, Tallent, Van Zandt, Sancious, and—arriving better late than never—Clemons all joined Springsteen for the recording sessions that took place at the 914 Sound Studios, a studio in Blauvelt, New York (a Rockland County hamlet) run by a friend of Appel, in June 1972.

Springsteen and company plugged in, literally, and created a microcosmic stir reminiscent of Dylan at Newport '65. Appel was cognizant of—and perhaps partially responsible for—the fact that Hammond viewed Springsteen as a singer-songwriter in the Bob Dylan mold, and the label was already preparing a promotional campaign that would position Springsteen as the latest "new Dylan." "Look, this is supposed to be a folk record and that is a rock 'n' roll instrument," Appel reportedly told Springsteen, pointing to his electric guitar.[58] Again, Springsteen stood his ground. Although he tried his hand playing acoustic sets in Greenwich Village folk haunts, as he later pointed out, "I'd been playing rock 'n' roll music in bars for eight years."[59]

The album took three weeks to record. At some point, Springsteen had delivered what he thought was a finished product to Columbia, but label president Clive Davis said it lacked radio-ready hits and sent Springsteen back to the studio. Springsteen responded by writing two of his best songs to that date: "Blinded by the Light" and "Spirit in the Night."

Springsteen's debut album, *Greetings from Asbury Park, N.J.*, was released on January 5, 1973. The nine songs on the album add up to a fresh but uneven—and sometimes awkward—mix that suggest a rookie in the recording studio, an emerging street-punk poet caught between solo aspirations and band dynamics, between the folksinger/songwriter paradigm and genuine rock and R&B influences.

Some of the songs don't work. Two of the slower numbers, "The Angel" (a portrait of a *Wild Ones*–type motorcycle outlaw) and "Mary Queen of Arkansas" (a ballad that might be about a drag queen) are pretentious failures. But many of the songs offer an infectious charm. "Growin' Up" (which evolved from a musically identical song with different words titled "Eloise") offers a coming-of-age retrospective that became a signature tune for Springsteen in concert. "Does This Bus Stop at 82nd Street?" is a succinct street vignette inspired by an uptown bus trip Springsteen had taken to visit a girlfriend in New York City. The first-person voice of street braggadocio in "It's Hard to Be a Saint in the City" (a song which, according to Appel, Springsteen had to be persuaded to include on *Greetings*)[60] is more successful than the distant, third-person narrator of "The Angel" in portraying a leather-clad, Brandoesque "king of the alley" tempted by Satan, who appears to him "like Jesus through the steam in the street."

"For You," a song from the point of view of a male protagonist singing to his suicidal girlfriend, manages to be lyrically feverish—sometimes too feverish—and musically understated—sometimes too understated—at the same time. "Lost in the Flood," perhaps the most emotive song on the album, opens with a dramatic chord progression on piano (along with feedback produced by Van Zandt kicking an amp) and tells what Jimmy Guterman calls a "postapocalyptic" narrative. A drag racer named Jimmy the Saint faces off against a New York City cop ("Bronx's best apostle") in a street shootout as a "storefront incarnation of Maria" (either a Virgin Mary statue or possibly just a virginal sales girl) looks on from a storefront. Most memorable are the nuns who run "bald through Vatican halls pregnant/pleading Immaculate conception."

Clearly, the lyrics are what make the album. Lines such as "Wizard imps and sweat sock pimps/Interstellar mongrel nymphs" (from "82nd Street") show a gleeful inventiveness that would have made Bob Dylan envious. In his *Rolling Stone* review, Lester Bangs astutely summarized: "Some of 'em mean something socially or otherwise, but there's plenty of 'em that don't even pretend to, reveling in the joy of utter crass showoff talent run amuck and totally out of control."[61] In *Crawdaddy!* Peter Knobler declared "There hasn't been an album like this in ages . . . There are individual lines worth entire records . . . There is the combined sensibility of the chaser and the chaste, the street punk and the bookworm."[62]

The album's opening track, "Blinded by the Light," is undoubtedly one of the record's lyrical delights. Its opening lines ("Madman drummers, bummers and Indians in the summer with a teenage diplomat/In the dumps with the mumps as the adolescent pumps his way into his hat") establish a unique structure of couplets—each line containing three words rhyming internally, with the ending of each line in the couplet rhyming externally—that, for the most part, is maintained throughout the song. The dizzying array of characters introduced in the song, ranging from a "fleshpot mascot," a "silicone sister," "young Scot with a slingshot," and "go-cart Mozart," demonstrated Springsteen's ability to describe everyday characters in rough yet poetic language. He explained during his 2005 *VH1 Storytellers* performance that the first line referred to "Madman" Vini Lopez, himself (the "bum"), and the name of his old Little League team, the Indians.

Sometimes, though, the album shows Springsteen more in love with wordplay than in writing songs. Songs such as "For You" and (even with its rhyming dictionary gymnastics) "Blinded" ramble and lose focus at times, as if Springsteen had needed an editor. (Manfred Mann's Earth Band would fill this role years later; with lyrics trimmed and the music injected with amped-up testosterone, they scored a number-one U.S. hit with their remake of "Blinded"—the only Springsteen song to ever reach number one—and an FM radio hit with their version of "For You.")

If the lyrics took center stage, the musical performance seemed relegated to the footlights. Neither Springsteen, Appel, nor Cretecos were experienced producers. Only one song, "Spirit in the Night," shows the band coming together as a unit. "Spirit" is a vignette of Bacchanalian youth that describes an impromptu trip of the singer, his girlfriend, and four buddies to a watering hole called Greasy Lake, which is located "on the dark side of Route 88." (According to author Bob Crane, Vini Lopez claims that the mythical Greasy Lake is actually a composite of two places that band members used to frequent: Lake Carasaljo, which was near the intersection of Routes 9 and 88 in Lakewood, New Jersey, and an unnamed swampy lake just off *Exit* 88 of the Garden State Parkway; Knobler told Crane that it was an "article of faith among local fans" that Greasy Lake's real-life origin was Freehold Pond—formerly Lake Topanemus in Freehold.[63])

From Clemons's bouncing sax riff and Lopez's high-hat drumming as the song begins, to the joyful call-and-response of the chorus, to the earthy bass line throughout (provided by Springsteen himself, as Tallent had gone south along with some other band mates after the first run in the studio),[64] it's clear that Springsteen reaches a peak not only in telling a story but also in fitting a narrative into the larger musical landscape.

Steve Simels in *Stereo Review* noted that the album reminded him of "what Van Morrison might be doing if he ever stopped whining," and the magazine ranked *Greetings* in its Top 10 albums of 1973.[65] But *Greetings* sold poorly, a fact that can be explained only partially by the backlash that many radio DJs felt toward Columbia's attempt to market Springsteen as the new Dylan. Even had it benefited from a more effective marketing strategy, the album was an uneven effort—the vinyl equivalent of a forty-niner's unsifted yield, nuggets of gold buried in sonic ore.

More than 30 years later, *Greetings* pales in comparison to most if not all of the Springsteen catalog. What is undeniable, though, is that the album shows the shape of things to come, the promise of a new voice in rock music, and the vast and yet untapped potential of an artist on the verge of finding his voice.

* 2 *

The Follow-Up, the Future of Rock 'n' Roll, and a Farewell to Asbury Park

The Wild, the Innocent & the E Street Shuffle (1973)

In July 1973, the same month that Bruce Springsteen opened for Bob Marley and the Wailers for a week of shows at Max's Kansas City in New York, Springsteen and his ragtag fleet of musicians returned to 914 Sound Studios to begin recording the follow-up to *Greetings*. Heading into the sessions, Springsteen was, as he remembers in *Songs*, "intent on taking control of the recording process ... I was determined to take the reins and go in the creative direction I wanted." Whereas *Greetings* is "primarily an acoustic record with a rhythm section," Springsteen's goal for his sophomore effort was to retain the lyricism of the first but to cut more of a rock record. "I had made my living primarily as a rock musician," he remembers. "For this record, I was determined to call on my songwriting ability and my bar band experience."[1] He wanted his second record to represent the past eight years in his musical life. The underlying story was that he wanted to break free from the "new Dylan" mantle that his record label had placed upon him.

The Dylan thing: Although Springsteen had indeed been a fan of the sixties Dylan, he had not actively presented himself as the successor to the Dylan throne. Springsteen had spent the overwhelming majority of his career performing styles that were far removed from Dylan's folk revival records, and by the time he began writing songs in the singer/songwriter milieu, Dylan was not as big an influence for Springsteen as what he heard on Top 40 radio. In 1974 he told Paul Williams: "In 1968 I was into *John Wesley Harding*. I never listened to anything after *John Wesley Harding*. Listened to *Bringing It All Back Home, Highway 61, Blonde on Blonde*. That's it. I never had his early albums and to this day I don't have them, and I never had his later albums."[2] Springsteen confided to Williams that he had missed many of the albums, by Dylan or anyone else, that came out after 1967 because his parents had taken the family turntable when they moved west.

Nevertheless, corporate America does nothing if not make continual trips to the well until it runs dry, and ever since Hammond's "discovery" of Dylan in 1961 had brought the label its first legitimate star of the sixties, Columbia had actively sought his folk-rock reincarnation. So zealous were Clive Davis and the CBS Records machine in promoting their rookie artist as the new Dylan that they had unwittingly released an album with built-in backlash. To be fair, the runaway lyricism evidenced on *Greetings* was, at the very least, reminiscent of Dylan's work. (By the early 1970s, some would have said that Dylan's own recent albums were merely reminiscent of his own earlier work.) But grizzled rock-radio veterans had seen a whole flock of singer-songwriters labeled as New Dylans—including Phil Ochs, Tim Buckley, John Prine, even Janis Ian—and had grown a protective layer of skepticism to such hype. Disc jockey Dave Herman at New York's WNEW-FM, the biggest rock station in the metro area (and, as such, the station that would have been the most likely to give *Greetings* airwave momentum) admitted: "I didn't even bother to listen to the album. I didn't want Columbia to think they got me."[3]

Thus, as Springsteen entered the studio in the spring of 1973, he was motivated to break free from New Dylan expectations. He also felt pressure to deliver the goods to his label, which was beginning to doubt if its recent signee would pay off. (Columbia executives might have kept in mind that Dylan himself had been described, in-house, as "Hammond's folly" prior to Dylan's second release.) But with *Greetings* having been a disappointing seller, at least Springsteen did not have to cope with fears of a sophomore slump. Rather, his second album would be the result of an artist still on his way up, still hungry, striving for a goal not yet reached.

Springsteen and company entered the studio with the experience of having one album session under their belts. While *Greetings* shows an artist (and producers) struggling to take a group more accustomed to playing live and translating its various parts within the technology of the recording studio, the new material from the summer of 1973 demonstrated a been-here-before, doing-it-right-this-time feel. Springsteen was no longer just a lead singer in front of a band, but rather the *leader* of a rock 'n' roll–style big band. Lyrically, Springsteen had evolved little from his rookie effort—which is not to say that he was not writing great lyrics, but rather that he was still writing a *lot* of great lines and, it sometimes seemed, jamming them *all* into his songs. In some cases, this mode of songwriting resulted in songs with obscure, sometimes indecipherable meaning. For one, there is "Bishop Danced," a song that Springsteen was performing live. (It was included on *Tracks*, the 1998 four-disc box set of unreleased tracks.) The song, described on stage by Springsteen as a "nonsense song," is a folk-rhythm jaunt driven by acoustic guitar and by Danny Federici's circuslike accordion. With the opening image of a bishop dancing with a "thumbscrew woman," doing a "double-quick back flip" and then sliding across the floor, the listener is never sure what the song is really saying, but in the tradition of such songs as "Whiter Shade of Pale" (with its 16 vestal virgins and tripping of the light fandango), it at least *feels* like it's saying something.

"Santa Ana," a track that Springsteen recorded in the studio that summer, was inspired by a trip that he had taken with his father to Tijuana. Describing the song, Springsteen addressed the incongruity between realistic and artistic representation, saying, "I was able to shrug off the reality of the situation."[4] Indeed, a song like "Santa Ana" shows Springsteen the lyricist finding a voice more concerned with surrealism than realism.

Here, we find a Southwest indebted more to Zane Gray than Steinbeck. As with "Bishop Danced," there are moments of brilliance that outshine actual meaning, and plot takes a backseat to pastiche. In "Santa Ana," the "Giants of Science" look to tame the New Mexico wildlands, Sam Houston's ghost is "fighting for his soul" in Texas, and the singer bids a jukejoint "contessa" to leave the bandana-wearing playboys behind. "French cream won't soften your boots," he tells her. "French kisses will not break your heart." At the end of that line, the singer breaks off into a joyous cry as if he's just put forth a line that no playboy can beat, and then the band joins in an ascendant chord progression that renders the scene triumphant, even epic.

These were the days when Springsteen was entering his epic mode, dealing with a larger-than-life theatricality found in the everyday and mundane. Two other songs from these sessions, "Thundercrack" and "Zero and Blind Terry," also spring from this mode. The first is about an ex-lover who has come back to town, her return announced by the crack of thunder. "This time she'll tell me how she really feels," the singer anticipates, perhaps to no avail. She'll bring him "down to her lightning shack." Maybe she will, maybe she won't; the point is more that the singer *feels* it to be true—so true that her return is enveloped in thunder and lightning. Musically climactic and clocking in at eight and a half minutes, the song was a set closer for Springsteen performances in 1973. But Springsteen left it off what became his second album, probably because the song "Kitty's Back" (which made side one of the new record) dealt with the same theme of an object of desire come back to town.

"Zero and Blind Terry" is an epic tale of outlaw love. Zero is the leader of the Pythons, an Englishtown, New Jersey gang that has rolled into town to face off against a rival gang. After Zero "rides like twilight" out of the "darkness that breaks like dawn" and runs away with his girlfriend, her disapproving father calls the state troopers, who chase the lovers across the railroad tracks. The song is written from a future perspective, telling the legend of Zero and Terry, who may or may not have gotten away from the police. The latter seems more likely given the bittersweet music and wistful tone of the singer, but it's almost beside the point, as the Romeo-and-Juliet-of-the-street story fades into urban legend. "If you look hard enough" like "young pilgrims" and "old timers" do, the singer muses, you'll see the lovers and the Python gang still doing battle across the tracks. The epic dimensions of the song depict not just a song of lovers on the run but of a town where people relive stories like this over and over, forever adding to the legend.

In songs like "Zero and Blind Terry," Springsteen displays the ability to fit his wild, runaway lyrics within the musical grandeur required to sustain such epic lyricism. Songs such as "Blinded by the Light," "For You," and, really, most of the rest of *Greetings* were lyrical heavyweights but musical lightweights. (He remembers in *Songs* that he wrote the lyrics for *Greetings* before he wrote the music, a practice he would move past for his follow-up album.) From this point on, however, Springsteen would maintain the balance he'd achieved in "Spirit in the Night." As Jimmy Guterman notes in *Runaway American Dream,* "In songs like 'Santa Ana' and 'Zero and Blind Terry,' you can hear Springsteen find ways to marry his love for stuffing as many words as possible into each song and still have a song with a groove."[5]

In 1975, Springsteen would release "Jungleland," a thematic descendant of "Zero." Closing side two of the landmark album *Born to Run,* "Jungleland" would represent the peak of his epic songwriting mode. But in 1973, Springsteen was still two years away from this turnpike opera and its New York City setting. His second album, titled *The Wild, the Innocent & the E Street Shuffle,* would be that figurative bridge over the Hudson.

In the chapter from his book titled "Side Two" (perhaps the most definitive essay I've come across on any Springsteen album) Guterman observes, correctly, that songs such as "Santa Ana," "Thundercrack," "Zero," and two other songs from the session, "The Fever" and "Seaside Bar Song," might have formed "the core of a strong record."[6] "The Fever," a slow, sultry jazz number loosely based on the Eddie Cooley/John Davenport standard "Fever," gained a following on the airwaves radio after Appel leaked it to stations. But Springsteen dropped all of them from the final track listing of *Wild.* Granted, the seven songs included—ranging from 4½ to 10 minutes long—were about all that could fit on vinyl pressings. (Springsteen remembers: "I wrote several wild, long pieces . . . that were arranged to leave the band and the audience exhausted and gasping for breath."[7])

Springsteen had not acquired nearly enough cachet for Columbia to even consider releasing a double album. In fact, *Wild* almost didn't come out. According to Appel associate Bob Spitz, when Appel played an early version of the album for CBS executives Charlie Koppelman and Kip Cohen, Koppelman said, "Fellas, we may have run to the end of our days with Bruce Springsteen. This is not an album we are going to put out." When Appel reported back to Springsteen, Springsteen "restructured" the album and "got rid of the filler."[8] Columbia released the album on September 11, 1973.

Taken together, the seven songs on *Wild* comprise a unique combination of long, often epic songs that nevertheless hold together as a concept album more tightly than even *Sgt. Pepper's Lonely Hearts Club Band* (forever dubbed by the rock press as the archetypal concept album). Contrasted with the vague theme of day-to-day life that one may find in *Sgt. Pepper,* on *Wild* the listener encounters a double-sided tale of residents of the fading New Jersey shore, and of the New York City that calls to them from the skyline.

The opening song, "The E Street Shuffle," is rooted musically in the traditions of soul and R&B. (Fittingly, the title alludes to E Street in Belmar, New Jersey, where David Sancious—by then a full-time member of the band—had once lived.) Springsteen says he based the song on a 1960s soul hit by Major Lance titled, "Monkey Time," which has a somewhat similar bouncing melody. As Guterman describes, "E Street Shuffle" begins the album with the sound of horns "caught mid-tuneup" and then moves into "a brief and funny blast that feels like a New Orleans funeral march."[9] Funeral march quickly shifts to frenetic, syncopated jazz and soul: "Van [Morrison] is everywhere here: in the vocal excitement, in the horn lines, in the 'Wild Night' rhythms," Guterman observes. "The mood is loose, exuberant, the soundtrack to a party." The song arrives at a raucous, cacophonous "false ending" and then the band returns for a frenzied coda because they're "having so much fun they can't end it yet."[10]

Unlike anything on *Greetings,* the focus of "E Street Shuffle" is on the music, not the lyrics. Sure, the world of the song is populated with many colorfully named characters. (Everyone in the Springsteen universe seems to have a nickname at this point in his career.) We meet Power Thirteen and Little Angel, along with a supporting cast of "boy prophets," "schoolboy pops," "teenager tramps in skintight pants," "phantoms in full star stream," and "blonde girls pledged sweet sixteen." But more importantly, these characters are present to give a collective call to dance. "I wanted to invent a dance with no exact steps," Springsteen commented.[11]

The gaze turns shoreward on the second song, "4th of July, Asbury Park (Sandy)." The song's title and lyrics, replete with images of fireworks, boardwalks, pier lights, beach bums, pinball machines, fortune tellers, and the south beach drag, locate it squarely in Springsteen's adopted hometown, as do the carnivalesque melodies of Danny Federici's accordion. In truth, "4th of July" captures Asbury Park better than any song on *Greetings* does. More grandly, although the singer begins by evoking the image of Little Eden, the song describes a twilight of paradise. The arcades are dusty, the local fortune-teller, Madam Marie, has been closed down by the police ("busted . . . for tellin' fortunes better than they do"), and the singer's been dumped by the waitress he was seeing. This very personal, post-lapsarian postcard develops the essence of a dead-end shore town decades removed from its heyday.

The song is deceivingly complex, though, as the singer is addressing the song's namesake, a girl named Sandy—whose name renders her a metaphor for the Asbury Park shore. (Springsteen said that Sandy is a composite of some of the girls he'd known along the Shore.)[12] Indeed, she seems to be more of a metaphoric Muse than a girlfriend; as he sings to her of the waitress who "said she won't set herself on fire" for him anymore, he further alludes to growing tired of the "factory girls" he used to chase underneath the boardwalk. Sandy sounds more like a friend, which makes the singer's proposition seem more an act of desperation than romance. "Love me tonight for I may never see you again," he cautions her. In her essay on the album for *Stranded: Rock 'n' roll for a Desert Island*, Ariel Swartley jokes, "You'd think he was ruining his chances with the girl: he can't stop telling her about his humiliations, about the girls who led him on, about the waitress that got tired of him. He can't even hand her a line without blowing it: 'I promise you I'll love you—forever?' Springsteen's adolescent voice squeaks incredulously."[13] It's unclear whether the narrator of "Sandy" has any more insight than the singer at the beginning of Meat Loaf's "Paradise by the Dashboard Lights." The singer's pledges of eternal love are transparent, though, as he ultimately decides to quit the Boardwalk scene (and tells Sandy she should do the same). Fittingly, Springsteen wrote this song after he'd been evicted from his Asbury Park apartment and had moved in with a girlfriend in Bradley Beach five minutes away.

Sandy, the girl we might leave behind, is followed sequentially on the album by Kitty, the girl who left *us* behind. On "Kitty's Back," Springsteen sings from a distance that he maintains for most—though not all—of the song as he ponders the fate of a friend whose girlfriend left to marry a New York City pretty-boy from Bleecker Street. The song is musically playful, an extended and "distorted piece of big band music" intended to serve as a centerpiece for Springsteen's band's live performances.[14] Recalling the music and the lingo of cool jazz, the song develops an extended metaphor of the neighborhood men as alley cats. It's been "tight on this fence," the singer says, ever since Kitty left and "them young dudes" took to "musclin' in."

"Kitty's Back" offers the illusion of a happy ending as Kitty returns to the old neighborhood. We don't know if she's back for good or just visiting, but the song captures the breathless anticipation of "Cat" (and, we get the feeling, every other loser in the alley, including the singer himself) as they see Kitty coming from the distance. Will Kitty ask Cat to take her back? We don't know. Would Cat take her back? Resoundingly, *yes*. The song ends with the admission that Cat knows his Kitty has been untrue, that she'd "left him for a city dude/But she's so soft, she's so blue," he's powerless to resist her. "Ooh, what can I do?" he wonders, resigned to his fate.

After leading us through the dance of "The E Street Shuffle," the album has presented us with one story of a boardwalk denizen dreaming of his escape, and another story of a girl who leaves the beach boys behind. In "Wild Billy's Circus Story," we come to a traveling circus that, by song's end, packs up and leaves New Jersey. The song was inspired by memories of the Clyde Beatty/Cole Bros. Circus that came to Freehold every summer;[15] years before, The Castiles had opened a gig at The Left Foot by playing a circus march. "Wild Billy" is one of the few rock songs (or more accurately, one of the few songs by a rock artist) built around an extended tuba solo; its deep notes bounce lightly throughout the song as we meet the Ferris wheel operator, sword swallower, a man-beast, Little Tiny Tim, fat lady Missy Bimbo, tightrope ballerina, human cannonball, the flying Zambinis, the ringmaster, circus boy, barker, elephants, and strong man Sampson. Springsteen describes the song as "a black comedy . . . about the seduction and loneliness of a life outside the margins of everyday life."[16] "Wild Billy" turns the traditional childhood dream of running away to join the circus on its head; the circus characters seem grotesque, something out of Wallace Stevens's "The Emperor of Ice-Cream." By the time the circus boss leans in to a little boy, "Hey, son, you wanna try the big top?"—a line that Springsteen delivers with more of a guttural growl than the "whisper" implied by the lyrics—the listener might very well cringe at the idea. In the end, though, the circus may leave town, but the dream of somehow getting away still remains.

On vinyl pressings of the album, "Wild Billy" closed side one. When listeners turned the record over to side two, they encountered a surprising three-song suite that today ranks as one of the best album sides in rock history. Guterman says that, "As full-side concepts go, only Van Morrison's *Astral Weeks* (pick either side) surrenders a comparable musical and emotional intensity,"[17] and as superlative as that sounds, it's hard to argue with him. Clocking in at 7:45, 7:02, and 9:56, respectively, "Incident on 57th Street," "Rosalita (Come Out Tonight)," and "New York City Serenade," comprise three acts of a rock operetta that spans jazz, folk, R&B and—for the first time on a Bruce Springsteen record—hard-driving rock 'n' roll.

"Incident" opens with the epitome of an early Springsteen antihero: a male prostitute named Spanish Johnny returns to midtown, bruised and broken from failed attempts to turn tricks for rich girls. He's hassled by pimps before meeting a girl whom he dubs Puerto Rican Jane. They spend the night (or at least part of the night) together, but then he leaves her, called back to the streets and its temptations for making some "easy money." The scenario is simplistic, but Springsteen elevates their stature by describing them as a "cool Romeo" and latter-day "Juliet," and by employing language that is heightened, sometimes beyond belief. Johnny calls down to kids on the street and says, "Hey little heroes, summer's long but I guess it ain't very sweet around here anymore." When Jane realizes Johnny is leaving her in bed to return to the street, she muses, "Those romantic young boys/All they ever want to do is fight." For many, such introspective words will be hard to accept coming from a failed gigolo and the desperate Latina who throws her love at him, but that seems to be the point. The action is stylized, the setting romanticized, and even ignoring the blatant Romeo-and-Juliet-in-New-York-City connection to *West Side Story*, it's clear that "Incident" raises the lowest of lovers to the most epic.

The juxtaposition of "Incident"/"Rosalita" ranks with "Heartbreaker"/ "Living Loving Maid" from the vinyl printings of *Led Zeppelin II* in that it feels incomplete to hear the first song end without then hearing the second one immediately follow. David Sancious's delicate piano line segues into the rapid-fire notes of an electric guitar chord ring out, announcing the first great rock 'n' roll song in Springsteen's recorded career.

The plot of "Rosalita" is simpler still: a hopeful rock musician looking to persuade his girlfriend to run away with him. As in "Spirit in the Night," when the narrator takes Crazy Janey and their friends to Greasy Lake, the would-be lovers of "Rosalita" would share their itinerary with their friends: Little Dynamite, Little Gun, Jack the Rabbit, Weak Knees Willie, Sloppy Sue, and Big Bones Billy. And as in "Zero and Blind Terry"—if not the entire collective body of all rock 'n' roll—there are the disapproving parents: the mother who doesn't like the singer because she thinks he's a hood, and the father who just doesn't understand and locks Rosie in her room like a rock 'n' roll Rapunzel. The singer sees himself as her rescuer, but he refuses to climb her window. "Windows are for cheaters," he tells Rosie. "Winners use the door." This is no rewrite of "Back Door Man"; the singer wants Rosie to walk out the *front* door, an act that would legitimize their relationship. Hand in hand with the singer's search for romanticism is a search for acceptance. He even seeks her father's blessing: He tells Rosie to let her father know that this is his "last chance to get his daughter in a fine romance." Then the singer lets loose his big news: "The record company, Rosie, just gave me a big advance." It's a joyous declaration, but one that pales in comparison to the song's climax. After dreaming of a San Diego café to where they can run—setting up romantic images of a cross-country road-trip for the lovers—the singer bids, "So hold tight baby 'cause don't you know daddy's comin'," and then lets loose in a primal rock scream that is so triumphant, one senses that it almost doesn't matter if Rosie goes with him.

The chorus is repeated one last time, and by the time the ringing of Danny Federici's organ subsides into the distance at song's end, the band has sustained a frenzied, out-of-control energy throughout more than seven minutes. As Guterman puts it, "the song ends with the sound of six very happy grown men collapsing in a heap."[18] And Springsteen has, if only for one song, fulfilled his promise as rock's Great Young Hope. Dave Marsh writes, "If anybody had doubts that Bruce Springsteen would someday write a classic rock song, 'Rosalita' dispelled them."[19] Marsh is often accused of being more Springsteen hagiographer than biographer, but he's right on the money when he describes "Rosalita" as one of the "precious moments in rock when you can hear a musician overcoming both his own limits and the restrictions of the form."[20] In *Songs*, Springsteen describes the song as his "musical autobiography." He himself had scored his "big advance" just the previous year (though it may very well have run out by then) and this was his "getting out of town" song, his "kiss-off to everybody who counted you out, put you down, or decided you weren't good enough."[21]

In the same vein, Springsteen describes the final song of the album, "New York City Serenade," along with "Incident" as being "romantic stories" of a city that had been his "getaway from small-town New Jersey" since he was 16.[22] Again, Sancious provides the link between songs, tickling the ivories with an introduction that morphs from distinctly classical to slyly jazz. Then Springsteen enters with the subtle strumming of his acoustic guitar, described by Swartley as "soft and startling like an unexpected kiss."[23] When he begins to sing, his voice is hushed and raspy, and the song completes the journey from Philly/Jersey Shore soul ("The E Street Shuffle") to the cool jazz of New York. The song is free-form, driven more by pictures than plot, a pastiche of "midnight Manhattan" life— Billy and Diamond Jackie parked in a car by the railroad tracks, the "fish lady" who should leave the tenement and get on the train out (but won't), the jazz man dressed in satin who sings amidst trash cans in the alley. (The song was known as "Vibes Man" in an earlier version.) "Listen to your junk man," Springsteen sings, and then whispers. As the curtain comes down, Springsteen sings the line, "He's singing, he's singing..." which grows from a hushed meditation into a powerful crescendo, and then the street-trash romantic cycle comes to a close. "Last record out you could hear the Dylan in him," Guterman writes. "Half an hour ago it was all Van Morrison. Now, as 'New York City Serenade' goes out on a one-note fade, Springsteen has moved past comparison."[24]

In many ways, *Wild* is the album on which Bruce Springsteen became Bruce Springsteen—and emerged from the shadow of Bob Dylan. Reviewing the album, Janet Maslin (later a film critic for *The New York Times*) remembered the previous winter, when Columbia had touted him as "a contender on those tired-out 'Next Bob Dylan' sweepstakes," and concluded, "Bruce just might turn out to be more interesting than that."[25] In his *Rolling Stone* review, Ken Emerson wrote that while Springsteen's first album had "sounded like [Dylan's] 'Subterranean Homesick Blues' played at 78 . . . *The Wild, the Innocent and the E Street Shuffle* takes itself more seriously. The songs are longer, more ambitious, and more romantic; and yet, wonderfully, they lose little of *Greetings'* rollicking rush."[26] *Real Paper* columnist Jon Landau (then married to Maslin) called *E Street Shuffle* "the most under-rated album so far this year, an impassioned and inspired street fantasy that's as much fun as it is deep," though he noted that Springsteen "ought to work a little harder on matching the production to the material, round out a few rough edges and then just throw some more hot ones on the vinyl."[27]

Looking back on his second album, Springsteen himself remembers, "I started slowly to find out who I am, and where I wanted to be. It was like coming out of the shadow of various influences and trying to be yourself."[28] Ironically, in their unconventional instrumentation and sheer length, the songs on *Wild* are even further away from the AM/Top 40 style for which he had the most affinity. During this period in his career, though, Springsteen still felt that he needed the forum of the extended, epic song to say everything that he wanted to say.[29]

Wild failed to achieve the commercial success sought by Springsteen and Columbia. It wouldn't even crack the charts until two years later, when it would benefit from the success of *Born to Run*. But the album's material further contributed to the band's growing performance repertoire. "Rosalita" replaced "Thundercrack" as the song with which Springsteen and the band, now known as the E Street Band, would close their sets.[30] "The E Street Shuffle," "4th of July, Asbury Park," and "Kitty's Back" all became crowd favorites in live sets.

The winter of 1973–74 had the band touring clubs and colleges throughout the East Coast and into the South with dates in Lexington and Nashville. In March, they played three stops in Texas and then hit Phoenix for one night before returning to the northeast for 14 gigs in April. In May, Springsteen and the E Street Band played college gigs in New Jersey, Ohio, and Pennsylvania and then pulled into Cambridge, Massachusetts, to open up for Bonnie Raitt at the Harvard Square Theater.

A bootleg recorded by someone in the crowd that night preserved the Harvard Square performance for posterity. Springsteen comes out and feels his way through a tentative version of "New York City Serenade."

Then the full band kicks in for a rousing version of "Spirit in the Night," followed by a comical number, "I Sold My Heart to the Junk Man," which Springsteen prefaces with a tongue-in-cheek confession about a girl who'd broken his heart. (Springsteen's anecdotal introductions and mid-song monologues were by then becoming intrinsic features to his live performances, often to the backing of lyrical music to further draw in the audience). The band dips back into *Greetings* for two more songs, "Does This Bus Stop at 82nd Street?" and "It's Hard to Be a Saint in the City," goes back to *Wild* for its title track, then closes with its two big concert numbers: "Kitty's Back" (interpolated with snippets of the jazz standard "Bright Lights, Big City") and "Rosalita." (Other sources have suggested that "Born to Run" and "She's the One" made debuts this night, but neither song appears on the Cambridge bootleg, and the editors of the book *Backstreets* note that neither song can be confirmed as part of the May 9 setlist.[31])

Jon Landau, also working then as an editor for *Rolling Stone*, had first seen Springsteen back in 1973 at Max's Kansas City. After sending writer Stu Werbin to cover Springsteen at Max's, Werbin had been so impressed that he insisted his editor accompany him the following night.[32] Landau saw Springsteen again in April at Charley's Bar in Cambridge. That night, Springsteen was standing outside reading a Xerox of Landau's review that had been placed in the window.

Landau went up and asked Springsteen what he thought of the review.

"Well, it's okay," Springsteen said.[33] Landau introduced himself to Springsteen, and the two talked for a while.

Landau attended the Harvard Square performance in May. Then he went home and wrote a concert review that would resonate throughout the rock world.

In truth, his piece for the May 22 issue of *Real Paper*, titled "Growing Young with Rock 'n' roll," was not just a concert review; it was an almost painful confession of disillusionment with rock music (and writing about rock music) and of the Saul-on-the-road-to-Damascus conversion he experienced in Cambridge that night.

Then 27 years old, Landau wrote of feeling old and of the classic platters from the sixties that had become personal time capsules, reminders to Landau of how things had once been different. But he went on to write of a new performer who had inspired him to write about music the way he once had:

> Tonight, there is someone I can write of the way I used to write, without reservation of any kind. Last Thursday, at the Harvard Square theatre, I saw my rock 'n' roll past flash before my eyes. And I saw something else: I saw rock 'n' roll future and its name is Bruce Springsteen. And on a night when I needed to feel young, he made me feel like I was hearing music for the very first time.[34]

The "rock 'n' roll future" line is, perhaps, the most quoted line from a music review ever. Looking to pump life into Springsteen's paltry sales track, Columbia would latch onto Landau's prophetic line and milk it for all it was worth in their promotional efforts on Springsteen's behalf. The review helped generate media interest in Springsteen, but it could not conceal the fact that he had yet to record a hit record. Like the New Dylan tag line, the label of being rock 'n' roll's future would prove to be yet another mantle that Springsteen the recording artist would have to bear as he returned to the studio, looking to fulfill his unlimited but still-unrealized potential.

* 3 *

Thunder Road Revue

Born to Run (1975)

January 1975 saw Bob Dylan return to the forefront of popular music with the release of *Blood on the Tracks*. Featuring such songs as "Tangled Up in Blue," "Shelter from the Storm," and the seething kiss-off epic, "Idiot Wind," the album is an all-time classic—the height of Dylan in the seventies, and his first great album since *Highway 61 Revisited*. *Rolling Stone* was prompted to devote three articles covering the album's release, including one by Jon Landau. "Dylan's electric albums have often been pointlessly sloppy," Landau wrote. "*Blood on the Tracks* will only sound like a great album for a while. Like most of Dylan, it is impermanent."[1]

Going one-for-two in predicting rock 'n' roll future ain't bad.

Meanwhile, the man dubbed the embodiment of rock's future still looked for a breakout album. *The Wild, the Innocent & the E Street Shuffle* had been an artistic success, but Springsteen had written most of that album in an epic-romantic mode, producing songs that were too long and too unconventional for radio. Springsteen the recording artist was known only to die-hard fans—those who saw the E Street Band perform up and down the East Coast and those esoteric few who bought albums based on record reviews knew about it. In short, by early 1975, Bob Dylan had arrived *twice,* while the man once pegged as the next Dylan had yet to arrive once and was still toiling in relative anonymity with an East Coast cult following.

Post-*Wild* life on E Street began to look bleak. First, Springsteen fired Vini Lopez after some band infighting. Lopez was replaced by drummer Ernest "Boom" Carter, who had been a frequent member of the late-night jams at The Upstage in Asbury Park and was best friends with David Sancious. But Carter's stay in the band would be short-lived. Sancious, the group's most accomplished musician, left the band to form a jazz-rock fusion group called Tone in 1974, and he recruited Carter to join him. Meanwhile, one half of Springsteen's production team left when Jim Cretecos sold his share in the business to Mike Appel. At the same time, the record label was losing faith in Springsteen. Columbia began telling radio stations to forget about Springsteen and to devote air time to another promising artist on the label, Billy Joel.

Charlie Koppelman at CBS suggested that the so-called future of rock 'n' roll should go to Nashville to work with session musicians and outside producers.[2] Springsteen would have nothing of it. "I was not interested in a strictly professional setup because I didn't want to contain my talents in that box, because I didn't know where they were going to lead me at the time," Springsteen reflected 30 years later. "And at that time, my concern was this: I have these abilities. I don't *know* what they are, but I know that they're *there.* And I don't know where they're going to lead me. But wherever that is, I have to go even if it's down a bunch of blind alleys, till I find the one that I *do* want to go down."[3]

"At that age, you're a combination of things," he said. "I had the big ego, the belief in my abilities, the intensity of desire. But the flip side of that is, 'Man, am I about to be collared and sent back on a bus to where I came from?' "[4] Still, Springsteen remained committed to making the Great American Rock Record. He had entered the studio in 1974 looking to create an album with (conflating various recollections over the years) the soaring vocals of a Roy Orbison, the lyrical poeticism of Dylan, the classic guitar riffs of Duane Eddy, and the textures of Phil Spector's classic early sixties productions. "I had these enormous ambitions for it. . . . I wanted to make the greatest rock record that I'd ever heard. I wanted it to sound enormous, to grab you by your throat and insist that you take that ride, insist that you pay attention—not just to the music, but to life, to being alive."[5]

Springsteen looked to cast images of the Jersey Shore hot rod scene within a grand, panoramic vision. In the summer of 1974, Springsteen had bought his first car: a '57 Chevy with dual, four-barrel carbs, a Hurst on the floor, and orange flames painted across the hood—a classic car straight out of the retro-youth car culture of *American Graffiti*. Two avenues in Asbury Park that ran parallel to the Boardwalk, Kingsley and Ocean, formed a "sort of oval racetrack" known as the Circuit, and it literally framed the town's beach bar district.[6] As he sat on his bed one night in his West Long Branch house, the phrase "born to run" popped into his head. "At first I thought it was the name of a movie or something I'd seen on a car spinning around the Circuit, but I couldn't be certain. I liked the phrase because it suggested a cinematic drama I thought would work with the music I was hearing in my head."[7]

Earlier in the year, he had been listening to Duane Eddy's "Because They're Young," a 1960 hit record that featured a slow, twangy guitar riff. Springsteen began to experiment with a similar riff on his guitar[8]—a hybrid model with an Esquire neck and Telecaster body—and found something that stuck in his head. Coupling the riff with the "born to run" motif, Springsteen had the beginnings of a rock classic.

Springsteen began to perform early arrangements of the song with the E Street Band. But Springsteen—who had been known for live performances that exuded an energy that had yet to be truly captured on record—had a vision of the song that could only be constructed in the studio. "It was the first piece of music I wrote and conceived as a studio production," Springsteen remembers.[9] Appel went as far as to meet with Jeff Barry, who had cowritten many of Spector's hits (and who also had cowritten a song with Jim Cretecos titled "Lay a Little Lovin'," a Top 10 hit for original *Hair* cast member Robin McNamara). Barry clued in Appel to some tricks that Spector had used to create his famous "Wall of Sound" atmosphere on hits such as "Be My Baby" and "Da Doo Ron Ron." As described in a 1988 *Rolling Stone* piece, "The 100 Best Singles of the Last Twenty-Five Years," Appel and Springsteen used techniques like "keeping the piano pedal down to generate a heavy drone," overdubbing numerous guitar tracks, "laying on heavy echo and reverb," and even adding a "Spectorish glockenspiel."[10]

After the band recorded the basic guitar/drums/bass track, Springsteen and Appel experimented with overdub tracks. The recording of "Born to Run" alone became an adventure in attempting to match recording studio technology to the infinite possibilities of rock 'n' roll mythology. They created mix after mix, with a symphony of overdubbed tracks combining electric guitar, layered acoustic guitars, piano, organ, a Fender Rhodes electric piano, synthesizer, saxophone, tambourine, drums, bass, and a glockenspiel, along with a string ensemble and female backing vocals on alternate mixes.[11] Springsteen even envisioned using sound effects, such as the noise of motorcycles peeling out during the instrumental break in the middle of the song, though that idea was eventually scrapped. Musically, the song was deceivingly complex, combining elements of early rock 'n' roll and hard rock with rockabilly, jazz (a syncopated drum riff that Carter's successor could never replicate), even Tin Pan Alley.

Depending on varying accounts, the band took anywhere from three to six months working on the song "Born to Run." (The song might have gone by the title "Tramps Like Us" early on, as Springsteen introduced the song under that title during his landmark gig at the Bottom Line in 1975.) Carter, who was still with the band for the recording of "Born to Run," remembers, "We would leave, go on the road and do shows, and then come back and record some more, all on that one song."[12] The intensity of efforts on the song would set a pattern for the rest of the album.

It was clear that "Born to Run" was something that the band had never done before. From Carter's opening drum roll and Springsteen's ringing guitar chords to Clemons' power-charged saxophone solo to Springsteen's wailing cry to close the song, "Born to Run" packs all the rock 'n' roll power of "Rosalita" and more, condensed almost into single-length format.

Almost. At nearly four-and-a-half minutes long, "Born to Run" was substantially shorter than "Rosalita" but still too long for AM radio, where the Top 40 hierarchy was shaped by the short-and-sweet format that held listeners' attentions and allowed for more ads in between. So when Appel played the song for Irwin Segelstein, the new president of Columbia, Segelstein rejected it; one aide reportedly dubbed it "Born to Crawl."[13] Already viewing the recording sessions as a money pit, Columbia cut off funding. Springsteen and the E Street Band headed back on the road.

Attempts to trim the record's length proved futile. The record's mix was so complicated that editing it proved all but impossible. So Appel decided to force the issue and made tapes of "Born to Run" to distribute to FM stations in Boston, New York, Philadelphia, and Cleveland. His makeshift promotional campaign proved to be crucial to advancing Springsteen's career. Appel had done the same thing with "The Fever," a number Springsteen decided he didn't like, but which had undeniable pop-R&B charm. (It became a staple for Southside Johnny and the Asbury Jukes, who recorded a version of the song for their debut in 1976.) Springsteen's manager had secretly leaked copies of "The Fever" to select disc jockeys, and Springsteen was surprised to get requests for the song during subsequent concert dates in the Southwest. Similarly, thanks to Appel's covert publicity, "Born to Run" became a cult hit on FM radio stations in the Northeast such as WNEW (where it became an unofficial theme song) months before its official release.

Out in Cleveland, area rock musician Michael Stanley (of the Michael Stanley Band) sang Springsteen's praises to WMMS disc jockey David Spero, and Spero in turn told fellow WMMS DJ "Kid Leo" about Springsteen.[14] Soon, Kid Leo began to play "Born to Run" every Friday at 5:55 PM to officially ring in the weekend.[15] Allan Clarke from The Hollies liked the song so much that he recorded a cover version of the song and released it in France several months before Springsteen released it himself in the United States (providing the answer to a quintessential rock trivia question).

Fans began to request "Born to Run" on the radio and at shows. The song created some buzz for an album that was not remotely finished and looked like it might never be, and Columbia executives were not thrilled that the artist with which it had been patient finally had a hit—with a song that could not yet generate any record sales.

While playing in Rhode Island, Springsteen gave an interview to the Brown University school newspaper and complained that Segelstein wanted to drop him. As chance had it, Segelstein's son was a student at Brown. As chance further had it, he was a Springsteen fan, and he called his father to argue against his rumored plans to dump Springsteen from his label. Irwin Segelstein reportedly called Appel and chided him for his client's bad-mouthing, but ultimately, Columbia's squeaky wheel got the grease it needed to keep rolling: The sessions were back on.

After completing "Born to Run" and another song, "A Love So Fine," an upbeat R&B bar-band piece that never made it onto the album, Springsteen was stalled by writer's block. Writer's block gave way to spurts of creativity that produced songs that the writer quickly disregarded. Danny Federici remembered, "Bruce was writing about a song per day. It was crazy. It got so I didn't want to go to rehearsal, because every time there'd be this mess of new songs to learn. And they were all gone so soon. Bruce just goes, 'That's yesterday,' and throws 'em away."[16]

Springsteen and the E Street Band kept performing in between studio sessions. His agency, Williams Morris, foolishly booked him to play the Schaffer Music Festival in Central Park, opening for a mismatched Anne Murray (yes, *that* Anne Murray) on August 3. Reportedly, Appel told Murray's managers that Murray would be better off opening, but her managers refused. After Springsteen delivered a crazed performance, complete with encore, Murray was all but booed—or "*Broooced*"—off stage.

Back in the studio, though, sessions ground to a halt when Sancious and Carter left the band at the end of the summer. Springsteen/Appel placed a classified ad in *The Village Voice* for replacements: "Drummer (No Jr. Ginger Bakers) Piano (Classical to Jerry Lee Lewis) Trumpet (Jazz, R&B & Latin) Violin. All must sing."[17]

According to Springsteen's and Tallent's recollections, the band auditioned 60 musicians, playing a half hour with each one.[18] Among the group of applicants were drummer Max Weinberg and pianist Roy Bittan. Both men brought eclectic musical backgrounds to the E Street Band. Weinberg's experience ranged from rock bands to the Broadway pit, where he had played in *Godspell.* Bittan had played with the Pittsburgh Symphony and toured with *Jesus Christ Superstar.* Thus, one might say that the addition of Weinberg and Bittan was fitting given the singer-songwriter who had been prophesied as being rock 'n' roll's savior.

Violinist Suki Lahav also served as an unofficial member of the band, both onstage and in the studio. The wife of Louis Lahav, who served as engineer on Springsteen's first two albums and parts of the third, Lahav's heartstring-tugging violin lines added a bittersweet dimension to such concert favorites as "Incident on 57th Street," "New York City Serenade," and a new song that the band began performing in 1974, "Jungleland."

In the October 1974 issue of *Crawdaddy!,* interviewer Paul Williams complimented Springsteen on this new song, and Springsteen shared some of the lyrics with him: "Boys flash guitars like bayonets, and rip holes in their jeans. . . . In the tunnel machine, the rat chases his dreams on a forever lasting night. Till the barefoot girl brings him to bed, shakes her head and with a sigh turns out the light." ("Jungleland" would continue to evolve, and none of the lines quoted above would remain intact.) Williams suggested that a line from the song, "In the quick of the night, they reach for their moment," could be used as the album's title, and Springsteen admitted that he had thought of that.[19]

Springsteen would consider a number of titles for his third album, including *From the Churches to the Jails*; *The Hungry and the Hunted*; *War and Roses*; and *American Summer*. The first two phrases also were taken from lines in "Jungleland"; the first three phrases combine low and high planes—elements of baseness (crime, hunger, war) with spirituality (religion, metaphysical haunting, love). The combination of the sacred and the profane—or, perhaps more accurately, the sacred *within* the profane—had been an element of Springsteen's music ever since *Greetings*. While struggling through the third-album sessions, Springsteen sought a record that would be a commercial success while at the same time staying true to his vision—to the album that he heard in his head—while desperately trying to capture it on record.

"Lyrically," Springsteen recalls in *Songs*, "I was entrenched in classic rock 'n' roll images, and I wanted to find a way to use those images without their feeling anachronistic."[20] In Thom Zimny's documentary, *Wings for Wheels: The Making of* Born to Run, Springsteen says that "I worked very, very long on the lyrics of *Born to Run* because I was very aware that I was messing with classic rock 'n' roll images that easily turn into clichés." With this in mind, he reworked and refined the songs in his notebook. "I kept stripping away . . . cliché, cliché, cliché . . . I just kept stripping it down until it started to feel emotionally real." In addition to classic rock 'n' roll imagery, Springsteen was inspired by the "noir-ish, B-picture titles" he was hooked on at the time. "The initial lyrics would have been like 'bad B-picture,' where I always thought the end product was supposed to be kind of 'good B-picture,' and then imbued with a certain spiritual thing."

Even though the album was Springsteen's first serious venture into rock 'n' roll record territory, he wrote all of the songs for the third album on piano. Marsh notes, "The mass of guitars on 'Born To Run' made the album seem guitar dominated, although in fact the most important instruments are Roy Bittan's piano and Clarence Clemon's [sic] saxophone." Springsteen remembered, "We decided to make a guitar album, but then I wrote all the songs on piano."[21] The distinction is not mere trivia. The songs' origins on piano gave them a particular melodic feel. As Tallent keenly notes in *Wings for Wheels*, "There's a great difference when you write on the piano and you write on the guitar, especially if you are sort of, you know, tentative about how to play. I think that oftentimes you can discover things on the piano you wouldn't necessarily discover on guitar."

Although Tallent doesn't elaborate in the documentary, one can imagine that the process of writing on piano as a secondary instrument, as Springsteen did, might produce a constructive discomfort—forcing the songwriter to focus more deliberately on melodic construction than he might otherwise have done. "I have a limited ability on [piano] but I can usually get pretty expressive with it," Springsteen told Jon Bream of the *Star Tribune* in 2005.[22] And as Springsteen wrote these songs on the Aeolian piano he had in the living room of his West Long Branch house, he strove for a particular epic quality in the music. The piano lines proved especially conducive to composing theatrical introductions to each song. "I was interested in setting the scene [in each song]," he explains. "It was part of the epic quality of the songwriting I was interested in. I was interested in writing these mini-epics, and the introductions were meant to make you feel that something auspicious was going to occur."[23]

But the sessions lagged along. After a show at Boston's Music Hall on October 29, 1974, Springsteen had called Landau, who lived in Boston. In his review of *Wild*, Landau had found fault with the production, so Springsteen started asking Landau questions about the role of a producer.[24] They spoke for hours that night. In the coming months, the Jersey shore native and the Brandeis graduate formed a friendship based on their love of classic rock records. Sometimes Springsteen would even crash at Landau's home after listening to 45 rpm records into the wee hours of the night.

He had Landau listen to a tape from the sessions and sought his advice. In early 1975, Landau joined Springsteen in the studio at the artist's invitation to serve as coproducer along with himself and Appel.

Much has been written on the clash of egos between Appel and Landau, which was almost immediate as soon as Landau appeared in the studio. (Dave Marsh and Eric Alterman would have us see Jon Landau as a rock 'n' roll John the Baptist, while Marc Eliot is an Appel apologist and Fred Goodman depicts Landau as a Svengali-like puppet master.) Appel, understandably, wondered what Landau—a music *journalist* who had taken less-than-successful turns in producing MC5, the J. Geils Band, and Livingston Taylor—was doing in the studio. Landau sensed Appel's resentment and, in turn, resented him for it. Personal and power squabbles aside, Landau did bring an outsider's fresh perspective that helped lift Springsteen out of the rut that he'd been in for months. "I think that if we talk about Jon Landau's most important contribution in my mind it was the fact that he was able to analyze each song, break it down into its component parts, and make it not seem such a big thing, Bruce," Appel said.[25]

In 1975, Springsteen told *Rolling Stone* that "[Landau] came up with the idea, 'Let's make a rock 'n' roll record.' Things had fallen down internally. He got things on their feet again."[26] He provided helpful suggestions on certain arrangements, such as another song that Springsteen had developed onstage, "Wings for Wheels." Originally, the song included a saxophone solo in the middle, but that didn't seem to work. Landau recommended the sax track be moved to the song's ending, and things fell into place. It was an important step in the evolution of a song that was eventually renamed "Thunder Road."

Landau also convinced Springsteen and Appel that they needed to leave the recording studio in Blauvelt, which Landau said "had seen better days," and move their sessions to the state-of-the-art Record Plant in New York City's Time Square.[27] Once situated at the Record Plant, Team Springsteen brought in a promising young recording engineer named Jimmy Iovine, who had worked with Phil Spector on John Lennon's album *Rock and Roll.* Iovine, who later became a producer and then founded Interscope Records, added a further layer of professionalism to the sessions.

Landau didn't always get his way, though. He thought a new song called "Linda Let Me Be the One" was Springsteen's best shot at a hit single.[28] But the song was left off the album in favor of "Meeting Across the River," which Landau thought little of but which Appel loved. Other session outtakes include "So Young and in Love," which is basically "A Love So Fine" with different lyrics; "Lovers in the Cold," a picture of two lovers walking through a snow-covered graveyard, set against a larger-than-life soundscape that somewhat resembles "Thunder Road"; and the boardwalk anthem "Lonely Night in the Park," which surfaced three decades later on satellite radio.

Although now working in a decidedly more professional setting, the sessions still dragged on laboriously. Danny Federici remembers, "We'd be there, sometimes we were there from nine, ten o'clock in the morning 'til five, six, seven, eight o'clock in the morning, around the clock. [We'd] just go on and on and drag and drag and drag."[29] "Springsteen had been bogged down in the project. He was having trouble getting the wide-screen sounds in his head onto record," Robert Hilburn writes.[30] Springsteen told one interviewer that year, "The tension making that record I could never describe. It was killing, almost; it was inhuman. I hated it. I couldn't stand it. It was the worst, hardest, lousiest thing I ever had to do."[31]

It was a bleak time. He was staying with Karen Darvin, his girlfriend from Texas, at a cheap hotel in Times Square, in the same neighborhood as pimps and prostitutes and junkies. Darvin knew no one in New York and stayed in their hotel room alone all day. When Springsteen came home, he was sometimes frustrated to the point of tears.

Springsteen had entered the dark side of the creative zone—having spent so many months in the studio, endlessly working and reworking the same songs to the point where every version sounded to him like an inadequate version of his imagined ideal. As he would describe later to Robert Hilburn:

> I was unsure about the album all the way. I didn't really know what I put down on it. I lost all perspective . . . the [sessions] turned into something I never conceived of a record turning into. It turned into something that was wrecking me, just pounding me into the ground.[32]

Staying at an inn on New York's West Side in the later stages of the album, as he described later to Robert Duncan of *Creem*, he became fixated on a mirror in his room, which seemed to symbolize the obsessive-compulsive atmosphere of the recording sessions: "the room had this crooked mirror . . . and every night when I'd come home, that mirror was crooked again. Every time. That crooked mirror . . . it just couldn't stay straight."[33] In another version, he remembered: "Couldn't get it to hang right. It just blew my mind after a certain amount of time . . . It was the album that mirror became—it was crooked, it just wouldn't hang right."[34]

With both an impending release date and a tour kicking off in Providence on July 20, the final days of the sessions proved hectic. Springsteen and crew worked frantically on the finishing touches. Band members shuffled between recording various album tracks for the mix and group rehearsals. The sessions ended mostly by necessity, on the eve of the tour.

Even after the definitive version of each was selected, the task of mastering the tapes proved arduous. "All I knew was it was the last thing I was going to have to decide before the record came out, and I was simply paralyzed."[35] Springsteen rejected a number of masters and even threw one out of his hotel room window. "I could only hear the things that were wrong with it at the time," he told Ashley Kahn of *The Wall Street Journal*.[36] Appel had to hold off the label executives while he waited for Springsteen to sign off.

Springsteen even toyed with the idea of scrapping the studio sessions entirely and releasing an album of live performances. " 'Maybe I might just scrap the whole thing—how 'bout that?' This is what he says," Appel remembers incredulously in the *Wings for Wheels* documentary.

Ultimately, Landau stepped in and jarred some sense into his prized fighter. "Look, you're not supposed to like it," he reportedly told Springsteen, arguing that an artist connected to his music is unable to enjoy it as does a fan who is separate from the material. "You think Chuck Berry sits around listening to 'Maybellene'? And when he does hear it, don't you think that he wishes a few things could be changed?"[37]

While Springsteen seemed to lose the forest through the trees, it became clear to those connected to the sessions that a remarkable album was in the works. Bolstered by what they were starting to hear (and perhaps thinking that it was now or never for its once promising artist) Columbia pumped $250,000 into promoting Springsteen and his new album.[38] The label released "Born to Run" as an advance single; on the flipside was another new song, "Meeting Across the River," a narrative that Mike Appel likened to the film noir classic *Night and the City,* told over piano, muted trumpet, and string bass. (Bassist Richard Davis, who played on Van Morrison's timeless *Astral Weeks,* made a cameo on the song. "*Astral Weeks* was like a religion to us," Van Zandt remembers.[39]) Even at its longer-than-ideal running time, "Born to Run" gained airplay and climbed the charts into the Top 20. Finally, Springsteen had the hit for which he, Appel, and Columbia had been waiting.

As anticipation built in late July and early August for the long-hoped-for breakout album, Springsteen and the E Street Band were out of town touring in Washington, DC, Virginia, Ohio, and Pennsylvania. They would return for five nights—two shows per night—at The Bottom Line, a nightclub in Greenwich Village. Columbia saw the venue as a perfect way to further spread the word on Springsteen and purchased more than a thousand tickets to the Bottom Line dates (approximately one-fifth of the total sold) and distributed them gratis to members of the rock media.[40] "Go and see him for yourself" became the label's mantra.

With this in mind, the Bottom Line dates became yet another step in Springsteen's career that would either make or break him. As chronicled in a special *Rolling Stone* issue on the greatest live performances in rock history, "Never had so much expectation been crammed into such a tiny space." Springsteen and his band returned to New York realizing just what rode on the Bottom Line shows. "We were right on the verge," Clarence Clemons remembered. "If we had flopped at the Bottom Line, it would have been very detrimental to us emotionally."[41]

They didn't flop. Instead, the band delivered a series of performances that would eclipse even the Cambridge "rock 'n' roll future" show in importance within Springsteen and the E Street Band's career. WNEW's Dave Herman, the DJ who had refused to buy into the Springsteen hype, showed up for the opening night date at The Bottom Line with what he would later admit was a "show me" attitude. Springsteen came out by himself, sat at the piano, and played a deliberate and impassioned version of "Thunder Road." The crowd was mesmerized and, as Herman remembered, moved to a standing ovation after the *opening number.* Then the E Street Band joined the singer on stage, and the rock 'n' roll portion of the show kicked in. "Within fifteen minutes," Herman said, "I realized I'd never seen anything like this before."[42] The DJ went on the station the next morning and delivered a *mea culpa* to his audience for having doubted the legitimacy of Springsteen's claim to the rock 'n' roll throne.

According to Clemons, the first night was "great" because of its initial "impact," but the following shows were better. On the third night, Dave Herman broadcast from backstage as WNEW carried the show live on-air. The band opened up with an autobiographical song from the forth-coming album, "Tenth Avenue Freeze-Out." Their set included high-charged covers of The Crystals' "Then He Kissed Me" ("she" substi-tuted for "he"), The Searchers' "When You Walk in the Room," and Gary U.S. Bonds's "Quarter to Three"; show-stopping versions of "Kitty's Back" and "Rosalita"; an intimate version of "4th of July, Asbury Park"; and a compact but frenzied version of "Born to Run" that a young punk group called The Ramones would have been hard-pressed to match across town in CBGB.

There must be something magical about the moment when an artist realizes he has finally arrived. After Springsteen came offstage following the final encore, he was "jumping up and down like a prizefighter after a big win, punching the air with both hands."[43] The performance has gone down as perhaps the most famous in the history of Springsteen and the band.

The Bottom Line performances showed rock fans and media alike that Springsteen was no creation of industry hype; he was the real deal. All that remained was the album that would officially announce his emer-gence onto the Big Stage.

The long-awaited album, *Born to Run*, was released on September 1, 1975. Advance sales had already put the album on the charts a week ear-lier. It shot into the Top 10 within the first month of its release, and by the end of October, it had gone gold. Springsteen's career would never be the same again.

As with *Greetings* and *Wild*, Springsteen's third album is ridden with Catholic/Christian imagery. There are references to ghosts, visions, and visionaries; crosses, churches, and prayers in the dark; original sin and at least one savior offering redemption; Mary, angels, wings, and heaven; soul crusaders and forced confessions; holy silence and holy nights; faith and the Promised Land. Yet any redemptive virtues that might be found within are tempered by darker images of an apocalyptic landscape: burned-out cars, a tattered graduation gown, chromed invaders, abandoned beach houses, suicide machines, kids huddled in the mist, dying in the streets, broken heroes, lovers in the cold, wasted and stranded midnight boys, empty homes, stolen sisters, and a death waltz. And while the album represents a height in rock romanticism—due in no small part to the contributions of newcomer Roy Bittan's melodies—the album's lyrics are more gritty than romantic, more city noir than teen beach romance. In the course of *Born to Run*'s eight songs, we meet "a killer in the sun," a faithless "tramp of hearts," a distinctly femme fatale angel who tells "desperate lies," two would-be hoods and a tough guy who doesn't dance, knife-fight victims, and a gang member dying (or dead) from gunshot wounds. These characters warn each other that no one rides for free; they make "secret pacts" and then curse each other for betrayals; rather than ascending to love, they "surrender" to it.

While the Springsteen of *Born to Run* still retains moments of youthful romanticism, from the first stanza of "Thunder Road" (with Mary fearing that "we ain't that young anymore") to the street toughs of "Jungleland" who end up "wounded/Not even dead," this Springsteen paints a landscape of lost youth. "It was the album where I left behind my adolescent definitions of love and freedom . . . [it] was the dividing line," he later reflected.[44]

The characters of *Born to Run* still display the same sense of rootlessness as the characters of Springsteen's earlier work, yet they are more *grounded*; facing the loss of their youth—and with it, the dreams of youth—they are tied more closely to earth. The album's opening track, "Thunder Road," has the singer telling Mary (named Angelina or Chrissie in earlier versions) that they should "trade in these wings for some wheels." As Springsteen described in his *Storytellers* performance on VH-1, "Thunder Road" was an "invitation" to an "earthly journey."

Springsteen originally intended the track sequence of *Born to Run* to add up to a concept album that collectively follows its character throughout the course of a day, and the finished album still conveys that sort of feel. (In his review of the album, Lester Bangs noted *Born to Run* "could almost be a concept album."[45]) Originally, "Thunder Road" was to appear in two versions—an acoustic one to open the album and then the full-band version to close it. But the song works intrinsically as an opener, not a closer. Marsh reports that Springsteen wrote "Thunder Road" in "a morning mood" and that he even played with the idea of beginning the song with "a clock radio clicking on and blaring Orbison's 'Only the Lonely.'" (The fourth and fifth lines of the song allude to a radio playing this song.) The uncharacteristically imagistic opening lines—"Screen door slams/Mary's dress waives"—initiate the action at daybreak. Then, as Marsh observes:

> The record moves through a series of encounters, some of which are flashbacks—"Tenth Avenue Freeze-Out," "Night," "She's the One"—but all of which are harrowingly current in their emotions. "Backstreets" ends Side One evoking the heat of the afternoon; "Born to Run" begins the second side with the early evening mist. By the time "Jungleland" is over, we have reached dawn of the next day. Much has happened, here in Nowhere, but nothing is finished. There is the feeling that these characters may be condemned to repeat such days forever.[46]

"Thunder Road" is "Rosalita" rewritten from the perspective of a less innocent, more realistic perspective. Again, the singer sits in his car in front of his girlfriend's house, calling for her to come out and drive away with him. But whereas "Rosalita" depicts a rock 'n' roll savior, the singer of "Thunder Road" warns that he *isn't* a savior, and that he offers no redemption save the chance to drive away. What's more, his invitation is distinctly unromantic: he tells Mary that she "ain't a beauty" but she's "all right," and he warns her that the ride he's offering her "ain't free." The last two lines of the song—"It's a town full of losers/And I'm pulling out of here to win"—could very well have been sung by the singer of "Rosalita," but the singer of "Thunder Road" seems more realistic about where he's headed.

"Backstreets," a painful, organ-drenched saga of a broken summertime romance and friendship, can be seen as Springsteen's answer to Dylan's "Idiot Wind." While the singer of "Backstreets" twice describes the departed girl, Terry, as a friend and never once as a lover, there's no mistaking the passion involved. Sung in retrospect, the song is about a relationship that was doomed to end. The lovers meet during a "soft infested summer." Marked by Original Sin (the "fire we was born in"), they were doomed to betrayal and expulsion. In the end, Terry has been stolen away by another man, and the singer is left to recall their pledge of "forever," and the image of her lying on his chest. He recasts in hindsight as

"Just another tramp of hearts/Crying tears of faithlessness." When it comes to songs about romance won and lost, Springsteen would never write a more powerful one, nor one more bittersweet.

Although the object of desire in "She's the One" goes unnamed, she could just as well be Terry. In fact, an early version of the song included the line, "I hated you when you went away," which was moved into the final version of "Backstreets." (Meanwhile, the references to French cream and French kisses in "Santa Ana" reappear here.) The girl of "She's the One" is also a liar; she has an "angel in her lies/That tells such desperate lies/And all you want to do is believe her." Musically, with its roller-rink piano and Buddy Holly rhythms, it harkens back to rock 'n' roll past, as does the song "Tenth Avenue Freeze-Out," the one and only song on the album with a distinct R&B feel. Although "E Street Shuffle" contains the band's name in the title, "Tenth Avenue Freeze-Out" (which refers in title to a Belmar avenue that intersects E Street) became the band's signature number. Even though the song is perhaps the least interesting of the eight songs, it lyrically calls out Clarence Clemons ("the Big Man joined the band") while musically announcing the arrival of Steve Van Zandt, who arranged the song's soulful horn section.

Two other songs, "Night" and "Born to Run," dip back into classic car culture. "Night" is a feverishly up-tempo track, sung in second person, of an Average Joe hot-rodder who endures his nine-to-five job until he can go out at night to drag race against "chromed invaders" on the circuit, and can search for his as-of-yet unfound love waiting for him somehow, somewhere.

A similar story is told in the album's title track. Again, the narrator works a dreary job by day, sweating out the "runaway American dream," while at night he joins a "chrome-wheeled fuel-injected" community. Of all the album's songs, "Born to Run" most embodies adolescent romanticism. The singer's car becomes a sexual metaphor around which he invites the girl, Wendy, to wrap her legs and strap her hands. Wendy's name renders the singer a rock 'n' roll version of Peter Pan, calling to her to run away with him. He wants Wendy to help him discover if his youthful notions of love are real, and in the best tradition of adolescent overstatement, he pledges his desire to die with her in the street, locked in an "everlasting kiss," and to love her "with all the madness in my soul."

"Born to Run" would become Springsteen's signature song, an accessible anthem that most compactly captured the themes of the sympathetic loser yearning for romance and escape. The characters of "Born to Run"—the title itself invoking the 1970s punk motto "born to lose"—are "tramps." Their lives, we're told, are marked by "sadness," and although the singer promises Wendy they will one day reach a romantic promised land, he can't tell her when. As in "Night," the theme of escape in "Born to Run" is undercut by a feeling of desperation.

Two songs after the tramps of "Born to Run" we move to the two-bit hoods of "Meeting Across the River." The unnamed singer plans an unnamed illegal deal with his partner in crime, Eddie. (The song's original title, "The Heist," and the thousands of dollars promised to the singer imply grand larceny.) The song's plot along with Randy Brecker's slick trumpet line implies the world of film noir, but these are not big-time characters. The singer warns Eddie that they can't "blow this one" and says that the word is out: this is their "last chance." The singer's instructions for Eddie to stuff something in his pocket to make it *look* like he's concealing a gun, and to change his shirt to convey the style they usually don't have, further convey the desperate acts of losers. The singer even warns Eddie to play it cool *or else*; if their job falls through, they'll be looking for Eddie, too.

Again, Springsteen renders his loser sympathetic. The singer of "Meeting" is trying to salvage his relationship with his girlfriend, who's threatened to leave him. We can assume she realizes that she's with a loser—especially since he's just hocked her radio for cash—and the planned heist is his last chance to impress her. He dreams of returning with the $2,000 payment he's been promised, and—more importantly—throwing it on the bed for her to see. "She'll see this time I wasn't talking/Then I'm gonna go out walking," he vows, convincing himself more than he convinces us. Given the song's title, the reference to "the tunnel," and the fact that Springsteen was still writing from a New Jersey perspective (he wrote most of the songs on *Born to Run* while living in West Long Branch), we emerge with the image of hoods from the New Jersey suburbs headed for a job in New York, a town too big for them. (Remember, New York is where Kitty ran off to when she was lured by her big-city lover.) If we had to take a guess, it would be that the singer and Eddie meet their end on the other side of the Hudson.

As Brian Hiatt reflects, "the song's tale of a Jersey guy risking it all for a big score in the city hit close to home." "By that time we'd been counted out, and it probably had something to do with that—a feeling I had about myself," Springsteen remembers. "It was that New York/New Jersey, big-time/small-time thing."[47]

"Meeting Across the River" serves as a prelude to the album's closing song, "Jungleland," which plants us firmly on that other side of the Hudson. It's hard not to notice similarities between the song and the one that closed *Wild*, "New York City Serenade." Both songs are extended opuses—grand finales set amidst the urban jungle. But whereas "Serenade" was more mood piece than narrative, this street-urchin story of "Jungleland" more closely resembles "Incident on 57th Street" and "Zero and Blind Terry," though it's superior to either song.

Roy Bittan's piano is the driving force of the song, as it is throughout much of *Born to Run.* "Jungleland" is introduced by Suki Lahav's bittersweet violin, accompanied by Bittan on piano. Lahav provides a classical element that helps create the sacred-within-the-profane motif that Springsteen had explored throughout his albums to date. Then, Lahav gives way to Bittan, who explores note sequences within a single chord. Only then does Springsteen enter to tell the story of the Magic Rat, a gang member who drives in from Jersey and flees the cops in Harlem with his unnamed "barefoot girl." After an organ rings out to underscore the holy silence found "From the churches to the jails" (again, juxtaposing the sacred and the profane), the band kicks in with its rock components of guitar and drums. As the gang members gather on the street at midnight, Springsteen again summons a theatrical sensibility: "Man there's an opera out on the turnpike/There's a ballet being fought out in the alley."

Bittan pounds out a fervent chord progression at the song's midpoint, and after the lovers disappear for the moment, Clemons's sax provides a soulful bridge to the song's conclusion. It's a stirring solo, and one that Springsteen took great care in working on with Clemons. Mike Appel remembers Springsteen "literally going through [singing] every note" for 16 hours with Clemons in the studio. Clemons describes it as "the most intricate solo" in all his years with the E Street Band.[48]

After Clemons's solo, the Rat and the barefoot girl are reduced to two hearts beating beneath the city. Her "whispers of soft refusal" give way to "surrender." It's unclear whether she is conceding to passion or, as with Spanish Johnny and Maria in "Incident," his leaving (or both). In the end, he does leave her to return to the streets and he is gunned down. He's carried away in an ambulance as she unknowingly turns off her bedroom light and goes to bed. (Unlike Spanish Johnny and Puerto Rican Jane, these lovers won't be meeting later on Lover's Lane.) Beneath a "wordless howl" that Springsteen improvised at the last minute,[49] Bittan delivers an ascendant chord progression to a resolution—the first and only in the song's nearly 10 minutes—bringing song and album to a transcendent ending.

Quite simply, *Born to Run* is a masterpiece. Its vocals don't soar as melodically as Orbison's, its lyrics are more Leonard Bernstein than Bob Dylan, and its musical core is derived from piano lines, not guitar riffs. But the record's elements were a recipe for a breakthrough blockbuster. The album not only gave Springsteen his first hit record, it transformed seventies rock music while pushing the boundaries of what a singer-songwriter could achieve within the rock genre. Hilburn writes,

> *Born to Run* breathed with the same kind of discovery that made Elvis Presley's *Sun Sessions* and Bob Dylan's *Highway 61 Revisited*, the two most important rock albums before it. Listening to all three works, you feel present at the forging of a major artistic vision. You sense the artist's excitement at finding something within himself that he hadn't known was there until it burst forth in the studio.[50]

The album made such a splash that both *Newsweek* and then *Time* came calling for feature stories. Appel had a rule of allowing interviews only to magazines that promised cover stories. Surprisingly—and unknowingly—both magazines agreed, and Springsteen appeared on the cover of the October 27 issue of both *Time* and *Newsweek*. While Appel had achieved an unprecedented publicity coup, to many, the dual covers smacked of yet more media hype.

To make matters worse, the *Newsweek* feature focused more on Springsteen as Hype than it did on Springsteen as Artist. The agenda of the piece, penned by Maureen Orth, with researchers Janet Huck and Peter S. Greenberg, is easily seen in the title of the piece, "Making of a Rock Star." For Orth and her colleagues, Springsteen was more media creation than rock 'n' roll salvation. The article focused on Columbia's promotional efforts and also cited a piece that Henry Edwards wrote for *The*

New York Times in October, titled "If there Hadn't Been a Bruce Springsteen, Then the Critics Would Have Made Him Up." (In his transparently
cynical article, Edwards dubbed Springsteen's lyrics an "effusive jumble,"
his melodies "second-hand or undistinguished" and his performance
"tedious" and cited "vigorous promotion" as the secret to the album's
success.[51]) The *Newsweek* piece reported that "some people are asking
whether Bruce Springsteen will be the biggest superstar or the biggest
hype of the '70s," and while stating that "most of the country...isn't
even aware of Springsteen yet," in the same breath it mentioned a "backlash" against Springsteen. "Women think he's sexy and it's likely he'll end
up with a movie contract," said Orth. She quoted an envious Warner
Brothers executive who described Springsteen as being merely "a kid with
a beard in his 20s from New Jersey who happens to sing songs," and who
lacked the stage presence of Elton John, couldn't sing any "sweeter" than
James Taylor, and couldn't write lyrics any "heavier" than Dylan's. "Hypes,"
the article concluded, "are as American as Coca-Cola so perhaps—in one
way or another—Bruce Springsteen *is* the Real Thing."[52]

Jay Cocks's piece in *Time*, "Rock's New Sensation," considered Springsteen with less cynicism and gave more space to a discussion of the
artist's work.

> His music is primal, directly in touch with all the impulses of wild hu-
> mor and glancing melancholy, street tragedy and punk anarchy that
> have made rock the distinctive voice of a generation....Casting
> Springsteen as a rebel in a motorcycle jacket is easy enough...but it
> ignores a whole other side of his importance and of his music....The
> sound is layered over with the kind of driving instrumental cushioning
> that characterized the sides Phil Spector produced in the late '50s and
> '60s. The lyrics burst with nighthawk poetry.[53]

Famed rock journalist Lester Bangs profiled Springsteen in the November 1975 issue of *Creem* with a brilliant article titled "Hot Rod Rumble
in the Promised Land." Writing from the Midwest, where Springsteen (he
noted) had yet to even tour, Bangs observed that "you can smell the backlash crisp as burnt rubber in the air." Yet Bangs seems to have understood
what Orth did not, arguing that Springsteen would "withstand the reac-
tionaries" because "street-punk image, bardic posture and all, Bruce

Springsteen is an American archetype, and BORN TO RUN will probably be the finest record released this year."

Although Bangs felt that Springsteen was not an "innovator," he noted that Springsteen's genius lies in the way in which he "rethought traditional sounds and stances" of early rock, teen rebel movies, and beat poetry. And although Bangs acknowledged a friend's criticism that Springsteen's depictions of New York City were more romanticized than realistic, he argued that perhaps that was the point behind Springsteen's rock vision: "Springsteen's landscapes of urban desolation are all height- ened, on fire, alive. His characters act in symbolic gestures, bigger than life [and his] music is majestic and passionate with no apologies." For Bangs, *Born to Run* was the work of a "gifted urchin cruising at the peak of his powers and feeling his oats as he gets it right, that chord, and the last word ever on a hoodlum's nirvana."[54]

In mid-October, Springsteen and the E Street Band touched off the West Coast wing of the tour with four dates at The Roxy in Los Angeles. That first night, celebrities abounded: Jack Nicholson, Jackson Browne, Wolfman Jack, a young Robert De Niro. At one of the dates, while playing "Quarter to Three" in the encore, Springsteen playfully taunted the audi- ence, asking: "Are you talking to me?" According to some sources (in- cluding Eric Alterman in *It Ain't No Sin to Be Glad You're Alive*) this bit of audience interplay became the inspiration for De Niro's famously impro- vised mirror soliloquy ("Are you talkin' ta me?") in the film he was shoot- ing at the time, Martin Scorsese's *Taxi Driver*.[55]

The following month, the band brought their act across the Atlantic for the first time. London's Hammersmith Odeon was the site of their European debut on November 18. The skeptical English critics were measured in their reception but the British fans went home happy; cov- ering the event for *Creem*, Simon Frith wrote, "He arrived as the most hyped-up American act in ages. . . . The audience clapped and cheered a lot but the critics were cagey."[56] According to the E Street Band mem- bers, Springsteen was angered by the hype for the event and was disap- pointed at the end of the night, apparently thinking he had bombed in his first English performance. (See my Afterword.) But after one-night stands in Sweden and Holland, they returned a week later to the Ham- mersmith Odeon on November 24 for an encore performance that, by most reports, blew the first one away. Then they brought it all back home to the United States, where the *Born to Run* tour concluded in Philadelphia on New Year's Eve.

The popular and critical acclaim for *Born to Run* would not be fleeting. Rankings of the all-time best popular music albums often place it in the Top 10. In 2003, a *ZagatSurvey* poll named it the best all-around compact disc recording in history.

Today, it is hard to evaluate the breakthrough that *Born to Run* was without being colored by hindsight. But it did not make his career. In the years that followed, Springsteen would encounter struggles within his own camp. And by the time he released his next record, his writing had evolved, delving deeper into the runaway American dreams that he first began to explore on *Born to Run*. From this point on, the writer of "Rosalita" and "Thunder Road" and "Born to Run" would begin to explore what his characters were running from, what they were running to, and if they had anything to run to.

* **4** *

Running into the Darkness

Darkness on the Edge of Town (1978)

Every blockbuster anticipates the follow-up. When an album like *Born to Run* emerges as if out of nowhere (as it must have seemed to all but the most hardcore fans) it creates the inevitable paradox: fans look ahead to see what the artist will do to top it, even though such a feat is almost always impossible. With insight unusual to an emerging star barely in his late twenties, Springsteen seemed particularly aware of this phenomenon and deliberated long and hard on plans for his fourth album. Appel wanted Springsteen to release the almost-obligatory live album celebrating the *Born to Run* tour. Landau reportedly advised Springsteen against this, saying Springsteen should go back into the studio to record a new album and build off the success of *Born to Run*. Unfortunately for his fans, after putting out three albums in two-and-a-half years, it would be another two-and-a-half years before Springsteen released another album of any kind.

The legal troubles that occurred between Springsteen and Appel after *Born to Run* have been much documented, debated, and deconstructed in the decades that followed. The point here is not to take sides, but the fact remains that in the wake of his sudden success, Springsteen, who up to then had been careless to the point of naïveté (or naïve to the point of carelessness) regarding financial matters, began to examine his contract with Appel. When he did, the artist discovered not only did he have a paltry royalty arrangement with Appel's Laurel Canyon company, but that all debts were charged against his (but not Laurel Canyon's) royalty account, and also that Laurel Canyon, not Springsteen, owned the publishing rights to all the songs from the first three albums. Not long after making this discovery, the relationship between Appel and Springsteen fell apart. Springsteen fired Appel and sued his ex-manager for fraud and damages; Appel countersued and informed Columbia that Springsteen contractually was prohibited from recording with anyone except Appel or someone sanctioned by him. Springsteen and his label planned to move forward with the next album anyway—with Landau as producer—but Appel obtained an injunction from New York State Supreme Court judge Arnold L. Fein preventing Springsteen from recording with Landau.

Beginning in the summer of 1976—ironically, when the nation was celebrating the bicentennial of its independence—Springsteen found himself ensnared in legal proceedings as he fought for the rights to his own music. Summoned to give a deposition before Judge Fein and attorneys for both sides, Springsteen gave a passionate testimony regarding ownership of his songs, stating his belief that Appel had promised Springsteen would retain intellectual property rights. Though certainly concerned with financial realities, Springsteen seems to have been even more outraged by the principle of the issue—that someone *else* could own the rights to his own creative outlet—than by the monetary implications. Springsteen testified:

> I don't own a fucking thing that I ever wrote. He told me . . . he told me I
> had half my publishing, and he lied to me. . . . I don't own any of that.
> Man, that is my blood in the thing. That is mine. I lived every fucking line
> of that song. Do you understand that? I lived every fucking line of that.[1]

In reading transcripts of the deposition, it becomes clear that Springsteen was out of his element in court, something which Appel's attorney, Leonard Marks, must have recognized. As Marks asked a series of question that seem intended to portray the artist as a pampered rock star, Springsteen became more and more frustrated with the implications of these questions. Eventually, Springsteen began to direct his anger toward Marks in emotional outbursts: "You can't use your name. How would you like to tell you that [sic]? You can't use your name."[2] Reaching a boiling point, he said: "I tell you one thing, you got a lot of fucking balls to sit there about my breaking my fucking word when he did to me, he fucking lied to me up and down."[3]

At one point, Fein had Springsteen accompany him to the judge's chambers. Although no transcripts exist of their discussion, Fein reportedly asked Springsteen if he realized that everything he was saying was going on the record and could be read back before a jury—of which the otherwise streetwise Springsteen was unaware. Afterwards, Springsteen controlled his temper, and the deposition proceeded in a more restrained atmosphere.

Barred from the studio, the band did the only thing they could do— they kept touring, though on a low budget. (Their 1977 dates took on the nickname of the "Chicken Scratch Tour.") Their touring kept them from falling off the map entirely, but it was a dark time for Springsteen. He reached a low point backstage before his concert at Detroit's Masonic Temple Auditorium in February 1977, when he was gripped with a terrifying feeling: he didn't want to go onstage. "At that moment," he told Robert Hilburn, "I could see how people get into drinking or into drugs, because the one thing you want at a time like that is to be distracted— in a big way."[4] Having fought so long to make it, Springsteen was suddenly confronted with the downside of having one's wishes come true.

Ultimately, *Springsteen v. Appel* did not go before a jury, as Springsteen and Appel reached a settlement in the spring of 1977. Essentially, Springsteen bought his way out of the Laurel Canyon contract. Appel received a sum of money plus a royalty split on the first three albums; in turn, Springsteen now owned the rights to his songs.

That June, Springsteen and the E Street Band entered the Atlantic Recording Studios in New York, this time with Landau acting as producer. On the first night, Springsteen laid down demos for roughly 20 new songs that he had stockpiled in the nearly three years since *Born to Run*. During their extraordinary run of performances in support of *Born to Run*, the band had debuted a number of new songs, including one song ("Something in the Night") that would eventually appear on the fourth album, and several others ("Rendezvous," "The Promise," "Frankie," "Don't Look Back," "Because the Night") that would be recorded during that album's sessions.

Springsteen and the band had dipped frequently into classic rock 'n' roll and R&B covers on stage. Keep in mind that this was the area of arena rock and album-oriented radio. Mid-seventies rock radio was dominated by blues-infused heavy metal and the excesses of progressive "art rock." Meanwhile, American bands like Kansas and Styx were spreading a form of catchy yet often pretentious "heartland" rock. At the same time, the emergence of punk rock on both sides of the Atlantic offered an apocalyptic view of rock 'n' roll as a dying, even quaint musical form. Yet Springsteen, the once-dubbed future of rock 'n' roll, remained charmingly if anachronistically dedicated to the rock roots of his childhood. He and the band covered such songs as Manfred Mann's "Pretty Flamingo," the soul standard "Raise Your Hand," and a medley of hits by Mitch Ryder and the Detroit Wheels. The "Detroit Medley" would become a staple of the live performances in the late seventies.

In one performance in February 1977, the E Street Band was joined by Ronnie Spector and Flo & Eddie to perform some classic Ronnettes tunes. Back in 1975 after *Born to Run* had hit, Springsteen had met Ronnie's ex-husband, the legendary Phil Spector, during one tour swing through Los Angeles. Marsh tells us that Spector invited Springsteen to watch a recording session for a new single by late-fifties/early sixties teen doo-wop idol Dion. Reportedly, Spector introduced Springsteen to the assembled studio musicians by saying, "Bruce Spring*street* is here. He's on the cover of *Time* and he's born to run, so let's show him how to make a record."[5] He also told Springsteen, ironically, that *Born to Run*— an album whose sound was inspired by Spector's own production style—sounded muddy, and that he (Spector) could fix that if he were Springsteen's producer—and, he said, Springsteen would sell five times as many records.[6]

The pairing never came about. Marsh suggests that those around Springsteen might have warned the singer about Spector's reputation for taking forever to produce an album. Or, just as likely, Springsteen simply might have found Spector too weird to work with. Although it is tempting to imagine what a Springsteen-Spector alliance might have yielded, we recognize in hindsight that Springsteen already was moving in a new direction musically, toward writing songs that would not have been conducive to the heightened romanticism of Spector's layered soundscapes. "Musically I wanted the [next] record to sound leaner and less grand than *Born to Run*. That sound wouldn't suit these songs or the people I was now writing about," Springsteen later wrote.[7]

Indeed, the characters that he was now writing about were, like Springsteen, a little older and a lot less youthful in their view of the world around them. Two hits that he had covered while touring, both by The Animals, reflected this new worldview. Springsteen told Will Percy in 1995:

> Up until the late seventies, when I started to write songs that had to do with class issues, I was influenced more by music like the Animals' "We Gotta Get Out of This Place," or "It's My Life (And I'll Do What I Want)"—sort of class-conscious pop records that I'd listen to.... They said something to me about my own experience of exclusion. I think that's been a theme that's run through much of my writing: the politics of exclusion. My characters aren't really antiheroes. Maybe that makes them old-fashioned in some way. They're interested in being included, and they're trying to figure out what's in their way. [8]

As we have seen in glimpses on *Born to Run*—in the weary, workaday world of "Night" and "Born to Run"—Springsteen's move toward a blue-collar class consciousness was already developing. In the songs he wrote for his next album, that class consciousness would come to the foreground. Springsteen explains: "I had a reaction to my own good fortune. I asked myself new questions. I felt a sense of accountability to the people I'd grown up alongside of. Also . . . I [had] stood the chance of losing much of what I had worked for and accomplished. All of this led to the turn my writing took."[9]

Perhaps the biggest indication that Springsteen's fourth album would be different was the song, "The Promise," a slow ballad that became popular on the tour supporting the fourth album, even though Springsteen had chosen to leave it off the album. The song presents a reassessment of Springsteen's lyrical world, recalling familiar names: Johnny, Billy, Terry. He mentions "Thunder Road" by name, recalling the song's road-bound romanticism and redemption, only to negate it in the same line: "There's somethin' dying on the highway tonight." The full-band version of the song is substantially different from the stripped-down version recorded for the 1998 *Tracks* box set; it proceeds deliberately, wistfully, almost mournfully. In a nod to the car culture celebrated on *Born to Run*, the singer remembers a Challenger he built by himself but (significantly in the Springsteen universe!) eventually had to sell when he needed money. The song's final line is a reminder of the dreams he and his friends once had, but which didn't come true: "Thunder Road . . . we were gonna take it all and throw it all away."

Reportedly, one reason Springsteen left "The Promise" off the forthcoming album was that listeners had assumed it was about his lawsuit with Appel. ("I don't write songs about lawsuits," he said at the time.)[10] It was not the only track from those sessions that would emerge with distinction from the cutting-room floor. There was also "Fire," a 16-line seriocomic ditty in which the singer tries to convince a reluctant lover to give into their passion.

Springsteen wrote the song for Elvis Presley (one bootlegged studio take of the song features Springsteen singing in a decidedly Elvis snarl) and even mailed a tape of it to Graceland. But it was not to be—Presley passed away on August 16, 1977. Days later, Lester Bangs wrote, "We will never again agree on anything as we agreed on Elvis." Greil Marcus would later concur but noted one possible exception:

> Rock and roll now has less an audience than a series of increasingly discrete audiences, and those various audiences ignore each other. . . . The fact that the most adventurous music of the day seems to have taken up residence in the darker corners of the marketplace contradicts the idea of rock and roll as an aggressively popular culture that tears up boundaries of race, class, geography and (oh yes) music. . . . A concert by Bruce Springsteen offers many thrills, and one is that he performs as if none of the above is true.[11]

Presley might very well have had yet another number 1 hit with the tailor-made "Fire"; instead, The Pointer Sisters took their version of the song to number 2.

A number of songs from the new sessions proved to be good material for other artists. "Because the Night," a blistering, seize-the-night anthem, became a Top 20 hit for punk rocker Patti Smith (who added lyrics to the unfinished demo that Jimmy Iovine had given her). Springsteen performed the song with Smith at a cameo at CBGB on December 30, 1977, and it remains a concert favorite among fans to this day. In 1993, Natalie Merchant's 10,000 Maniacs covered it during their appearance on *MTV Unplugged.*

Southside Johnny and the Asbury Jukes covered two songs from these sessions: "Hearts of Stone," a saxophone-drenched torch song about the "last dance" of an affair ("I can't talk now, I'm not alone/So put your ear close to the phone") and "Talk to Me," a jumping rocker with a self-explanatory message. Both songs appear on Johnny and the Jukes' *Hearts of Stone,* which *Rolling Stone* ranked among the Top 100 albums from 1967 to 1987. "Rendezvous" was a signature tune for the Greg Kihn Band years before the E Street Band's own version appeared on *Tracks.* The Knack covered "Don't Look Back," a great, straight-ahead Springsteen rocker that appears on both *Tracks* and on the E Street Band's reunion concert album *Live in New York City* (2001). "Jeannie Needs a Shooter," a quirky rumination on sexual healing that Springsteen cowrote with Warren Zevon (and recorded on his own in the studio), ended up on Zevon's 1980 album *Bad Luck Streak in Dancing School.*

The sessions for the fourth album represented the most prolific period in Springsteen's career, not just in the sheer number of songs he cut—all told, Springsteen and the E Street Band worked out a reported three dozen tracks during the studio sessions in 1977 and 1978[12]—but also in their quality. One that would rival "The Promise" in reputation as a legendary lost track was "Frankie," a beautiful song that harkens back to the layered sound of *Born to Run* and to the dying-town romanticism of *E Street Shuffle.* "Walk softly tonight, little stranger," the narrator tells his girlfriend. "Yeah, into these shadows we're passing through. . . . You make all my dream worlds come true." (As with "The Promise," a later version of the song would appear on *Tracks.*)

Springsteen also wrote and recorded three songs that he ultimately decided to save for his subsequent album. There was a playful bar-band rocker, "Sherry Darling"; "Independence Day," a son's parting statement of defiance to his father; and "Drive All Night," a painfully wrought song of desperate love, which James Mangold selected for use in his 1995 film *Copland.* To go along with these tracks, there was the stark "Iceman" and the playful "Give the Girl a Kiss" (both on *Tracks*) as well as countless others that have yet to see the light of day on an official release: a Spector-ish soul number titled "Get That Feeling"; the raucous "Break Out"; a Buddy Holly–inspired number, "Outside Lookin' In"; the deliberate, romantic ballad "Spanish Eyes"; and the haunting "Preacher's Daughter."

It could be argued that up to 20 songs that did *not* make the album merited inclusion. None of the above tracks (and there were more still) made the cut for the fourth album. Why withhold so many potential hits from an audience starved for a follow-up record? As Springsteen's behavior before and after *Born to Run* testify—his seeming obliviousness to financial matters, his refusal to sanction concert merchandise, his shunning sponsorship offers—he remained dedicated to a career shaped more by vision than by commerce. In 1978, Springsteen told Dave Marsh, "I got an album's worth of pop songs, like 'Rendezvous' and early English-style stuff. . . . But I didn't feel it was the right time to do that, and I didn't want to sacrifice the intensity of the album."[13]

Landau surmised, "When you consider he had, but didn't use songs like 'Fire' and 'Because the Night,' you've got to assume he didn't really want [his next record] to be that big."[14] Cynics might laugh at his manager's assessment, but Springsteen had been so disenchanted with the *Born to Run* hype and backlash that when he finalized the tracks for his next album, he asked Columbia to release it without any accompanying publicity. His idea was to have the album drop in stores one day, without any advance notice to fans or the media. (Eventually, he would compromise and allow Columbia to promote the album in select locations throughout the country.)

As he would later remember, "Right after *Born to Run* I asked myself, 'What do I really want?'" His answer: "'I want to be a rocker, a musician, not a rock & roll star.' There's a difference." A decade earlier, he might have laughed at the artist who considered such "problems"; but now, having broken through, he discovered the double-edged sword that comes with pop culture success: "The bigger you get the more responsibility you have. So you have got to keep constant vigilance. You got to keep your strength up because if you lose it, then you're another jerk who had his picture on the cover."[15]

Having endured the fallout of a publicity blitz, a media backlash, and the possibility of losing his own body of work, Springsteen looked to exert vigilant, perhaps even obsessive control over his artistic output. He demanded that the band work with him through countless takes of songs in the studio. According to the *Backstreets* compilation book, four songs selected for the fourth album required more than 40 takes each; four others took more than 20.[16]

The album almost came out in the fall of 1977 carrying the title *Badlands*, but then Springsteen decided it wasn't ready. The band went back into the studio, and songs were reworked into the following year. Eventually, Springsteen identified 10 songs for inclusion on the album, selecting the ones that, in his mind, best comprised the story he wanted to tell at that point in his career. "I wanted to put out the stuff that I felt had the most substance and yet was still an album."[17]

With some publicity, though nowhere near as much as had announced *Born to Run*, Springsteen's fourth album, *Darkness on the Edge of Town*, was released on June 2, 1978. The album cover, designed by Andrea Klein, visually announced a new Springsteen. The package is decidedly bleak: the title is presented in a typewriter font, and the Frank Stefanko photographs on both the front and back show Springsteen without a hint of his charisma—sans facial growth and with unkempt hair, staring at the camera with a disinterested, even off-putting expression on his face, looking (ironically) like a jerk on the cover—a punk version of Al Pacino in *Dog Day Afternoon*. Old-fashioned wallpaper and white venetian blinds serve as the background.

Paradoxically, this was a newer and older Springsteen, far removed from the back-alley ballets and nighthawk poetry of *Born to Run*. Considering lyrics and song structures together, the transition between *Born to Run* and *Darkness* is almost as striking as that of any two consecutively released albums in Springsteen's career. Granted, the release of 1982's *Nebraska*—an acoustic album sandwiched in between two made-for-stadium-tour albums, *The River* and *Born in the U.S.A.*—would represent a striking (and controversial) shift in musical genres, but lyrically, it could be argued that any song from one of these three albums could fit nicely onto one of the other two albums. Meanwhile, nothing on *Darkness* would fit on any of its three predecessors. Nor could Springsteen have written any of its songs until that particular point in his career.

The 10 songs on *Darkness* (along with the outtakes from the *Darkness* sessions) represent a movement toward the more succinct songwriting style toward which Springsteen had been striving. Eight of the 10 songs are less than five minutes long—a significant fact for a recording artist known for showstoppers such as "Kitty's Back," "Rosalita," and "Jungleland." Production-wise, the songs are also sonically stripped down when compared to the faux-Spector sound of *Born to Run*. Solo instrumentation often stands on its own, and musical phrases come and go, often amidst a silent background, without echo and reverb. Contrasted with Lopez's free-form eccentrics and Carter's "Born to Run" gymnastics, Max Weinberg's drums provide what amounts to a systolic and diastolic heartbeat throughout critical moments of *Darkness*. Even Springsteen's vocal style seems to have changed, at times sounding more meditative than passionate on songs such as "Racing in the Street," "Factory," and "Darkness on the Edge of Town."

At the same time, musically speaking *Darkness* is Springsteen's fiercest record to that point in his career—and his first album that is, song-for-song, a traditional rock album. Neither *Greetings* nor *Wild* can be considered rock albums, and while *Born to Run* is unquestionably a rock album, its piano-and-saxophone core and theatrical moments transcend the genre. *Darkness* presents a more conventional ten-song, five-song-a-side lineup, with songs like "Badlands," "Adam Raised a Cain," and "Candy's Room" that are driven by rock guitar; meanwhile, a number of critics have noted the reduced role of Clarence Clemons, whose work on the album has been described more in terms of cameos than solos. *Darkness* is the album in which Springsteen leaves R&B behind and plants himself firmly in the world of hard rock, seventies style.

Lyrically, *Darkness* shows a movement away from the grand narrative voice of earlier Springsteen. The voice of these songs is less that of a storyteller—only "Racing in the Street" truly tells anything resembling a story with a plot line—and more a singer-songwriter, working within the standard verse-chorus structure of popular rock song. Or as Hilburn observes,

> [*Darkness*] represented his first step toward a leaner, more accessible writing style. "Factory," for instance, has little of the flashy literary sweep of his early work.... Just as "Spirit in the Night" was a forerunner of his narratives, "Factory" was the precursor of sparse yet riveting tunes like "Stolen Car" and "Highway Patrolman."[18]

Whereas the choruses on past albums sometimes serve as speed bumps to the runaway lyrics, the choruses on *Darkness* stand as the rallying cries of the songs. Indeed, Springsteen admitted that these songs tended to emerge from the chorus outward: "The songs [on *Darkness*] were difficult to write. I remember spending hours trying to come up with a single verse. 'Badlands,' 'Prove It All Night,' and 'Promised Land' all had a chorus but few lyrics."[19] While a song like "New York City Serenade" had been an early break from plot-driven narrative, the songs on *Darkness*—with rousing verses on enduring the metaphorical badlands, affirming a belief in a metaphorical "Promised Land," and a masculine challenge to prove it all night—are more anthemic than poetic.

Also, the first three songs on the album are all, at least partially, written in the second person. Until this point, Springsteen's songs had almost always had an element of "I," "we," or "they"—that is, the voice was the protagonist, cast member, or third-person narrator. But here, Springsteen begins to sing to a general, proverbial "you" standing in for his audience. He dispenses advice in "Badlands," warning us against wasting time, and sings of the price we have to pay. In "Adam Raised a Cain," he positions the listener in the role of a son battling with his father. In "Something in the Night," he tells us we are "born with nothing" and—in lines that recall his legal disputes with Appel—observes, "Soon as you've got something/They send someone to take it away." The I/we/they still remains an important element throughout *Darkness*, but the emergence of a "you" is telling because it creates an interesting paradox: the listener is drawn into the events of the songs, yet (at the risk of invoking literary deconstruction, which has no place in rock 'n' roll) the recognition of a "you" also serves to draw a distinction—and, thus, a distance—between artist and audience. Eric Alterman argues:

> The "you" addressed on *Darkness* is always singular, never plural, much less communal. Hence the response to every defeat, every broken heart, and every dashed dream is always the same: the individual must simply will him- or herself the strength to go on.... There is the lone individual and there is the void: the "darkness on the edge of town."[20]

As Springsteen himself noted: "On the old stuff, there's a lot of characters and groups of people and as it goes along it thins out; people drop by the wayside until on *Born to Run;* it's essentially two; it's a guy and a girl. And then on *Darkness,* there's a lotta times when there's just one. In the end, on the last song, there's just one."[21]

If *Darkness* is less communal, it also offers less of the sense of place that characterizes his first three albums. *Greetings, Wild,* and *Born to Run* are all grounded in the Jersey Shore/Metro area. But as Daniel Wolff notes, the setting of the first two songs, "Badlands" and "Adam Raised a Cain," could be "any place that's racked with fear and in any family where a son inherits a father's sins." Wolff further notes that, after briefly returning to Asbury Park (identified with a reference to Kingsley Avenue) in the third song, "Something in the Night," the rest of the album "refers to other parts of the United States—the Utah desert, little towns in Louisiana—or, more often, leaves the landscape generic. Springsteen's 'streets of fire' run anywhere people are tricked and lied to; his 'mansions of pain' exist wherever the factory whistle blows."[22]

Springsteen does still deal with notions of escapism on *Darkness.* "I wanna spit in the face of these badlands," he sings in "Badlands," and he invokes notions of the ultimate Exodus in "The Promised Land." But it's interesting that the singer of "The Promised Land" insists that he's singing of a place—if only metaphorically—that he believes in. Again, we risk hitting the deconstruction button, but it's fair to note that the very act of insisting upon the existence of a promised land also acknowledges doubt—no longer is it assumed that there's something to which we can run. Wolff notes:

> Though he borrows the title of "The Promised Land" from Chuck Berry, Springsteen's song isn't nearly as specific—or as cheerful. Berry played on the idea that the payoff to the American Dream lay west, in California. Two rock & roll generations later, Springsteen defines his promised land in the negative: where you *aren't* "lost and broken hearted," where your dreams *don't* "tear you apart," where your blood *doesn't* "run cold."[23]

As Guterman notes, "The word believe shows up in both 'Badlands' and 'The Promised Land': The singer believes despite little evidence to justify it."[24]

The Promised Land-as-fraudulent myth motif comes straight out of John Steinbeck's *The Grapes of Wrath,* which John Ford adapted for the screen in 1940. Springsteen had developed an interest in American cinema, and especially the work of John Ford, including *Grapes*, *The Searchers*, and *The Man Who Shot Liberty Valance*. As he told Robert Hilburn:

> I became fascinated with John Ford movies, the fact that they were all westerns. I watched the early ones and the late ones. It was fascinating to me how he'd film the same scene—a dance scene or a confrontation—and make it different in every picture.
>
> There was a lot of continuity in his work. I liked that. You . . . go back to the previous movie and have a clearer understanding of where he was coming from. What he was saying in this film was changing the shape of what he said in another one.[25]

Fittingly, the lyrics of *Darkness* paint a number of scenes that have a cinematic quality. The album's first track, "Badlands," owes its title to the 1973 Terrence Malick film of the same name. In "Adam Raised a Cain" (a song inspired by another film adaptation of a Steinbeck novel, *East of Eden*) we see the father standing in the doorway as his son stands in the rain. The protagonist of "Something in the Night" rides down the avenue alone at night—much like the taxi driver in the discarded track "City at Night." We meet the heroine of "Candy's Room" at the end of a dark hallway, her pretty face concealing sadness like a postmodern damsel in distress. "The Promised Land" describes a "dark cloud rising from the desert floor." The men answering the factory bell in "Factory" could be characters out of Elia Kazan's *On the Waterfront*. The title track, which closes the album, includes the singer's plea for his ex-lover to meet him at a distinctly film noirish location: a spot under the bridge at the edge of town.

That "darkness" found at the edge of town is indeed reminiscent of the visual style of film noir, as Springsteen himself notes in *Songs*. A noir film, Robert Mitchum's *Thunder Road* (1958), had inspired the title of *Born to Run*'s opening track, but the film is, despite its bootlegging characters, more fatalistic than romantic. The film's vision is most effectively summarized in the exchange between Mitchum's character, Lucas Doolin, a bootlegger, and his singer-girlfriend played by Keely Smith. When she tells him, "I just want to be normal people. I just want to be somebody," he responds, "You are, honey. That's the big trouble. You are somebody."

The "big trouble" of being "somebody"—literally, living—is felt throughout *Darkness,* perhaps most poignantly by the girl in "Racing in the Street" who "hates for just being born." Film historians have noted that the origins of the film noir genre are rooted in French existentialism— perhaps about as far as you can get from Springsteen's early seventies romanticism. Before any philosophy department adjuncts go writing papers on Springsteen and Sartre, we must take note that the burden of existence felt by the characters on *Darkness* is decidedly religious in nature. On his fourth album, Springsteen (always the good lapsed Catholic) states that "it ain't no sin to be glad you're alive," speaks of washing sins from our hands, references the biblical Adam and Cain, alludes to "the fire we was born in" and the need to wash sins from our hands, and describes angels walking through streets of hellfire. In his *VH1 Storytellers* performance, he even hints that the story of Jesus' crucifixion can be seen symbolically as a "darkness on the edge of town."[26]

In the guitar-blitzing "Adam Raised a Cain," the singer reminds us, "In the Bible Cain slew Abel/and East of Eden he was cast." As in the novel—and the film that cast James Dean as the protagonist—the song portrays a contentious father-son relationship. Again, the lyrics work in a series of images, the most powerful one being the father, who spent his life working "for nothing but the pain" and is left to walk "empty rooms looking for something to blame." The situation depicted is more complex than that of a disapproving father; the listener is told that one is already paying for somebody else's sins: "You inherit the sins, you inherit the flames."

"Factory" is a more secular companion piece to the Genesis setting of "Adam Raised a Cain." The three four-line stanzas of "Factory" depict a factory-worker father, though in calling him "Man"—capitalized, with no preceding article—Springsteen renders him an Everyman character, one of many who work in "mansions of fear [and] pain." The line "Factory takes his hearing, factory gives him life" describes a grim cycle; Man's job in the factory allows him to be breadwinner for his family, but it also takes up his whole life. At the end of the day, the factory workers emerge with "death in their eyes." The singer concludes, "It's the working, the working, the working life."

While both "Night" and "Born to Run" had portrayed elements of blue-collar life, it is with *Darkness* that we notice a shift in Springsteen's lyrical focus toward the "working life." As Marsh argues, "for all the cars, the violence and the searching, the dominant image of *Darkness on the Edge of Town* is labor. There are lines about working in 'Badlands,' 'Adam Raised a Cain,' 'Racing in the Street,' 'The Promised Land,' 'Factory,' and 'Prove It All Night' and in three of the other four songs, there are references to wealth or the lack of it." Marsh also notes that, for Springsteen, the most striking scene from John Ford's *The Grapes of Wrath* is of the displaced Dust Bowl farmer who wants to find out whom he can enact revenge upon for his eviction, only to find out that the offender is not a man but a "faceless corporation." "Similarly, a vague, disembodied 'they' creeps into songs like 'Something in the Night,' 'Prove It All Night,' and 'Streets of Fire' to deny people their most full-blooded possibilities."[27]

While recent biographers and critics have gone a little too far in retroactively enlisting Springsteen in the ranks of Walt Whitman and John Steinbeck, it is true that *Darkness* represents a distinct move away from the theatrical world of *Wild* and the grittily romantic streets of *Born to Run*. As Springsteen said in evaluating the album:

> I think it's less romantic—it's got more, a little more, isolation. It's sort of like I said, "Well, listen, I'm twenty-eight years old and the people in the album are around my age." I perceive 'em to be that old. And they don't know what to do. . . . There's less of a sense of a free ride than there is on *Born To Run*. There's more of a sense of: If you wanna ride, you're gonna pay. And you'd better keep riding.[28]

That last thought—"If you wanna ride, you're gonna pay. And you'd better keep riding"—encapsulates the message that one receives in listening to the *Darkness* songs. On the one hand, there is a continual reminder of the price one has to pay, either literally or (more importantly) metaphorically. In "Badlands," broken hearts are the price one pays for living a full life every day. In "Adam," the son pays for the sins of the father. "Something in the Night" tells us that the price of having "something" is the threat of someone coming to take it away. In "Candy's Room," suitors from the city trade "fancy clothes and diamond rings" for Candy's affections. (In his book on Springsteen, Alterman—doing for Candy what Pope Gregory I did for Mary Magdalene—declares her a "prostitute," though this is not necessarily clear.) The father in "Factory" loses his hearing to the incessant noise of the factory. The girl in "Prove

It All Night" is told "this ain't no dream we're living through tonight/ Girl, you want it, you take it, you pay the price." In the album's last track, the singer has lost his money and his wife; he concludes he'll "pay the cost/For wanting things that can only be found/In the darkness on the edge of town."

Lest anyone think that Springsteen has totally gone off the dark edge in this, just his fourth album, we must remember the second part of his summary statement: "And you'd better keep riding." Despite the harshness that comes out of the world of *Darkness*, a "seize the day" message emerges from beneath the album. "Badlands" brings the message that we must endure the badlands until they start "treating us good." The singer of "Prove It All Night" urges the girl to put away her dreams and face real life. The *Darkness* cast seeks the essence of life's extremes: the heat and passion of the "hidden worlds that shine," or the "things that can only be found/In the darkness on the edge of town." The cast of characters that Springsteen wrote about in this period look to find an essence of life found only in its most extreme corners. Throwing in two outtakes, the narrator of "The Iceman" wants to "go out tonight," to "find out what I got" (a line that shows up in "Badlands"), and in "Because the Night" the singer says, "Take me now as the sun descends. . . . The time has come to take this moment."

But the seize-the-day/seize-the-night message of *Darkness* emerges more as defiance than escapism. On *Born to Run*, the desire to not be "just like all the rest" was introduced with "Backstreets." On *Darkness*, the adults of "Adam" and "Factory" have spent their whole lives working and end up with nothing to show for their work except broken bodies and broken spirits. Springsteen's fourth album is the first on which he depicts his own generation by contrasting it with the previous one. The spirits in these nights run not to run away from their parents, but to keep from *being* their parents. As the son tells his father in one of the session's deleted tracks, "They ain't gonna do to me/What I watched them do to you." Keep riding, pay the cost, Springsteen seems to be telling his generation, or else it'll end up like the last.

Darkness did well, reaching number 5 on the album charts, but as Eric Alterman summarizes: "Most of the critics who loved *Born to Run* loved *Darkness* as well, but not as passionately or perhaps as innocently."[29] Critical reception was favorable though somewhat tempered. *Time* magazine said, "*Darkness* passes the romantic delirium of *Born to Run*, cuts deeper, lingers longer," and *Crawdaddy!* termed it both "unsettling" and "staggering." *Rolling Stone* argued that while the new songs were about "experienced adults, they sacrifice none of rock 'n' roll's adolescent innocence." *Creem* called it an "artful, passionate, rigorous record that walks a fine line between defeat and defiance," but bemoaned that "it might have also been a great record" if it had showed more of Springsteen's "go-for-broke recklessness."[30] The *Chicago Tribune* declared that "like its predecessor, it favors bombast over subtlety, but this time the music is almost frighteningly brutal. . . . Springsteen brandishes his guitar and voice like blowtorches."[31]

Today, *Darkness* ranks as one of Springsteen's best, an excellent album that suffers only from comparisons to the classic album that it followed. Years later, *Rolling Stone* called *Darkness* "a pivotal album [for Springsteen]: on it he put aside both the multilayered sound and the mythic cityscapes . . . shortened his songs and toughened his outlook."[32] In 2003, a *ZagatSurvey* poll ranked it the seventh most popular album of all time.

Granted, despite its fierceness and economy, the album does suffer from occasional slow moments. A song like "Racing in the Street" can seem plodding at times. Christopher Sandford notes, "*Darkness*, by turns, could be measured or curiously flat; a matt coat where *Born* was all gloss."[33] While biographer Marc Eliot is guilty of a preposterous overstatement in saying, "*Darkness* is today considered by all parties involved to be an artistic failure, the worst of all of Springsteen's albums" (an evaluation no doubt colored by the fact that his book was written "in cooperation with Mike Appel") Eliot is not unfair in saying that Springsteen "has often spoken of his wish to somehow be able to redo it."[34] In retrospect, the album might have been his most arduous to record, even more so than *Born to Run* had been. Seven years later, Springsteen commented:

> The only record I ever really . . . I can remember working really hard on . . . without a lot of feeling like I had the help of some inspiration or something was *Darkness on the Edge of Town*. I remember I just used to sit in my room like eight hours a day and I had tapes of my songs and I just worked out each song, verse by verse, real specifically.[35]

After the lengthy recording phase, Chuck Plotkin was brought in to help with Jimmy Iovine's mix. Just a month before the album came out, Springsteen decided to add a Steve Van Zandt guitar solo to one of the songs on side two, which necessitated a remix for the entire album side. As Eliot notes, the album's final mix was never satisfying to the Springsteen camp. "That record really is a shame; it didn't sound very good," Steve Van Zandt has said. "It has some of his best and most important songs, some of his best guitar playing, and a terrible production."[36]

If *Born to Run* was the album that made Springsteen on record, the *Darkness* tour was the one that established him as an enduring live performer. The band touched off its tour on May 19 in Asbury Park's Paramount Theater, two weeks before the album hit stores. Danny Federici said, "I remember we finished the record and jumped in the trucks and got on the road as soon as we could after that." Steve Van Zandt later called this period "our fightin' years. We were gonna prove something." Max Weinberg recalled:

We did a couple of tours of places that nobody plays probably even to-day, I mean way down south and in the Midwest, you know, small towns, really putting out the message that we were here to stay: Forget what you read, and forget what you might think about Bruce Springsteen and the E Street Band. When we hit that stage, we were ready to rock.[37]

Armed with songs from four albums in 1978, Springsteen and the E Street Band put together set lists that approached three hours in length, and which often consisted of two, even three encores. "The idea was that the show should be part circus, part political rally, part spiritual meeting, part dance party," Springsteen said.[38]

Dave Marsh caught up with Springsteen that summer while profiling him for *Rolling Stone*. Of the July 8 show at the Veterans Memorial Coliseum in Phoenix, Marsh would write, "It's not that it's just another fantastic show.... It goes farther than the Roxy, with all of that show's intimacy, innocence and vulnerability, but with an added factor of pandemonium.... I've never seen anything like this in such a big hall." The promotional video of "Rosalita" from that night's set, shot by Arnold Levine, effectively captures the spirit of that night, as Springsteen—equal parts Elvis Presley, James Dean, Arthur Fonzarelli—is rushed onstage by a procession of women. (Before the encores were over, Marsh counted 17 girls who had darted onto the stage seeking a kiss on the cheek.) Springsteen remarked of one girl with braces, "This little girl, couldn't have been more than fifteen. . . . And she had her tongue so far down my throat I nearly choked."[39]

After touring the Northeast in August and September, the band took a hiatus in October. In *The Ties That Bind*, Erik Flannigan suggests that Springsteen and Landau spent this time mixing tracks for a rumored live album. The recordings were, reportedly, from the August 9 performance at The Agora in Cleveland. In the era of the double-live album—just two years after *Frampton Comes Alive!* had made Peter Frampton a sudden superstar—a live set of the Agora show (which now circulates as a three-disc bootleg) could have been a blockbuster. That song list of this hypothetical album would have begun with a cover of "Summertime Blues," then "Badlands," "Spirit in the Night," "Darkness on the Edge of Town," "Factory," The Promised Land," "Prove It All Night," "Racing in the Street," "Thunder Road," "Jungleland," "Paradise by the 'C'" (an instrumental), "Fire," "Sherry Darling," Buddy Holly's "Not Fade Away," Van Morrison's "Gloria" leading into "She's the One," "Growin' Up," "Backstreets" (nearly 14 minutes long) and "Rosalita" (ditto), "4th of July, Asbury Park," "Born to Run," "Because the Night," and two R&B covers, "Raise Your Hand" and "Twist and Shout." [40]

In November, Springsteen and the band headed back across the country again. In December, they played two dates at the historic Winterland in San Francisco. The *Winterland Night* three-disc bootleg, which documents the set from the December 15 show as broadcast on San Francisco radio station KSAN, is regarded by many collectors and traders to be the ultimate Springsteen performance. While performing "Backstreets," Springsteen broke off into a pseudo-dialogue to the song's absent Terry, recalling her promises and then reminding her, "But, baby, you *lied*." He repeats "*You lied*," hanging onto the words with all the sweet self-righteousness of a jilted lover. Author Charles Cross would say of that night's version, "I think it's the best thing Springsteen has ever done, the emotional zenith to his body of work. I can't listen to it without feeling a tear coming to my eye, a tug of a raw nerve on my heart."[41]

During the Winterland show, Springsteen dedicated "Darkness on the Edge of Town" to Vietnam veteran Ron Kovic. Earlier in the tour,

Springsteen had read Kovic's autobiography, *Born on the Fourth of July.* He met Kovic soon after in Phoenix, and afterward Springsteen went to a nearby Tower Records, bought all of his records, and left them outside Kovic's hotel room. On the *Darkness* record, Springsteen wrote, "If this album can affect you half as much as your book affected me, then I will have done my job."

Ultimately, *Darkness* represents a dividing and defining line in Springsteen's career. As good as the album is—and as good as his ensuing albums are—there remains an inherent sense of loss to it all. Years later, Mike Appel would bemoan the transformation of his former client: "His more recent stuff, while drawing on Hank Williams, Roy Orbison, and the like and still making it on their own as original music, just seems too simplistic to me, devoid of the unique art form he once possessed so completely."[42] Of course, it would be easy to dismiss what Appel says as mere bitterness over a lost client, but there is something to what he says. Gone were the genre-expanding free-form epics and boundless romantic theatricality that had once defined Springsteen as a songwriter and storyteller. As Don McLeese asked in the *Chicago Reader,* "Who would have thought that all the crazy, risk-filled exhilaration of *The Wild, the Innocent, and the E Street Shuffle* would lead to the numbingly ponderous clichés of 'Racing in the Street'?"[43]

Slate's Stephen Metcalf, for one, suggests that Landau—who shunned the "avant-garde" experimentation of Jimi Hendrix, The Velvet Underground, and White Album–era Beatles in favor of the more "primitive . . . pre-Beatles" hit records—pushed Springsteen toward more conventional "guitar driven intro-verse-chorus-verse-bridge-chorus songs."[44] Fred Goodman argues, "Just how deep an impression Landau was making on Springsteen became apparent with the release of *Darkness on the Edge of Town.* Aside from cleaving to Landau's preference for rock's traditional short-song format, the album was loaded with imagery and debts to sources Landau discovered as a film critic."[45]

Regardless, the maturation of an artist is not only inevitable but necessary, and in leaving behind one mode of songwriting and exploring another, Springsteen showed that he had grown as a writer. "By the end of *Darkness,*" he later wrote, "I'd found my adult voice."[46] As Goodman writes:

> Springsteen's previous songs told stories about ex-girlfriends who had run off with street hustlers and "city dudes"; on *Darkness on the Edge of*

Town those same women still rejected him, but now they were married and fading into the anonymity of suburban life in towns with comfortable, bourgeois names like Fairview while Springsteen prowled the less predictable perimeters of that world as an outcast in search of some redemption unnamed and unknown.[47]

The album would be the touchstone for the directions that Springsteen would take in his future career. Having grown older and experienced the inevitable loss of innocence, Springsteen had less romantic notions of redemption. But his characters still made declarations like, "I ain't a boy, no, I'm a man/And I believe in a promised land." The notion of the proverbial promised land remains, even though his characters have left their youth behind.

Reviews often cited the lyrics of *Darkness* as being grim, but Springsteen disagreed. Soon after its release, he pointed to a line early on in the album's opening track, "Badlands," that spoke about believing in "the love and the hope and the faith." That "relentless" belief, he said, is "there on all four corners of the album."[48] It is this relentless need to believe, even in the darkest corners in life, that Springsteen would explore in the coming years.

✳ 5 ✳

Double Shot

The River (1980)

In September 1979, Bruce Springsteen and the E Street Band performed on consecutive nights at the MUSE (Musicians United for Safe Energy) Concerts for a Non-Nuclear Future at Madison Square Garden. Springsteen, the latest East Coast rock-guitar hero, stood out among the West Coast soft-rock lineup that included Jackson Browne, Bonnie Raitt, Linda Rondstadt, Crosby, Stills, and Nash, the Doobie Brothers, and Poco. It was a mismatched lineup, and some of his fellow performers were resentful of the disproportionate attention paid to Springsteen— the one artist who had decided not to sign the antinuclear statement released by the MUSE coalition. Bonnie Raitt, Chaka Khan, and Tom Petty and the Heartbreakers all had to deal with anticipatory chants of "Brooooooce" from the crowd during *their* performances.

When Springsteen finally walked on stage on September 22, the crowd exploded. Kit Rachlis of the *Boston Phoenix* would describe their reactions as "the most frenzied I've ever heard."[1] By all accounts, Springsteen delivered a remarkable show. The band began by ripping into the power trio from *Darkness,* "Prove It All Night," "Badlands," and "Promised Land," then debuted a new song called "The River," followed by "Sherry Darling" and then three powerhouse favorites: "Thunder Road," "Jungleland," and "Rosalita." They finished off with three fit-for-encore covers: the Zodiacs' "Stay," their Mitch Ryder medley, and Buddy Holly's "Rave On."

His second-night performance had some awkward moments. He'd turned 30 that day, a problematic age for an artist who had once embodied the youthful promise of rock 'n' roll. (He joked with the audience that perhaps he couldn't trust himself anymore—echoing the counterculture axiom that warned not to trust anyone over 30.) When presented with a birthday cake, he threw it into the audience. There was also an uncomfortable onstage exchange between Springsteen and photographer (and ex-girlfriend) Linda Goldsmith, who was trying to photograph Springsteen from the pit. But filmed performances of three songs the band performed that night would go down not only as the highlight of the film that encapsulated the concert, but as some of the most noteworthy moments of rock music ever captured on the big screen.

In the *No Nukes* film, Springsteen and the E Street Band make their way through "The River" and "Thunder Road." The series of close-ups on Springsteen during these two numbers compellingly capture his charismatic stage presence. Then, he leads the band in a frenzied performance of Gary U.S. Bonds's "Quarter to Three," dancing, strutting, and gyrating like a punk rocker possessed by the ghost of Thin Elvis. As he leaves the stage amidst the final bars of the song, the crowd has witnessed not just a concert but a pop culture *event.*

A more-than-anyone-needed triple album of the MUSE nights was released in May 1980. The album has all but been forgotten today—of all the artists included on the recording, only Springsteen and the E Street Band and Tom Petty and the Heartbreakers (an emerging Florida band with a decidedly *Darkness on the Edge of Town* feel) would go on to bigger and better. The only tracks from the collection that are played with any regularity are both from Springsteen performances: "Stay" (a duet with with Jackson Browne), and the Mitch Ryder "Detroit Medley." The medley has gone down as one of the most energetic live recordings in all of rock, helped in no small part by some editing magic that cut out some extended midsong crowd interplay that wouldn't have worked on record. Marsh argues, "Although he had already sold out three nights at the Garden on his own, although he had often played better, MUSE placed Springsteen firmly and permanently in the pantheon of American superstars."[2]

He and the E Street Band had entered the studio back in April. A decade marred by Vietnam, Watergate, and most recently a recession and energy crisis, was coming to an end. As Marsh notes, while the band was in the studio laying tracks for the fifth album, "the very gas pumps that fueled the fantasies of *Born to Run* nearly ran dry."[3] (One song from the session, "Held Up without a Gun," describes two instances of white-collar rip-offs: the price of gasoline and—hmm—a cigar-smoking manager wielding a contract and a pen.)

Ironically, the biggest news of the day covered the perils of one alternative energy source. Just a week earlier, reactors at the Three Mile Island nuclear power plant near Harrisburg, Pennsylvania, had suffered a partial meltdown. The near disaster had almost forced local officials to evacuate the surrounding neighborhoods; nationwide, it served as a sudden and scary symbol of the dangers of nuclear power, and it inspired artistic action such as the MUSE efforts.

The first song that Springsteen and the band cut that spring was "Roulette," a roundabout response to Three Mile Island. Throughout his work, Springsteen had been focused more on human concerns than political ones. While the Woodstock Nation had sung of changing the world, Springsteen wrote more of changing lives, and even in a song inspired by a nuclear disaster, he does not deal overtly with nuclear politics but rather with the general sense of distrust and doom inspired by Three Mile Island. Set against a frenzied drum line straight out of The Safaris' "Wipeout," the song depicts the sudden flight of a Rikers Island fireman. He and his wife grab their kids, hastily pack their car and drive away in the wake of an unmentioned incident, leaving the toys "out in the yard" and their home "unguarded"—a nice touch in a song born of paranoia. The song exists in the foreground of a social order that is playing roulette—the driving metaphor of the song—with the singer's life, kids, and wife. While driving away, they run through a roadblock; the singer is arrested but escapes: "They said they want to ask me a few questions but I think they had other plans."

The "they" of these lines echoes the concerns that Springsteen was exploring more and more. As already discussed, the songs from *Darkness* had portrayed a community of "they" and "you"; but more and more,

Springsteen was examining the dichotomy of "they" and "we." In his lyrics, he began to examine the social forces behind the dangers of a Three Mile Island—and more expansively, the forces behind the economic conditions that seemed to threaten notions of the American social structure.

During the *Darkness* tour, he had read a paperback volume, the *Pocket History of the United States*, a populist history by Allan Nevins and Henry Steele Commager. While performing in England, he had delivered a book report on Nevins and Commager's revisionist revelations: "I started reading this book, *The History of the United States*, and it seemed that things weren't the way they were meant to be—like the way my old man was living, and his old man, and the life that was waiting for me—that wasn't the original idea."[4] Jim Cullen tells us:

> This is, of course, a somewhat simplified and romantic notion of American history. But it is not without its truth, especially when one considers the prominent place of "the pursuit of happiness" in the original republican vision. Nor is it surprising that this would be the moral Springsteen would extract from Nevins and Commager; first published in 1942, the book was a nationalist manifesto meant to draw an implicit contrast between the United States and Nazi Germany by emphasizing the pluralist, egalitarian elements in our history.[5]

While playing the Meadowlands in 1980, Springsteen would say of Nevins and Commager:

> They helped me understand how when I was a kid all I remember was my father worked in a factory, his father worked in a factory . . . And the main reason was that they didn't know enough. . . . They didn't know enough about themselves, and they didn't know enough about the forces that controlled their lives.[6]

On *Darkness*, Springsteen had sung not so much about his generation rebelling against the last but more so about his generation not wanting to be *kept down* like the past one. In contrast to The Who's "My Generation," Springsteen's statement with regard to his generation was not to express a

wish to die before he gets old but to prevent getting old before his time—
to not let *them* turn him old before his time, as *they* had done to his father.
("They ain't gonna do to me/What I watched them do to you.")

As Marsh summarizes, Springsteen's references to the "hidden American class system" were "profoundly *prepolitical.*"[7] Indeed, Springsteen's
political education at this point—found in part through a mass-market
paperback—seems grounded in a certain naïveté. And despite his par-
ticipation in the MUSE efforts, it seems that his political inspiration at
this point translated more to artistic than activist action. He seemed distant from the other, openly political artists; organizer and producer
Danny Goldberg remembers: "Bruce was the outsider at the concert. The
word was to give him as much space as he wanted, not to crowd him. He
was the big draw, no question, but he really wasn't part of the scene."

Nevertheless, Goldberg observed that, "Bruce was extremely in awe of
both Graham [Nash] and Jackson [Browne], of their being such big stars
and having all of this humanity and political concerns."[8] Springsteen's
declining to sign the MUSE manifesto came not from his disagreement
from the platform—it's doubtful he would have participated in the event
if he disagreed with its premise—but from an apparent resistance to his
music becoming co-opted by the world of politics. The sentiment of his
post–*Born to Run* songs seems to have come not from an established ideological platform but organically, from a growing populist awareness.

Hand in hand with his populist examinations was a growing interest
in country music. Country music was, in many ways, a decidedly heartland music about as far away (both literally and figuratively) as you could
get from Springsteen's Jersey Shore music roots. Yet the Americana roots
of country music had much in common with the populist viewpoint that
he'd begun to explore. As he told *Double Take* magazine in 1995: "I'd been
really involved with country music right prior to the album *Darkness on
the Edge of Town* [1978], and that had a lot of effect on my writing because I think country is a very class-conscious music." And as he notes in
Songs, "I liked the fact that country dealt with adult topics, and I wanted
to write songs that would resonate down the road."[9]

One of his most adult songs, in fact, has roots traceable to the father
of contemporary country music, Hank Williams. Lines from Williams's
"Long Gone Lonesome Blues" served as the building blocks for one of

the highlights of the new album sessions, a song inspired by Springsteen's younger sister, Ginny, who was pregnant and married by age 17
and struggled when her husband lost his job.

That song, "The River," remains one of the best songs he's done—
certainly one of his post–*Darkness* best. It's a starkly beautiful tale that
resembles "old tyme" folk balladry in its lyrical voice. The narrator comes
from "down in the valley" where (he sings while addressing a "mister")
you are raised to do "like your daddy done." The song comprises the
painful reminiscing of the narrator looking back on the days when he
and Mary would drive down to the river and go swimming: "I remember
us driving in my brother's car/Her body tan and wet down by the reservoir." We're in a rural setting—about as far as we can get from the world
of Spanish Johnny, Maria, Eddie, or the Magic Rat. But this is no pastoral
romance; the narrator impregnates his girlfriend, and his birthday presents for turning 19 are "a union card and a wedding coat." The courthouse wedding described is about as unromantic as you can get: a
joyless event with no flowers, no wedding dress, no smiles. With the description of the judge putting it "all to rest," this sounds more like a funeral than a wedding, but that's precisely the point. The *youth* of these
characters has died, and when the singer loses his construction job—
the singer comes out and blames the "economy," an unlikely word for any
popular song—and is unable to support his family, he is left to bemoan
the curse of unfulfilled dream. Is it "a lie," he wonders, or is it "something
worse"?

The sentiment closely resembles Langston Hughes's question of what
happens to "a dream deferred." And while Springsteen's question is
posed from an economic perspective and Hughes's from recognition of
racial divisions, both "A Dream Deferred" and "The River" deal with existence outside of accepted society. Springsteen's consideration of the
dream at the heart of America—the American Dream—would provide
material for famous concert raps. In 1981, while touring Europe in support of the fifth album, Springsteen told a Stockholm audience:

In America there's a promise that gets made, and over there it gets
called the American Dream, which is just the right to be able to live
your life with some decency and dignity. . . . But over there, and a lot of
places in the world now, that dream is only true for a very, very few peo-

ple. It seems if you weren't born in the right place or if you didn't come from the right town, or if you believed in something that was different from the next person, y'know.[10]

Joel Bernstein visited the band in the studio as they recorded the first takes of "The River," and his notes that day provide a valuable look at the band's recording processes: "The band all loosened up by vamping history-of-rock hits. Then Bruce strapped on an acoustic and went through the basic riff. Roy Bittan scored it. Next the drums and bass, and last the whole group came in. But everyone was tired and in the end they only hit it twenty times that night."[11]

In addition to the experiences of his youngest sister, the wedding of E Street lighting director Mark Brickman, held at The Whisky in Los Angeles in 1979, provided a backdrop for the song. Springsteen and the band attended the wedding and even performed a number of songs—some old, some new, nothing borrowed nor blue. The wedding and especially the words of the presiding rabbi would touch Springsteen profoundly; he later told Brickman that the wedding played a part in about half the songs that showed up on the fifth album.[12] It's a slight exaggeration, but the effects of Brickman's wedding can certainly be heard in such songs as "I Wanna Marry You" and "Two Hearts (Are Better than One)," both destined for the forthcoming album.

E Street Band dynamics figured prominently in these sessions, proving integral to a search for a new sound. For one, Springsteen was focused on getting just the right drum sound. In the early stages of the sessions, Springsteen took Weinberg aside and told him that he needed to pick up the level of his drum work. Weinberg later admitted, "He could have got someone else. But he gave me time to find myself."[13] Weinberg would provide a ringing backbeat throughout the album.

Steve Van Zandt, meanwhile, emerged as a strong presence on both sides of the mic. Van Zandt provides a strong accompanying vocal to Springsteen's, practically performing duets on such songs as "Two Hearts" and "Out in the Street," with Springsteen's and Van Zandt's voices weaving in and out to create an effect greater than the sum of its parts. For the first (and only) time to date on a Springsteen album, Van Zandt served as a credited member of the production team, and not surprisingly, a good portion of the album captures the upbeat spirit that dates back to Van Zandt's shore-R&B roots. "*The River* was the first record where I felt comfortable enough to start capturing what the band was all about," he said.[14]

Meanwhile, other artists continued to solicit Springsteen's songwriting talents. In 1980, he met Welsh roots-rocker Dave Edmunds backstage at a London gig and played a song for him called "From Small Things (Big Things One Day Come)." "From Small Things" is a rockabillyish number with deceivingly dark lyrics about a girl who marries a guy she meets at an all-night hamburger stand, has two children, but then runs away with a real estate agent, whom she shoots dead because "she couldn't stand the way he drove." Edmunds recorded the song and released it on LP in 1982.

There was no shortage of material. Springsteen even strayed from the classic rock 'n' roll and country spectrum and experimented with reggae rhythms in songs such as "You Gotta Be Kind," "Down in White Town," and a reggae version of "You Can Look." The *Essential Bruce Springsteen* collection includes Springsteen and the E Street Band's performance of reggae star Jimmy Cliff's "Trapped" from the 1980–81 tour.

Bob Marley, who would release the final album of his lifetime, *Uprising*, in 1980, didn't come calling, but the legendary New York City punk-rock group Ramones did. On the surface, it seemed an unlikely partnership— the writer of overblown rock mini-operas and the group known for two-minute punk rock classics such as "Teenage Lobotomy" and "Blitzkrieg Bop." But like Springsteen, the Ramones were steeped in the history of pop rock and also covered songs such as "Surfin' Bird," "Needles and Pins," and "Warm California Sun." For them, Springsteen wrote a song about an absent husband and father with a terminal case of wanderlust ("Got a wife and kids in Baltimore, Jack/I went out for a ride and I never went back.") "Hungry Heart" would have been an odd topic for the group, yet the surprisingly catchy, pop-friendly, roller-rink melodies of the song, not to mention its concise stanzas and uncharacteristic brevity, would have been well suited for the Ramones. When Jon Landau heard it, though, he liked it so much that he convinced Springsteen to hold onto it for inclusion on the forthcoming album.

The working title for the album was *The Ties That Bind*, after a song that the E Street Band had debuted during the *Darkness* tour. The projected lineup of tracks for the album was: *Darkness* leftover "The Ties That Bind"; a melodic love song titled "Cindy"; "Hungry Heart"; "Stolen Car," a stark ballad about a self-destructive loser at love; and a relatively conventional invitation for commitment, "Be True," on side one; and on side two, "The River"; a tear-it-up song of sexual frustration in "You Can Look (But You Better Not Touch)"; a world-weary ballad, "The Price You Pay"; "I Wanna Marry You"; and "Loose Ends."[15] "Loose Ends," which showed up later on *Tracks*, is surprisingly strong given the awkwardness of the metaphor: "It's like we had a noose and baby without check/We pulled until it grew tighter around our necks/ . . . Well baby you can meet me tonight on the loose end." Yet the song's melodies are so good, Springsteen's singing so rich, and the band's performance so tight that it comes across as one of his best deleted tracks.

There's that *d* word again. The projected *Ties That Bind* lineup would have made a strong enough album. But after playing the MUSE concerts, something about the experience—perhaps it was witnessing the passion of fellow artists in their support of a cause—inspired Springsteen to go back into the studio and reevaluate the album. He arrived at the conclusion that *The Ties That Bind* lacked . . . something. He says in *Songs* that the album lacked the "unity and conceptual intensity" he sought for his albums.[16] (It should be noted that Springsteen even had spent hours selecting the *track sequence* for *Darkness*.) So he continued to record demos at his Holmdel, New Jersey, home and with the E Street Band back in the Power Station studio.

In the end, Sandford tells us, the band worked on some 90 songs during the complete sessions.[17] And as with *Darkness*, a number of album-worthy songs, including "Bring on the Night," "Dollhouse," and the jubilant "I Wanna Be with You," would remain unreleased for nearly two decades.

Again, the guiding principle for Springsteen in sifting through these 90-some songs was finding an overall concept to give the album a sense of cohesion. One important concern for him was how to come to terms with the complexities and contradictions of his own work. He told Robert Hilburn:

> Rock and roll has always been this joy, this certain happiness that is in its way the most beautiful thing in life. But rock also is about hardness and coldness and being alone. With *Darkness* it was hard for me to make those things coexist. How could a happy song like "Sherry Darling" coexist with "Point Blank" or "Darkness on the Edge of Town"? I couldn't face that.[18]

In planning the revised lineup for the album, Springsteen "finally got to the place where I realized life had paradoxes, a lot of them, and you've got to live with them."

And as he explains in *Songs*, after the "seriousness" of the *Darkness* record, he'd wanted to explore more of an "emotional range" in his songs and to represent the full spectrum of his live shows:

> All the years I'd been performing, I'd often start the show with something that sounded like it came out of the garage. In the past, these were two kinds of songs that fell by the wayside when we went into the studio to record. For *The River*, I wanted to make sure this part of what I did wouldn't get lost.[19]

It was fitting, then, that Springsteen decided to make his fifth record a double album. Not only had he and the band recorded enough strong material to merit a double release, but both practically and symbolically, a double album would allow him to explore this dual-sided nature of rock 'n' roll. It was a long time in coming, but on October 10, 1980, the album, titled *The River*, was released.

Jimmy Guterman suggests that what distinguishes *The River* from what the planned *Ties That Bind* release would have been is a "sense of extremes," and it's a fine observation given the emotional and musical range in the material that was added.[20] "Sherry Darling," "Two Hearts," "Out in the Street," "Crush on You," "Cadillac Ranch," "I'm a Rocker," and "Ramrod" evoke the most playful heights of bar-band/garage-band joy, while "Jackson Cage," "Independence Day," "Point Blank," "Fade Away," "Drive All Night" and "Wreck on the Highway" deal wistfully (and often painfully) with moments of loneliness, fear, and desperation. Don McLeese summarized that the album's songs fit into two categories: outtakes from the *Darkness* sessions or songs recorded soon after, which aimed at "some sort of mythic resonance," and the "straightforward stuff...all copyright 1980." ("Sherry Darling" dated back to the *Darkness* days.) Of the former, McLeese observed: "Since the production never attempts the studied grandiosity of *Born to Run* or the epic heavy-handedness of *Darkness*, themes that might previously have been overladen with bombast are rendered more powerful through understatement." Of the latter: "There's a feeling of spontaneous combustion about songs such as

'Cadillac Ranch,' 'Ramrod,' and 'You Can Look (But You Better Not Touch),' sparks of influence from countless one-shot supernovas from our collective subconscious. Less Kierkegaard, lots more Kingsmen ['Louie, Louie'] and Bobby Fuller Four ['I Fought the Law']."[21]

From the opening note (Max Weinberg on the snare drum), of the first song "The Ties That Bind," it was clear that this was a different kind of Springsteen album. A first listen to *The River* brought a crispness, clarity, and liveliness—everything that had been lacking on *Darkness*. Springsteen remembers being concerned after his fourth album about moving too closely toward what he termed the "sterility of '70s production": "I had a clear idea of what I wanted to hear. I wanted the snare drum to explode and I wanted less separation between the instruments."[22] The location of the sessions had gone a long way toward achieving this goal. As Sandford notes:

> Springsteen had tended to work in low-slung rooms like 914 or the CBS studio in Manhattan. Even the Record Plant could evoke, and often did, the marquee-jam of a sold-out dive. The Station held no such terrors. Anyone entering the converted church on West 53rd Street was met with soaring, steeply angled ceilings in a neat ecclesiastical touch. The acoustics revealed themselves, to the connoisseurs of such matters, as "true." There were no dead spots.[23]

According to guitarist and coproducer Van Zandt, "extensive room mics" were used to effect the live sound that Springsteen sought.[24] Springsteen and company felt it so important to continue work in the Power Station after Springsteen found his post–MUSE muse that they pushed The Clash to another studio to work on their follow-up to *London Calling*. The Clash chose to make their next release, titled *Sandanista!*, a triple album partially to mock Springsteen's *River*. *Sandanista!* failed to crack the Top 20. *The River* became Springsteen's first album to reach number one.

Like the best double albums, *The River* had something for everyone. Marsh places it in historical context, finding a dual-sided nature to *The River*'s four sides:

> The landmark double-disc rock albums are Bob Dylan's *Blonde on Blonde* and the Rolling Stones' *Exile on Main Street*, the former recorded by an

artist just reaching maturity, the latter made by artists trying to figure out what to do with theirs. Springsteen's exists between these two archetypes. Its first two sides are a chronicle of people awakening to the fact that they aren't young anymore, that their futures are no longer limitless. . . . The last two sides, on the other hand, describe one version of how someone bred on rock and roll dreams comes to terms with the knowledge that he has aged.[25]

The comparison to Dylan's and the Stones' albums is apt. *Blonde on Blonde* is hardly Dylan's best album, nor is *Exile* the Stones' best work; yet both albums stand as landmarks for these music legends not just for the sheer selection of songs but because they mark transitions in their career. Likewise, *The River* lacks the transcendent moments of *Wild* side two, let alone the entire *Born to Run* record, yet it is with good reason that it became his most commercial album at the time.

Side one begins with two tracks that date back before the *River* sessions. "The Ties That Bind" is a challenge to a hurt woman to not forsake love but rather accept the ties of relationships. "Sherry Darling" is the flipside, with the narrator having to cope with the complaints of his girlfriend's mother "yappin' in the back seat" as he drives them to get her unemployment check. "I didn't count on this package deal," he tells his girl, complaining of a tie-and-bind he could do without. Yet the song is defiantly fun; amidst voices talking and singing in the background, as if we're in a bar, the singer takes solace in dreaming of kicking his wouldbe mother-in-law to the curb. He warns his girlfriend that her mother is one complaint away from taking the subway back to the ghetto.

The River comes at you in song clusters, opening with "Ties" and "Sherry," two ruminations on the interpersonal ties of relationships. "Out in the Street" (which evolved from "Out on the Run," an even more raucous song), "Crush on You," and "You Can Look (But You Better Not Touch)" provide a triple-shot of garage raunch rock in the same vein as garage-rock classics like "Double Shot of My Baby's Love" and "96 Tears." Immediately afterward come two marriage songs, "I Wanna Marry You," in which the singer professes his love for a single mother, and "The River," a sobering tale of a young couple prematurely forced into the roles of father and mother. On side three, two playful rockers, "Cadillac Ranch" and "I'm a Rocker," are followed by two starkly beautiful tales,

"Fade Away," sung by a lover who doesn't want to disappear from his love's life, and "Stolen Car," about a car thief who fears he will disappear into the darkness one night. *The River* ends with a poignant parting shot: "Drive All Night," a spurned lover's desperate vow to his ex, for whom he would drive all night just to buy her shoes, and "Wreck on the Highway," a ballad about a man haunted by a fatal car wreck he witnesses in the night.

That sense of fear pervades the album. If *The River* is Springsteen's most playful album, it's also his most depressing, and it's not simply a question of some songs being one way and other songs being another. Springsteen himself has termed "Ramrod"—an overtly *fun* song that includes the autoerotic metaphor "She's a hot stepping hemi with a four on the floor/She's a roadrunner engine in a '32 Ford" and which Marsh describes as "an even more joyous counterpart to 'Born to Run'"—as being "one of the saddest songs I've ever written."[26]

One can only guess what exactly Springsteen meant by such a line. So let's do so: In the song, the singer tells the object of his affections of a "cute little chapel nestled down in the pines." Say the word, he tells her, and they'll "go ramroddin' forever more." This sounds very much like the sentiment of "Rosalita" and "Born to Run." But remember, Springsteen is now 30 years old, more mature and less innocent than the voice who told Rosie to drive away with him to a southern California café, who told Mary that redemption was found underneath the hood of a car, and who told Wendy that they were both tramps born to run. This is also the same Springsteen who has simultaneously authored tales of broken relationships, at least one defeated relationship, and the fragile mortality of another. Perhaps any sadness we can find in "Ramrod" comes in knowing what the singer in the song doesn't yet know—that the chapel in the pines doesn't necessarily offer a happy ending.

It is this conflict of dreams and reality that pervades *The River*. Songs throughout the album ponder the sense of loss when dreams are lost. The woman in "Jackson Cage" is even more imprisoned than her convicted lover, and like the couple in "The River," they are both imprisoned by dreams of a better life. In "I Wanna Marry You," the singer reminds the girl that "true love can't be no fairy tale." In "Point Blank," a song with the message of you're born dying, the singer looks back at an ex-lover and dreams that they were still together—but they aren't: "I was gonna be your Romeo you were gonna be my Juliet/These days you don't wait on Romeos/you wait on that welfare check." In "Stolen Car," the singer remembers: "We got married, and we swore we'd never part/Then little by little we drifted from each other's heart." "The Price You Pay" delivers a second-person proverb on facing the costs of life and love. Along with these album tracks we can add "Be True" and "Restless Nights," which both contrast the romance of life in movies with the loneliness of real life; and "Loose Ends," which compares the young lovers' expectations for their love with how it actually turns out. The dichotomies of dreams and reality add yet another dimension to Springsteen's songwriting from *The River.*

Truthfully, although the initial popularity of *The River* was probably due more to its "fun" songs—the first single, "Hungry Heart," became Springsteen's first Top 10 hit—the album's most poignant moments come from examinations of lost dreams and lost love. "Fade Away," a song that has since been all but overlooked despite its breaking the Top 20 when released as a single in early 1981, is both romantic and fatalistic in the best tradition of the baby-don't-go song. Springsteen sings at the limits of his range, Van Zandt (whose voice, let's face it, is so rough that he makes Springsteen sound like Smokey Robinson) accompanies him powerfully, and Danny Federici's right hand dances along the edge of the keyboard, providing a melody that almost weeps from beginning to end. Borrowing a line from Derek and the Dominoes' "Bell Bottom Blues" (off rock's best double album, *Layla and Other Assorted Love Songs*) the singer tells his already-gone lover, "I don't wanna fade away." But from the beginning of the song, when we're told she's found someone else, we know that she *is* gone and he *will* fade away.

The very cinematic image of fading away was on the mind of Springsteen the cinema buff when he wrote two other (unreleased) songs from this period: "Slow Fade" and "Fade to Black." The former is an earlier version of "Fade Away," whereas "Fade to Black" could've been included as an entirely distinct song. In it, Springsteen uses the cinematic fade as a metaphor for the dissolution of a relationship. (The couple even meets in a movie theater.) After a bad fight, the final verse mirrors a movie script: "The sunlight falls like a bright veil/A camera pans an empty room/The picture dissolves and slowly pulls back."

The trio of "Stolen Car," "Drive All Night," and "Wreck on the Highway" provide a heart-wrenching flipside to the more jubilant road songs "Out in the Street," "Cadillac Ranch," and (despite Springsteen's own reading) "Ramrod." The car thief of "Stolen Car" has sunk into self-destructive sadness after the dissolution of his marriage. The version of "Stolen Car" on *The River* evolved out of a longer one, appearing on *Tracks*, in which it's clear that the marriage is long over, the singer left to dream in vain of a reunion.

"Drive All Night" is a deliberately paced reunion of ex-lovers, dating back to *Darkness*. Aside from the reference to "machines and . . . fire waiting on the edge of town," the song is characterized by the plodding pace that marked songs like "Racing in the Street." Yet Springsteen's emotional intensity on "Drive All Night" sustains the song until the end. The climax is his declaration that his lover has his "love, heart and soul." He sings "heart and soul" three times in a heart-wrenching manner and (to be frank) oversings the first two times badly, losing control of his voice. Technically speaking, these moments are the worst of Springsteen's vocal work captured on record, but he probably chose to use the take that appears on *The River* for reasons both practical and artistic: the song was recorded at the last minute before the album's release, and his vocal vulnerability does underscore the painful intensity of the song. Marsh observes:

> At the end of "Jungleland," as that girl switches off her bedroom light, she is totally unknowing about the world beyond her walls. Her lover lies bleeding in the street, but she remains innocent. The image recurs at the end of "Drive All Night," but this time, the couple together know everything that's out there, and they're quite deliberately protecting each other from it—for a time.[27]

Similarly, the singer of "Wreck on the Highway," a countrified song that borrows its title from a Roy Acuff tune, wishes for the ability to protect his lover from the world outside. The structure of the song is the stuff of folk balladry with four five-line stanzas, each roughly adhering to a rhyme scheme of A-B-C-C-B. The plot is simple: While driving home on a deserted county road after work one night, the singer passes a wrecked car on the side of the road with the driver lying on the ground among glass and blood. The singer calls an ambulance, which takes the wounded (and probably dying) man to the hospital. As it does, the singer imagines a state trooper having to knock on the door of the man's girl-friend or wife and inform her of his death. In the last verse, the singer tells us that he suffers from nightmares of the incident and awakes to see his lover lying next to him. "I just lay there awake in the middle of the night," he sings, "Thinking 'bout the wreck on the highway." Having once steeped himself in youth-inspired car culture, Springsteen ends his fifth album with a song that depicts the road as an image of mortality.

The River drew the widest range of reviews of any of his albums to that time. Musician called it his best album to date, and Stephen Holden of the Village Voice called it "Bruce Springsteen's dictionary, encyclopedia, and bible of rock and roll." Cleverly, Holden notes, "Springsteen said the same things just as eloquently before, but there wasn't much joy to offset the pain. It's The River's lighter moments that give it the edge over Spring-steen's earlier albums." Time magazine said, "Four sides, 20 songs, a clarity and artistic ease and breadth of passion unequaled by any other rock record this year."[28]

But others felt Springsteen had lost his creative edge and had started to recycle his own material. Creem headlined its panning review "Born to Stall." In New Musical Express, Julie Burchill—perhaps missing the point in a way that only a British reviewer can while commenting on Springsteen—said The River was "great music for people who've wasted their youth to sit around drinking beer and [are] wasting the rest of their lives too." In Trouser Press, Ira Robbins declared, "Unable or unwilling to cast off the clichés of his past records, The River's attempt to Make a Statement is buried in an avalanche of repetition and evident lack of inspiration."[29] "Out in the Street" and "Ramrod," after all, do echo themes that date back to "Rosalita," and certainly, the car and road imagery that had shone in his past albums now risked becoming heavy-handed. On The River or in River session outtakes later released on Tracks, one encounters a dark highway, the blacktop, the street, the open streets, and the last block; lovers parking at a rendezvous, lovers parking at the reservoir, a lover driving all night, and a lover haunted by a car crash; the county line, a deserted stretch of a county two-lane road, the interstate, a sunny Florida roadway, and the place where the highway ends and the desert breaks; Eldredge Avenue, Riverside Avenue, 53rd Street, Union Street; Breakers Point, and Highway One; gas pumping, an Exxon station, and a Texaco station; whitetails, roaring engines, a ramrod, at least one bumper, someone's brother's car, a hot-steppin' hemi with a four on the floor, a road runner engine in a '32 Ford, a black Cadillac, an El Dorado Grande, El Dorado fins, a Hong Kong special, James Dean's Mercury '49, Burt Reynolds' black Trans Am, and the Batmobile; a roadblock, police cruising by in black-and-whites, a stolen car, a wreck on the highway, an ambulance, the outlands, and a rider in a black night.

For some, Springsteen was furthering the lexicon of his own urban mythology. For others, it was all a bit much. As Frances Lass asked in *Time Out:* "What would he have done if he'd failed his driving test?"[30]

Yet Springsteen was also venturing off the highway and onto the backstreets, as it were, developing a recurring cast of blue-collar characters. There are policemen, a fireman, a salesman, a factory worker, construction workers, welfare mothers, an unemployed gas station attendant— even a car thief and a bootlegger. If, for some, *The River* might have served up four sides of pre-owned cars, it was also the album with which Springsteen firmly entrenched himself within the blue-collar ethos and began to shift away from the Atlantic shore toward America's heartland.

And on the ensuing tour, Springsteen and the E Street Band took their legendary status as performers to the next step. For the first time, they touched off an album tour outside of the Northeast—at the Crisler Arena in Ann Arbor, Michigan, on October 3. The band didn't play the East Coast until late November with two nights at the Capital Centre in Landover, Maryland, followed by two nights at Madison Square Garden. The band was now playing big arenas, and the shows themselves were getting bigger, regularly including more than 30 songs a night. Ticket demand increased, and the E Street Band returned for two more nights at the Garden in mid-December, followed by three nights at the Nassau Coliseum in Uniondale, New York. The third night, on New Year's Eve, has gone down as the longest concert in the history of the band to date: a four-hour marathon that miraculously maintained a high level of energy from beginning to end through 38 songs.

The soundboard tapes of this record-setting show reveal several idiosyncrasies: "Sherry Darling" with a vague ska feel; the emerging tradition of the crowd singing the first verse of "Hungry Heart"; an extended version of "Fade Away" with a wonderfully soulful introduction; and some beautiful Roy Bittan interludes in which his keyboard work rings out like chimes. Comically, during the first line of "Jungleland," the New York

Islanders' faithful in the crowd (whose team was in the midst of its four consecutive Stanley Cups) actually booed the reference to the "Rangers" gang members. (These aren't hockey players having a homecoming in Harlem, folks!)

The tour was just beginning. After playing Toronto and Montreal, the band played several arena dates in the Midwest and South and then took off for Europe in April 1981. That month, Gary U.S. Bonds (who originally charted with "Quarter to Three" back in 1961) released a comeback album with a lot of help from Bruce Springsteen and his friends. For the album *Dedication,* Springsteen wrote three songs: "This Little Girl," "Your Love" and "Dedication," and reworked an arrangement of Moon Mullican's Cajun-flavored "Jolé Blon," on which he sang a duet with Bonds. Bonds gave Springsteen an opportunity to record material such as "Jolé Blon," of which the E Street Band had recorded a version during the *River* sessions. Songs like "Dedication" (with its purposefully silly spelling out of "D-E-D-I-C-A-T-I-O-N") wouldn't have fit on that album, but it made sense on a record of party and bar-band tunes.

Years before, Southside Johnny had given Springsteen an outlet for his more R&B-oriented material. On his first three albums with the Asbury Jukes, Southside Johnny had covered eight songs written by Springsteen, including gems like "Trapped Again" and "Love on the Wrong Side of Town." Now, Bonds reaped the benefits of Springsteen's castoffs. Himes suggests that, "Springsteen often approached his own albums with the uneasy awareness that he should be careful because he might be making a rock classic. By contrast, he approached Bonds's disc as a loosy goosey party record and his band let it rip as they seldom had on vinyl."[31]

Dedication was an unofficial E Street Band record, really, with the band backing Bonds throughout and Steve Van Zandt and Springsteen acting as coproducers. Together, they helped shape *Dedication* into a rock-revival record that blended the best elements of classic rock 'n' roll and R&B and scored a surprising commercial success in the early 1980s music climate. "This Little Girl," on which Springsteen sang backing vocals, broke the Top 20 singles chart—19 years after Bonds's last hit (setting a record).

In 1982, Bonds would release his follow-up, *On the Line,* with even more help from the E Streeters. Springsteen wrote seven of the album's 11 songs: "Hold on (To What You Got)," "Out of Work" (a Top 40 hit), "Club

Soul City," a passionate "Love's on the Line," "Rendezvous," "Angelyne," and "All I Need." Springsteen performed "All I Need" during a sound check at the Meadowlands in July 1981—a soulful and melodic number that harkened back perfectly to the pop crooner tradition of Bonds and his contemporaries.

The tour returned to the United States for the summer of 1981. Springsteen and the E Street Band played the famed Hollywood Bowl in June and then six shows in July to christen the new Brendan Byrne Arena in East Rutherford, New Jersey. On September 14, 1981 in Cincinnati's Riverfront Coliseum, the tour came to an end after 144 shows.

The tour was a remarkable success, though it also included some somber moments. In early December 1980, while the band played the first of two nights at the Spectrum in Philadelphia, John Lennon was shot and killed outside the Dakota Hotel in New York City. Coincidentally, New York DJ Vin Scelsa was playing "Jungleland" on WNEW when an Associated Press teletype transmission reported that Lennon had been shot. "I didn't want to believe it," Scelsa told the *Daily News* 25 years later. "But by the time 'Jungleland' was over, 10 minutes later, AP had sent another bulletin saying John Lennon was dead."[32]

The following night, Springsteen debated calling off the show but then decided against it. He opened the show telling the Spectrum crowd why he thought it appropriate to play that night, and then the band put on a 35-song set ending with "Twist and Shout," a song once famously covered by The Beatles.

A month earlier, America had swept former-actor-turned-politician (and former-Democrat-turned-Republican) Ronald Reagan into the White House. Performing at Arizona State University the day after the election, Springsteen commented, "I don't know what you thought about what happened last night. But I thought it was pretty terrifying."[33] Then he led the band into "Badlands," the title of the song suddenly taking on ominous meaning. For Springsteen, who just a year before had resisted making an overt "No Nukes" statement, his words that night in Tempe stand as a convenient sign that he was becoming more outspoken in the political realm. They also foreshadowed the complex relationship that Springsteen would have as a popular culture icon in Ronald Reagan's America.

∗ 6 ∗

A Meanness in This World

Nebraska (1982)

In 2004, author Tennessee Jones published *Deliver Me from Nowhere*, a collection of 10 short stories that together comprise a song-for-song interpretation of Bruce Springsteen's 1982 album *Nebraska*. Although the concept seems forced and smacks of fan-fiction fanaticism, Jones's stories aren't bad. (The book seems to have opened the door for a new genre of Springsteen-inspired fiction—Exhibit A: *Meeting Across the River: Stories Inspired by the Haunting Bruce Springsteen Song*, edited by Jessica Kaye and Richard J. Brewer.) The *Deliver Me from Nowhere* collection came four years after Sub Pop Records, an independent label known more for alternative bands such as Soundgarden and The Shins, released *Badlands: A Tribute to Bruce Springsteen's* Nebraska, featuring such artists as Dar Williams, Ani DiFranco, Son Volt, Ben Harper, Aimee Mann, Michael Penn, and Johnny Cash.

Today, *Nebraska* is considered a classic. But back at the time of the album's release in 1982, even long-time, dedicated fans had been ill prepared for Springsteen's sidetrack from rock 'n' roll.

After the conclusion of the *River* tour, Springsteen returned to New Jersey to plan his next record. As he describes in *Songs*, he had grown weary of spending so much time and energy in the recording studio, where he found the atmosphere "sterile and isolating" and where he "rarely got the right group of songs" he wanted "without wasting a lot of time and expense." Looking for a way to make the process less arduous and more economical, he decided that he wanted to not only write but hear any new material before he took it into the studio again.[1]

In December 1981, he called his guitar tech, Mike Batlan, and discussed this new process. Batlan brought a four-track Tech tape machine to Springsteen's house in Colts Neck. There, Springsteen sat in a chair with an acoustic guitar and worked through Spartan versions of new songs, singing/playing into two microphones. After laying down these two tracks, he then added harmony vocals, "hit a tambourine," or added a second guitar line, using the remaining two available recording tracks.[2]

Springsteen thought he merely was recording demo tracks for a new album to be recorded with the E Street Band. But the nature of these new songs was distinct. As he describes in *Songs*, the new material "tapped into white gospel and early Appalachian music, as well as the blues." Such artists as Robert Johnson and John Lee Hooker—artists whose records "sounded so good with the lights out"—provided guiding influences, as did the folk balladry of Woody Guthrie. Springsteen remembers, "I wanted to let the listener hear the characters think, to get inside their heads, so you could hear and feel their thoughts, their choices."[3]

Springsteen sent a cassette tape of his 15 favorite songs from the Colts Neck sessions to Jon Landau, along with two notebook pages of handwritten commentary. The lineup of songs on the tape was:

1. "Bye Bye Johnny"
2. "Starkweather (Nebraska)"
3. "Atlantic City"
4. "Mansion on the Hill"
5. "Born in the U.S.A."
6. "Johnny 99"
7. "Downbound Train"
8. "Losin' Kind"
9. "State Trooper"

10.   "Used Cars"
11.   "Wanda (Open All Night)"
12.   "Child Bride"
13.   "Pink Cadillac"
14.   "Highway Patrolman"
15.   "Reason to Believe"

Soon after, Springsteen gathered the E Street Band in the studio to record band versions of the songs. But something was different about these songs; they didn't seem to lend themselves to full-band, electric arrangements. Though larger in instrumentation and volume, Springsteen judged these amped-up versions to be inferior to the original acoustic versions recorded as demos. He tried recording the songs by himself in the studio, but even these solo arrangements didn't capture the stark ambience of the Colts Neck demo tape.

At this point, he tabled these tracks and recorded some other new material with the band. These newer songs definitely *were* rock songs, and they pointed toward the possible release of a new album with the E Street Band. It was rumored that Springsteen's next album would be titled *Murder, Incorporated,* named after a hard-driving new song about a man who stands up to organized crime only to be killed in the final verse. (More generally, "Murder, Incorporated" explored paranoia in the face of indomitable social forces, the same territory as "Roulette.")

While Springsteen kept working with the band on a growing list of new rock 'n' roll songs, he remained committed to the songs that he had written alone in New Jersey, which he considered "some of my strongest songs."[4] He selected nine songs from the demo tape that he felt held together best as a group. He also added one more, a very personal song called "My Father's House." These 10 tracks were released as the album *Nebraska* on September 20, 1982.

The publication of Jones's *Deliver Me from Nowhere* brought the album's literary influences full circle. Sitting in his rented house in Colts Neck, New Jersey, prior to recording the material that would comprise the album, Springsteen had been reading Flannery O'Connor. (Stephen Metcalf is just one writer who suggests that Jon Landau was the one feeding Springsteen an "American Studies syllabus heavy on John Ford, Steinbeck, and Flannery O'Connor."[5]) A Catholic writer in the Southern

Gothic vein, O'Connor had captured Springsteen's imagination after he saw John Huston's 1979 film adaptation of her novel *Wise Blood*. The influence of O'Connor on Springsteen can be seen in a number of instances. For one, he used the title of two O'Connor short stories, "The River" and "A Good Man Is Hard to Find," for songs (the latter, an unreleased song that surfaced on *Tracks*). As Geoffrey Himes observes, Springsteen learned from O'Connor the "value of plainspoken language." Himes argues, "It was better to describe young men out on the weekend in language they themselves might use ... than to describe them in kind of high-falutin' language never heard in a barroom—as he does on 'Born to Run.'"[6] O'Connor's stories also served as a model of narrative economy for Springsteen. "They were a big revelation. She got to the heart of some part of meanness that she never spelled out, because if she spelled it out you wouldn't be getting it," he told Will Percy—the nephew of Walker Percy, another Catholic author in whom Springsteen had become interested—in 1995. "In small detail—the slow twirling of a baton, the twisting of a ring on a finger—they found their character."[7]

O'Connor's Catholicism, an uncommon faith among Southerners, held additional interest for Springsteen. O'Connor's view of Catholicism was a complex one. As Himes summarizes, "She retained an unwavering faith in Christian redemption, but nearly every story she wrote tested that faith against examples of crime, cruelty, delusion and failure of every kind."[8] In Springsteen's own words: "Her stories reminded me of the unknowability of God and contained a dark spirituality that resonated with my own feelings at the time."[9]

This "unknowability of God" is a theme with which O'Connor dealt in a number of her stories. In "The River," the child narrator mistakes the metaphor of river baptism with literal reality and drowns while trying to find God for himself:

> The river wouldn't have him. He tried again and came up, choking. This was the way it had been when the preacher held him under—he had had to fight with something that pushed him back in the face. He stopped and thought suddenly: it's another joke, it's just another joke! He thought how far he had come for nothing and he began to hit and splash and kick the filthy river.... He plunged under once and this

time, the waiting current caught him like a long gentle hand and pulled him swiftly forward and down.[10]

Likewise, in "Good Country People," Hulga tells a con man, "We are all damned . . . but some of us have taken off our blindfolds and see that there's nothing to see. It's a kind of salvation."[11]

In "A Good Man Is Hard to Find," the family comes to a fateful end after meeting a killer known as The Misfit. After he has the rest of her family shot—a fate that she herself seals by unwisely identifying The Misfit—she tries to appeal to him in Jesus' name, but The Misfit tells her:

"Jesus was the only One that ever raised the dead," The Misfit continued, "and He shouldn't have done it. He thrown everything off balance. If He did what He said, then it's nothing for you to do but throw away everything and follow Him, and if He didn't, then it's nothing for you to do but enjoy the few minutes you got left the best way you can—by killing somebody or burning down his house or doing some other meanness to him. No pleasure but meanness," he said and his voice had become almost a snarl.

Desperately grasping at straws, she denies Christ, saying, "Maybe he didn't raise the dead."

"I wasn't there so I can't say He didn't," The Misfit said. "I wisht I had of been there," he said, hitting the ground with his fist. "It ain't right that I wasn't there because if I had of been there I would have known. Listen lady," he said in a high voice, "if I had of been there I would of known and I wouldn't be like I am now."[12]

Himes adds, "One of the great devices employed by O'Connor and such fellow Southern writers as William Faulkner and Eudora Welty was to tell stories through the eyes of a child." As he points out, children serve a unique purpose within fictional worlds because, as narrators, they *observe* but don't always *understand* what happens in front of them—often leaving it up to the reader to interpret the events narrated, to "fill in the missing information." [13]

As Springsteen wrote songs in Colts Neck, he became interested in the perspective of childhood. He explains in *Songs* that the songs from this period were "connected" to his childhood more so than any other record to that point, not just in narration but in the "tone of the music." The Colts Neck songs would show the influence of these childhood memories. Three songs, "Mansion on the Hill," "Used Cars," and "My Father's House," were all told from a child's perspective, all, as Springsteen assessed, "stories that came directly out of my experience with my family."[14]

"Mansion on the Hill" is another song with a title that Springsteen borrowed from Hank Williams. In *A Race of Singers,* Bryan Garman notes that Williams's song describes a "romantic relationship thwarted by class distinctions."[15] Springsteen's song is deceivingly complex, and it deals with class distinctions, though in a different context. The lyrics describe a mansion that both rises above and looms over the rest of the town. The narrator remembers parking with his father and looking up at the mansion; in summers, he and his sister hid in cornfields and listened to rich people having fun at parties inside the house.

In "Used Cars," the singer remembers the family's purchase of a used car and, more importantly, the humbling nature of the experience. The salesman stares at the father's hands, undoubtedly worn from years of manual labor, which have nevertheless left him with little income. (The salesman says he wishes he could give the family a break on the car's price.) After buying the car, the "neighbors come from near and far" to see the family drive in their "brand new used car." The paradoxical description of the car hints at the complexity of the scenario: the mix of pride felt in purchasing an automobile, and shame at having the purchase of a *used* car be a celebratory moment. Shame triumphs over the singer, whom we can picture cringing as he walks alone and hears his little sister blowing the horn of the car, "The sounds echoin' all down Michigan Avenue." In the end, he clings to a bitter, unrealistic dream of winning the lottery, after which he vows, "I ain't ever gonna ride in no used car again."

"My Father's House" is the most poignant of the three songs. It opens with the singer recounting a dream in which he is a child, running through a dark woods of "wild . . . tall" pines, amid the rustling wind, hoping to make it home before "darkness falls." There are "ghostly voices" and, in an echo of Robert Johnson's "Hellhound on My Trail," the "devil snappin' at [his] heels." At dream's end, the singer falls shaking but safe in his father's arms. But awoken from the dream, we learn the singer is estranged from his father. The dream inspires him to resolve the things that had "pulled [them] apart"; he gets dressed and drives out to his father's house. When he gets there, a woman (a stranger) speaks to him through a chained door and tells him that his father doesn't live there anymore, and the sins between father and son "lie unatoned" across the dark highway between the singer's current home and that of his childhood.

The significance of homes in both "Mansion on the Hill" and "My Father's House" is inescapable. The descriptions of both are archetypal and, it can even be said, psychoanalytic in their dreamlike imagery. In the former, the mansion emerges from out of childhood memory, standing beneath a "full moon rising." In the latter, the father's former residence "shines hard and bright . . . like a beacon." The two houses are guarded by a steel fence and chained door, respectively; each instance establishes the house and everything that it represents—social and familiar acceptance—as unattainable.

In *Songs*, Springsteen prefaces the lyrics to *Nebraska* with memories of his grandparents' house, where his family lived until he was six. Springsteen remembers the "lack of decoration, the almost painful plainness" of the house:

> Our house was heated by a single kerosene stove in the living room. One of my earliest childhood memories was the smell of kerosene and my grandfather standing there filling the spot in the rear of the stove. All of our cooking was done on a coal stove in the kitchen. As a child, I'd shoot my watergun at its hot, iron surface and watch the steam rise.[16]

It's not a stretch to find profound psychological dimensions in both songs, especially with regard to images of the home and fatherhood, and how they reflect issues with which Springsteen had to deal. As Springsteen would later say of the creative space from which the song came, "that was [the] bottom . . . I'd hope not to be in that particular place ever again."[17]

The most shocking lyrical perspective, though, is evidenced in the song, "Nebraska." The song is based on the true story of Charley Stark-weather, who killed 11 people between Nebraska and Wyoming in 1958–59 while traveling with underage girlfriend Caril Ann Fugate. Springsteen was directed to the story first by the movie *Badlands*, a fictionalized account of Starkweather and Fugate that Terrence Malick directed very much in the same "antihero" genre as Arthur Penn's *Bonnie and Clyde*. Springsteen was so fascinated by *Badlands* that he was moved to call journalist Ninette Beaver, the author of *Caril*, a nonfiction book on the Starkweather murders, to learn more about the case. From his research sprung the song, "Nebraska," which he called the "record's center."[18]

The song is told from the killer's perspective, the image is straight out of Malick's *Badlands*, and the economy of language harkens back to O'Connor: "I saw her standin' on her front lawn just a-twirlin' her baton/Me and her went for a ride sir and ten innocent people died." After they're caught and the singer sentenced to death, he remains unrepentant. His last wish is that his girlfriend joins him in the electric chair, and he blames his inexplicable actions on the "meanness" of the world.

"Johnny 99" is a companion piece to "Nebraska." The song is another jailhouse narrative, but this time the focus is not as much on the crime—the narrator, Ralph, kills a night clerk while in a drunken rage—as it is on the factors leading up to it. Bryan Garman writes that "Johnny 99" combines the narratives of Julius Daniels's "Ninety Nine Year Blues" (1927) and Carter Family's "John Hardy Was a Desperate Little Man" (1930)—both from the Folkways *Anthology* that Springsteen had been delving into at the time—but Springsteen's song is not really like either one, especially when considering the character's motives.[19]

Johnny (his name is Ralph, but he's dubbed with his titular nickname after receiving a life sentence) gets drunk on Tanqueray and wine while attempting to drown his worries; he loses his job when the Mahwah automobile plant where he's employed is shut down. After committing the murder, he ends up in the rough side of town ("where when you hit a red light you don't stop") waving a gun. An off-duty cop sneaks up on him and cuffs him. Johnny appears with a court-appointed defender before a hanging judge, "Mean John Brown," and is sentenced to 99 years. Unlike the perpetrator in "Nebraska," Ralph/Johnny shows remorse—he doesn't claim to be innocent and he says he'd be "better off dead"—and elaborates on his road to ruin: debts that "no honest man could pay" and the house he stood to lose to foreclosure. The moral climax of the song comes at the end of the penultimate verse: "I ain't sayin' that makes me an innocent man/But it was more 'n all this that put that gun in my hand."

Jim Cullen argues, "As he himself admits, Johnny is responsible for his crime. But he also implicates the CEO of the auto company, the board of the bank, and state and federal regulators, i.e., anyone who helped create a situation in which people are saddled with debts they cannot honestly repay." In addition, the "fact that Johnny's rage unfolds in a dangerous part of town calls attention to the social forces that serve as a backdrop for, and perhaps shape, his actions."[20]

While Cullen suggests that the arrest being made by an *off-duty* policeman implies "a sense of responsibility that is more than official or contractual,"[21] perhaps more to the point is that the incident illustrates a keen awareness of narrative detail; only a cop dressed in civilian clothes would be able to get anywhere near a gun-wielding criminal while still having the wherewithal to apprehend him. Although the off-duty policeman acts on behalf of law and order—a cause to which we are surely sympathetic—putting ourselves in Ralph/Johnny's shoes, we can imagine his sense of betrayal at getting captured by one of his blue-collar brethren. Cullen points out that Springsteen

> begins the song by yodeling—an eerie, melancholy wail. This wail, an act of musical homage, conjures up the ghost of Jimmie Rodgers, the beloved "Singing Brakeman" of Mississippi who left the railroad to become the first major country and western singer in the 1920s. Even before he's said a word, then, Springsteen connects his story to a great working-class musical tradition.[22]

It can be said that in the six years since *Born to Run*, Springsteen had moved from street-urchin opera to blue-collar soap opera. "Atlantic City" is set amidst gang warfare, and to a haunting folk melody with Springsteen providing an additional vocal track of wailing harmony. The death of the "Chicken Man from Philly" refers to the murder of Philip Testa in 1980. The protagonist, like Ralph/Johnny, has "debts that no honest man can pay," and recalling the singer of "Meeting Across the River," he tells his girlfriend of a guy he met and how he's going to "do a little favor for him." But unlike the small-time hoods in "Meeting," the protagonist of "Atlantic City" seems to possess an awareness that they didn't. "Well now everybody dies baby that's a fact," he tells her philosophically. "But maybe everything that dies someday comes back."

Prior to *The River*, when Springsteen had written of characters committing crimes—such as Spanish Johnny in "Incident" and the small-time crooks in "Meeting"—they came across as romantic flirtations with the wrong side of the law. Now, however, we can see how the driver from "Stolen Car" is a psychological relative to characters in "State Trooper" and "Highway Patrolman" on *Nebraska*.

Like "Stolen Car," "State Trooper" is told from the point of view of a car thief. ("License, registration, I ain't got none/But I got a clear conscience 'bout the things that I done.") Unlike the driver in "Stolen Car," though the driver in "State Trooper" has no secret wish to be caught. Each of the first three stanzas ends with the driver's plea to a state trooper—who is either tailing him or is imagined—not to stop him as he drives past the glow of oil refineries on the New Jersey Turnpike during a rainy night. Like Springsteen's imagined listener, the driver is alone in the dark, yet this is not a peaceful solitude. As in its unlikely inspiration, "Frankie Teardrops," a 10½-minute song from the 1977 debut album for synth-punk band Suicide, "State Trooper" has a sense of minimalist desperation. Fervently strumming a monotonous guitar line, Springsteen sings hauntingly. His narrator imagines the approaching trooper to have a nice family and says "the only thing that I got's been both'rin' me my whole life." He can't even get music on the radio, which plays only "talk show stations." In the end, the singer casts out an empty plea for somebody to hear his "last prayer," to "deliver me from nowhere."

The song "Highway Patrolman" has obvious connections to "State Trooper"; the protagonist, Joe Roberts, is himself a trooper. But the song bears a closer resemblance to "Losin' Kind." In that song, Frank Davis picks up a prostitute outside a barroom, and after they spend time together in a Best Western motel room, Frank robs a roadside bar and beats the bartender. Frank and his date-for-the-night ride away, and in an ending reminiscent of the noir classic *Out of the Past*, he wraps his car around a telephone pole during a high-speed chase. Frank and the girl are able to crawl out of the wreckage, but when the patrolman tells Frank he's "lucky to be alive," Frank says, "Well, sir, I'll think that one over if you don't mind/Luck ain't much good to you when you're the losin' kind."

In "Highway Patrolman," Joe has a brother, Franky, and "Franky ain't no good." In rhyming couplets, we learn of a recurring story of Joe getting a call on the police radio reporting of trouble with Franky downtown. "Well if it was any other man," Joe muses, "I'd put him straight away/But when it's your brother sometimes you look the other way." But this time, Franky commits a serious crime: he leaves a kid lying on the floor of a roadhouse with a girl—probably someone they were fighting over—crying nearby at a table. She tells Joe it was Franky; Joe gets in his patrol car and spots Franky "out at the crossroads" driving a (probably stolen) car with Ohio plates. Joe chases him to within five miles of the Canadian border; realizing Franky intends to flee the country, Joe pulls to the side of the road and lets him go, watching the taillights of the Buick disappear in the night.

Beneath the plot are many layers. We learn that in 1965, Franky joined the army, while Joe got a farm deferment and married Maria, the woman with whom (as Joe recalls in a flashback chorus that paints a sentimental scene before lost innocence) they took turns dancing to the song "Night of the Johnstown Flood." Note, then, that although we are told that one man is "honest" and the other "no good," their fates are largely shaped by a social construct—the farm deferment. With it, Joe marries Maria, and (when wheat prices keep falling until they were "gettin' robbed") then takes a job as a highway patrolman. On the other hand, Franky comes home from the army in 1968 without social ties; because Joe is married to Maria, Franky is left to fight for other men's women in roadhouse bars. True, Franky is no good, but Joe, the reluctant cop who claims to do his job "as honest as I could," does *not* do his job and does *not* bring in his brother. The final irony is that Joe, who claims that any man who "turns his back on his family . . . just ain't no good," must turn his back on his brother—and his own job—to let his brother go.

To listen to *Nebraska* is to take a trip through a treacherous moral landscape. Springsteen's narrative ballads present characters who make important decisions—often the wrong ones—and the direction of the listener's sympathies is often problematic. Christopher Sandford said that one of the relatives of Starkweather's victims called the explanation of "there's just a meanness in this world" from the title song "crap." Similarly, one interviewee—a policeman who professes admiration for Springsteen—in Robert Coles's controversial *Bruce Springsteen's America*, questions the focal points of songs like "Johnny 99," "Highway Patrolman," and "State Trooper." Of "Johnny 99," the policeman asks:

> But who's thinking of that night clerk—he's mentioned for a half a second only at the start: "got a gun, shot a night clerk." . . Are we supposed to start sobbing, I want to know, because a guy has lost his job—and decides to go on a killing spree after he's tanked himself up with that Tanqueray stuff! . . . Maybe I've been in too many courtrooms, and seen the families of the *victims* in there, crying their bloody hearts out! Where are *they* in that song of the Boss?[25]

The policeman terms the description of the song's presiding judge as "Mean John Brown" as a "setup": "Bruce, pal, how about mean Johnny 99?" he asks.

Our man in blue also questions "Highway Patrolman" and "State Trooper" as songs that, by their titles, might imply an interest in a policeman's perspective. As he says about the latter, "There's not a single word about the state trooper, about him, his life, even though folks like me, they'll read that title on the album and go right for it!"[26] (For the former, his objection is vaguely stated, but we can understand it given the song's portrayal of a reluctant patrolman who lets his brother escape the law.) Coles's policeman does not necessarily offer esoteric insight, and his perspective is undoubtedly influenced by his occupation. But his comments do highlight the complexities that would continue to develop between Springsteen and his fans.

On an album filled with songs about a murderous road trip, the damnation of used cars, and both ends of the highway chase experience, "Open All Night" emerges as the one and only fun-filled offering on *Nebraska*. Many of the lyrics date back to a song from the *River* sessions called "Living on the Edge of the World," a light, up-tempo number. "Open All Night" is stripped down instrumentally, of course, but it retains the fast tempo of its predecessor, as well as the all-out joy evoked by "fun" *River* songs such as "Cadillac Ranch" and "Ramrod." It can be seen as a more hopeful version of "State Trooper," with which the song shares many similarities: some identical lines, a pesky state trooper, a radio jammed with talk (here, gospel) stations. The driver in "Open All Night" is also alone, driving through industrial north Jersey in the early morning, where the refinery towers appear surreal, "like a lunar landscape." But here, the narrative tension derives from the singer's desire to make it home in time to see Wanda, whom he'd met at her job at the Bob's Big Boy on Route 60. (His boss doesn't dig him, we're told, so the singer was put on the night shift.) The song is lightheartedly serious: the singer repeats the prayer to be delivered from nowhere, but here the prayer is offered to the local deejay, asking for rock 'n' roll music to provide company on the remaining three hours of his drive. This is a more serious concern than the state trooper he passes while speeding by; even though the trooper hits his "party light," the singer simply says, "Goodnight, good luck, one two power shift" and leaves him behind in the middle of the song.

Nebraska closes on a note of circumspect hope with "Reason to Believe." The four verses of the song introduce us to a cast of characters that seem to come out of O'Connor's fiction. We see a man poking a stick into a dead dog on the highway, looking like he believes that "if he stood there long enough that dog'd get up and run." We meet two jilted lovers: one, who waits in vain at the end of a dirt road for her lover to return, the other, a groom left at the altar. We witness a baby being baptized in a river while mourners stand over a dead man's grave, praying that the Lord will help them make sense of the man's death. In each case, the singer offers the same conclusion: "Still at the end of every hard earned day people find some reason to believe."

Again, we come back to O'Connor and the persistence of faith amidst trials. Twice, the singer says it "Struck me kinda funny" before observing how "people find some reason to believe." In each case—even the river baptism scenario, which resonates with the knowledge that a boy drowns at the end of O'Connor's "The River"—we are not given any affirmation of faith; in fact, the singer labels these illustrations of faith as being "kinda funny." Yet as Springsteen had once said, you'd better keep riding. The point in "Reason to Believe"—and, in fact, throughout the entire album—is that people endure, that they struggle against all evidence to the contrary, because it's the only thing that they can do—or else they end up dead, spiritually or literally.

After *The River, Nebraska* came as a shock. For fans on the periphery, those who had come to know him through "Born to Run" and "Hungry Heart," the album's acoustic-folk sound must have seemed dreary, its lyrics disarmingly depressing. Ironically, the album did spawn Springsteen's first standard-release video (not counting the 1978 "Rosalita" video, which was really just a concert clip), though even this was not a fully commercial move. The "Atlantic City" video is a starkly atmospheric, black-and-white video featuring street scenes in which neither Springsteen nor any of the E Street Band members appear. Arnold Levine, who'd shot the "Rosalita" footage, had asked Landau about possibilities for shooting a video of the song. Springsteen was unavailable for the shoot—he was headed to California to work with Chuck Plotkin in mixing some new rock 'n' roll tracks—but signed off on the project with just two conditions: it should be "kind of gritty-looking" and "it should have no images that matched up to image in the song."[27]

Nebraska is by nature the least commercial release Springsteen had done since his debut record, but it would not be accurate to call the album a commercial failure. Even lacking a radio-friendly single, it reached number four on the album charts and attained gold-record status soon after its release—this in the midst of an early 1980s recession. Many critics praised the album's sincerity. The *New York Times* called it Springsteen's "most personal record, and his most disturbing." *Time* described it as "an acoustic bypass through the American heartland . . . like a Library of Congress field recording made out behind some shutdown auto plant," and *Rolling Stone* said, "This is the bravest of Springsteen's six records; it's also his most startling, direct and chilling." In *Musician*, Paul Nelson said the album sounded "demoralizing" and "murderously monotonous . . . deprived of spark or hope." In the *Los Angeles Times*, Mikal Gilmore— whose older brother Gary was executed on January 17, 1977, for the murder of a Provo, Utah, hotel manager—described the album as "dark-toned, brooding and unsparing" but said it was "also the most successful attempt at making a sizable statement about American life that popular music has yet produced." Greil Marcus said it was "the most complete and probably the most convincing statement of resistance and refusal that Ronald Reagan's U.S.A. has yet elicited from any artist or any politician."[28]

Nebraska continued an evolution of style and substance that began with *Darkness* and continued with *The River.* But if fans worried that the album signaled Springsteen's farewell to the popular rock music genre, they would soon learn that this was anything but the truth. In fact, the album that was Springsteen's least commercial of the 1980s shared roots with the album that proved to be the most commercial of his entire career.

* 7 *

Nebraska Becomes Electric

Born in the U.S.A. (1984)

Of the several nonmusical works that have influenced Springsteen, one rarely discussed is Robert Frank's *The Americans*, a book of photographs originally released in 1959. In 1995, Springsteen told Will Percy:

> I was twenty-four when I first saw the book—I think a friend had given me a copy—and the tone of the pictures, how he gave us a look at different kinds of people, got to me in some way. I've always wished I could write songs the way he takes pictures. I think I've got half a dozen copies of that book stashed around the house, and I pull one out once in a while to get a fresh look at the photographs.[1]

Frank had traveled the country in the 1950s on a Guggenheim grant, photographing everyday people in everyday situations and, in the words of John Szarkowski, "established a new iconography for contemporary America, comprised of bits of bus depots, lunch counters, strip developments, empty spaces, cars, and unknowable faces." Elizabeth Kunreuther tells us, "Photography before Frank was pristine: carefully focused, carefully lit. Frank would intentionally lose focus, his work was shadowy and grainy, full of unconventional cropping and angles. He broke the rules in order to be true to his vision of America he saw in his travels across the country in 1955 and 1956."[2]

Peter Marshall describes the use of visual motifs in *The Americans:*

> the recurring element of the flag, the orator followed by the listeners . . . the car and the American Dream . . . Frank concentrates on the ordinary, the things you see on the road and along its edges, but he also deals with real issues, whether of race . . . or spiritual emptiness. . . . A petrol station forecourt, the pumps like figures in a religious procession, carrying a tall banner that says "S A V E" in heavy capitals. . . . a Fourth of July celebration in New York, where the giant hanging flag is shown to be patched, torn and threadbare.[3]

In the 1980s, Springsteen found himself more and more interested with the theme of spiritual emptiness found on Main Street, U.S.A. One early demo from Colts Neck, "Vietnam," was an up-tempo tune built around a bouncing acoustic guitar line. In this song, a returning vet discovers that he's lost his factory job to a slow economy, and has also lost his girlfriend (or wife), who's run away with the singer of a rock band. Like many returning veterans, he experiences a sense of isolation from the society he returns to. Walking down Main Street, U.S.A., the veteran says, "All I seen was strangers, watchin' a stranger pass by/And that stranger was me." In a line that is more affected than realistic in its blunt cynicism, a factory foreman tells him, "Now don't you understand, you died in Vietnam."

Springsteen reworked the lyrics while keeping the basic plot for a new song. The title and chorus of this new song came from the name of a film script that director Paul Schrader had sent Springsteen in 1981. The plot revolved around a blue-collar rock band in Cleveland, and Schrader had hoped Springsteen would write music for the film. Something about the title of the script, *Born in the U.S.A.,* resonated with Springsteen. Obviously, Springsteen's breakthrough album had begun with the same word, and as Geoffrey Himes summarizes, a string of recent music and movies— from "Born on the Bayou" to "Born to Be Wild" to "Born to Lose" to "Born

to Boogie" to *Born to Kill* and *Born Free*—had established artistic statements of inborn identity as an artistic subgenre of sorts. And there was
also "Back in the U.S.A.," a Chuck Berry song that Springsteen and the E
Street Band had covered in their early days.

More relevant were the resemblances to the title of Ron Kovic's *Born
on the Fourth of July,* a book much more closely related to the subject matter that Springsteen explored in "Vietnam," and to the song it evolved
into, called "Born in the U.S.A." After reading Kovic's story and meeting
him, Springsteen had become especially interested in the struggles of
Vietnam vets. He also met Bobby Muller, a veteran who founded Vietnam
Veterans of America with future Democratic presidential nominee John
Kerry. In August 1981, the band had played a benefit concert at Los Angeles's Sports Arena for the Vietnam Veterans of America. Dating back to
his Steel Mill days, and in early songs like "Lost in the Flood," Springsteen had explored the topic of returning Vietnam veterans. Meeting
Kovic and participating in the 1981 benefit concert seems to have rekin-
dled his interest, and he worked that into songs such as "Vietnam" and
"Born in the U.S.A."

Although the *Tracks* version of "Born in the U.S.A." is performed with
a feverish intensity, it doesn't exactly work as an acoustic song. Landau
didn't think much of the song at the time. But as Team Springsteen was
struggling with its attempts to record an electric *Nebraska,* Springsteen
had the band take a turn at this one. And as history would prove, unlike
the other Colts Neck songs that weren't conducive to full-band arrangements, "Born in the U.S.A." was destined to be a rock 'n' roll song.

The studio version of "Born in the U.S.A." that millions of fans would
soon know begins with a single piano-and-bass note. Then Max Weinberg
kicks in, his drum beat keeping time for a martial, six-note phrase on synthesizer, which provides the melodic hook throughout the song. Then
Springsteen joins in, singing of a character from a "dead man's town"
who's given a choice: serve in Vietnam or (we can assume from references
to his "hometown jam") serve time. He chooses the former, goes off to "kill
the yellow man," returns from war, and can't get hired back. But he's the
lucky one; his brother went to Vietnam and never came back.

The song's lyrical structure shows just how far Springsteen had
evolved from the extensive lyricism of his first three albums. "Born in the
U.S.A." tells its story in quick, four-line stanzas. The couplet "Come back

home to the refinery/Hiring man says 'Son if it was up to me,'" is exemplary of Springsteen's economic lyrics. We learn that the protagonist worked at a refinery before the war, that he is unable to get his job back upon his return, and (most importantly) that his foreman can't hire him back due to the larger economic situation—all without the singer telling us any of this explicitly. Similarly, one line about his brother (a "buddy" in the "Vietnam" version) packs a lot of punch: "They're still there, he's all gone." In just one line, we have an implied KIA and (again, more importantly) a damning assessment of the entire war's futility: his brother, and the other Vietnam fatalities, died in vain because "they" (the Vietcong) remain—as the world would learn conclusively by the end of the decade, the Domino Theory rationale for the Vietnam War proved false.

The final verse and chorus reprise include unexpected references to, respectively, Martha and the Vandellas' 1965 hit "Nowhere to Run" and Hank Williams's 1948 song "I'm a Long Gone Daddy." The first is a song about the heartbreak of lost love; the second, a leaving lover's final tell-off. The reference to "Nowhere to Run" serves as a callout to the Top 40 hits on which Springsteen grew up (the "three-minute records" he sings about in the song "No Surrender"). Himes explains the Williams reference:

> Springsteen drops the leaving but retains the swagger, using "gone" in that beat-poet sense of being "cool" or "far out." "I'm a long gone daddy in the U.S.A.," his protagonist sings, as if confident that all the hypocritical judges, hard-assed sergeants, and head-shaking personnel officers in the world can't break his spirit.

Likewise, we take the same sense of indomitable spirit from the singer's oft-repeated declaration, "I was born in the U.S.A." As Himes notes, it's as if Springsteen is echoing "Woody Guthrie's assertion that 'this land is my land,' that no one can chase him off, that the nation belongs as much to him as to anyone."[4]

The album's title track records one of the classic impromptu in-studio moments in rock music. As the song was winding down, Springsteen yelled to Weinberg to keep the drums going, and Weinberg let loose with an extended roll that allowed the band to collect its energy before kicking back in for the song's conclusion. As Springsteen remembered: "We played it two times and our second take is the record. That's why the guys are really on the edge. You can hear Max—to me, he was right up there with the best of them on that song."[5]

And that song would go right up there with the likes of "Born to Run" and "Rosalita" as one of Springsteen's signature songs. It would also provide the title, the moral center, and even the packaging of Springsteen's seventh album. In *Songs*, Springsteen notes that the song "set the mark and feel" for the other songs on *Born in the U.S.A.*

Tellingly, he also says it "more or less stood by itself. The rest of the album contains a group of songs about which I've always had some ambivalence." He almost looks back on *Born in the U.S.A.* as being an artistic failure of sorts. "I wanted to take [*Nebraska*] and electrify it," he writes. "But it really didn't flesh out like I had hoped it would."[6]

With that said, it's interesting to jump ahead a year or two, by which time *Born in the U.S.A.* had become far and away Springsteen's best-selling album—indeed, one of the bestselling albums, period. It sold 20 million copies worldwide and spawned *seven* Top 10 hits (this from an artist who had scored only two to date, and those seemingly in spite of himself), not to mention several heavy-rotation MTV videos, a mammoth, worldwide tour, household-name status for Springsteen, a copycat Chrysler commercial, and even a presidential campaign controversy. All of this came from a collection of 12 songs, most of which Springsteen would later come to regard with "ambivalence."

This might seem ironic, but it's really not. Ever since *Born to Run*, Springsteen had been struggling with competing motivations within himself: the desire to be a popular musician versus the ramifications of becoming popular. The former is self-explanatory; the latter is more complex. For Springsteen, his concern seems to have been not so much with protecting his privacy in the face of intense media glare—though that would surely become an issue in his life and career—as it was with not having his work co-opted by the popular culture and society. This concern would prove hard to manage with the release of *Born in the U.S.A.*, an album designed to reach the broadest common denominator of American popular culture.

As Marsh records, the night in May 1982 that the band recorded "Born in the U.S.A." was when "they knew they'd really begun making an album." Over the next few weeks, Springsteen and the E Street Band hit their stride, recording a number of new songs live in the studio, with minimal overdubbing.[7]

"Working on the Highway," which grew out of "Child Bride" from the Colts Neck tape, provides a nice study of how Springsteen moved toward a wider audience with U.S.A. The earlier "Child Bride," another sung-from-behind-bars tale, is written from the perspective of a man who falls in love with an underage girl and runs away with her (consensually) down to Florida. But the girl's brothers track them down and call the cops, and the man is sent to jail for violating the Mann Act.

"Working on the Highway" retains the story of the man in love with a girl too young, along with several lines from the original song's lyrics. But in its full-band arrangement with its rockabilly rhythm, firecracker percussion, and five-note organ phrase, the story is transformed from a brooding acoustic tale into a snappy, almost *happy* song. Some lines providing further exposition on the young couple's love are deleted, and the tragedy of this ill-fated love is lessened. When the singer ends up on the Charlotte County road gang at song's end, the effect is less of a hurt song than that of a blue-collar ditty, with the singer merely answering a different "work bell clang" than he had when he used to wave a red flag on county road 95.

"Child Bride" might have worked on an album like *Nebraska*. (And as Springsteen site webmaster Flynn McLean notes, if the producers of the *Lost Masters* bootleg volume that includes "Child Bride" were ever brought up on charges of copyright infringement, "they could play Child Bride back to back with Working on the Highway and they would be acquitted.")[8] But with its appeal to both blue-collar rock and good ol' boy country fans, "Working on the Highway" works much better as a popular song, and it provides an excellent album track, maintaining a level of energy and fun on side one of *Born in the U.S.A.*, bridging from the sing-along *sha la las* of "Darlington County" to the painful dream-love of "Downbound Train."

"Darlington County" dates back to *Darkness*. I've never heard the original version of the song, but all one has to do is to hear the cowbell at the beginning of the track on U.S.A. to realize that it must have evolved musically quite a bit from the original version. "Darlington County" is another song steeped in countrified blue-collarism, with the singer and his friend Wayne driving down from New York City into South Carolina in search of union jobs. In a 180-degree twist on "Kitty's Back," our dual protagonists are city boys looking to score some local girls. But these two aren't pretty boys like the one who stole Kitty; they're more mischievous than anything else. They speed through eight hundred miles of road "without seeing a cop," and when they reach their destination, they try to work some girls by waving rolls of cash and claiming that each of their fathers owns one of the Twin Towers. (The song stands as a relic of the pre-9/11 world.) And as the singer leaves Darlington with a "little girl" at the song's conclusion, he spots Wayne "handcuffed to the bumper of a state trooper's Ford." Jimmy Guterman says, "It's unclear whether the Ford is moving," and although that suggestion feels a bit too extreme for the song, it illustrates his point that, "You could dance and shout to them or you could wonder what was going on beneath all those 'Sha-la-la's.'"[9]

"Downbound Train" might be the best song on the record. (In her 1984 review, Debby Bull called it "the saddest song he's ever written," which might explain why it was never released as a single.) In its *Nebraska* incarnation (aka the "Son You May Kiss the Bride" version, named after some lyrics that were later deleted), it doesn't quite work. (The up-tempo approach of that version doesn't quite fit its bittersweet story.) Slowed down and with full instrumentation, though, the *U.S.A.* version is a standout. The opening strums of a minor-chord guitar melody lay the foundation for one of Springsteen's most bittersweet songs. Like the protagonist of "Stolen Car" or any number of songs on *Nebraska*, the teller of "Downbound Train" once had a job, had a wife—but then it all fell apart. After he gets laid off from his job at the lumberyard, his wife leaves him; he sings to us alone, working at a car wash "Where all it ever does is rain." It's a nice metaphor for the car wash, but it's also an echo of Credence Clearwater Revival's "Who'll Stop the Rain?"—which has nothing to do with weather and everything to do with mental hardship. Bull declared, "It's a line Sam Shepard could have written: so pathetic and so funny, you don't know how to react."[10]

The whistle of the nearby Central Line reminds the singer of his ex-wife's departure as he goes to sleep at night. A mournful synthesizer introduces a dreamlike musical element to the song. The singer hears his lover crying for him. He follows her voice through the woods to a clearing, where their "wedding house" emerges, shining in the moonlight. He runs into the house and up the stairs, but when he gets to their bed-room, it's empty—then, heartbreakingly, the train whistle awakes the singer from his dream. The singer concludes grimly: "don't it feel like you're a rider on a downbound train."

From the cold-sweat passion of "Downbound Train," the album moves to the heated passion of "I'm on Fire," a two-and-a-half-minute ode to adulterous lust. The song was recorded in the minimalist country-folk style of Johnny Cash and the Tennessee Three. (Cash covered the song in a stirring version that was included as a bonus on the *Badlands* compila-tion.) According to Himes, Springsteen came across the song in his note-book and recorded it with Roy Bittan and Max Weinberg one evening while the rest of the band was on dinner break.[11] Springsteen sings in a sonorous, Cash-like voice. The music is understated—Bittan's synth lines are restrained and Weinberg's drumming like the ticking of a clock—and the words are what give the song its heat. "Hey little girl is your daddy home?" the singer asks, and when he asks if her "daddy" can do the same thing to her that *he* can, we know this song has nothing to do with incest. Nor is it a simple statement of who's-your-daddy-ism. When the singer confesses that he feels like someone "cut a six-inch val-ley/through the middle of my soul," and that he wakes up in the middle of the night soaked with sweat, it's clear which person is really in charge of the other.

On side two, the songs speak more of nostalgia than passion. "Glory Days" best exemplifies what made *Born in the U.S.A.* work as a pop record. With its descriptions of the one-time high school baseball star sitting at a bar remembering his (long-gone) glory days, as well as the once-beautiful girl who is now a divorcée raising two kids, the song touches upon the "best years of our lives" cliché that, nevertheless, rang true to many of Springsteen's listeners. It's not a happy song. The singer finds himself hoping that he won't "sit around thinking" about his own lost glory days when he gets old, and he concedes, "But I probably will." As Marsh says, "Despite its giddiness, 'Glory Days' is as much about the fear of death as anything on *Nebraska.*"[12] Yet the song *is* a happy song. From the let's-get-this-party-started guitar intro to the faded beauty's ability to deal with her lost direction in life—"when she feels like crying/she starts laughing"—the song emerges as a communal statement of en-durance.

Between the summer of 1982 and the spring of 1983, Springsteen had recorded a number of demos (24-track mixes, more polished than the Colts Neck Teac tapes) at the garage studio in his Hollywood Hills bungalow. A number of them had a rockabilly or country feel: songs such as "Betty Jean" ("Honey you're cute, but you sure are mean/Oh, Betty Jean"), "One Love" (a simple statement of love), "Sugarland" (a despairing farmer sings, "I'm sittin' down at the Sugarland bar/Might as well bury my body right here"), "The Klansman" (from the view of a child raised in a racist family), "Delivery Man" (a comic song culminating in a truck crash and the narrator chasing chickens across a parking lot) and "Don't Back Down" (a "buck up" song that Springsteen ran through in at least ten different takes). There was also "Follow That Dream," a reworking of the 1962 Elvis Presley single by the same name, and "Baby I'm So Cold (Turn the Lights Down Low)," itself a rewrite of Springsteen's "Follow That Dream" with new lyrics.

A number of the so-called Hollywood Hills tracks had a *Nebraska*-like folk tenor. Like "Losin' Kind," "Fugitive Dreams" is inspired by *Out of the Past:* a tale of a man whose "satisfied" life with his wife and children is disrupted by the appearance of a mysterious visitor who mentions something he'd "done a long time ago." And like "Losin' Kind," the narrators of "James Lincoln Deere" and "Richfield Whistle" begin by stating their name and then touch upon a similar territory as "Johnny 99."

"Richfield Whistle" tells the story of James Lucas, a parolee from an Indiana prison. Lucas marries, and he and his wife "worked as hard as two people could," but we're told, "This didn't do no good." Lucas gets a parolee job making deliveries for a rich business owner, but he starts skimming off the top of his cargo and selling it on the side. Although he admits he "didn't like" what he was doing, he says, "I didn't lose no sleep at night." But then his boss discovers Lucas's crime. That night, he fights with his wife, and he goes off driving, apparently headed on a downward spiral like the driver in "Stolen Car." He pulls into a liquor store, and (in a nice touch of O'Connoresque detail) leaves his motor running— signaling a planned getaway for an intended robbery. But when the narrator stands before the store cashier, he changes his mind, turns around and heads out. He goes home, reconciles with his wife, and they lie in bed, listening to the prison whistle blow in the distance.

In "James Lincoln Deere," James Deere sings from within Richfield

Prison, looking back on the days when he was free—"Just a kid, no better or worse than you," he tells the listener—and the crime that took away his freedom. Unlike Lucas, Deere says he and his wife Terry "got by all right," but Deere is tempted by his brother-in-law, who would show off rolls of money he made by selling stolen farm equipment. (Note the proximity of the narrator's name to the name of the leading farm equipment vendor, John Deere.) He resists temptation until he loses his job. The two rob a Stop & Shop supermarket, and Deere shoots a store boy while getting away.

In retrospect, we can see how "Johnny 99" works better than either two Richfield songs. "Richfield Whistle" tells a compelling narrative, but the couple's financial woes seem glossed over in the end. Meanwhile, Deere's crime—shooting a boy in the face, and while clear-headed and sober—is jarringly gruesome even when compared to Ralph/Johnny's act of drunken violence. Most significant, perhaps, is that in both songs, the protagonist's wife sighs and tells him, "We can have anything we want." Her sigh casts her statement in dubious light—not to mention the fact that, in both songs, the protagonist finds himself living under his in-laws' roof. Interestingly, both contain a line that touches upon while at the same time questioning the heart of the American dream.

In "James Lincoln Deere," the narrator hears a foreman say, "These jobs are goin' boys/And they ain't comin' back." The line would resurface in another song, "My Hometown," which closes the *Born in the U.S.A.* album. It's a very personal song, inspired by Springsteen's own hometown of Freehold. The first verse, based on Springsteen's memories of driving with his father through town, is surprisingly sentimental given the songwriter's treatment of fathers from "Adam Raised a Cain" to "Independence Day" to "My Father's House." As the father drives his eight-year-old son through town, he "tousles" his son's hair and says "Son take a good look around/This is your hometown."

In the song's final verse, the singer (now grown) finds himself telling the same thing to his own son as they drive through town. But with the middle verses referring to an incident of racial violence in 1965 and then the "whitewashed windows and vacant stores" on Main Street and the textile mill that's closing, the singer's message to his son is no longer a simple statement of pride (as his father's had been) but advice to look around and remember something even as it's fading away.

As he was working on *Born in the U.S.A.*, Springsteen may have felt the same thing about his own career. The album would be the last one for nearly two decades in which Steve Van Zandt would have any part. Van Zandt, more given to R&B than the country-twang pop toward which Springsteen was migrating, was leaving the E Street Band to pursue different musical directions. This would be no small loss for Springsteen ("Buon viaggio, mio fratello, Little Steven," say the liner notes to the album) and two songs on the album, "No Surrender" and "Bobby Jean," served as musical farewells to Van Zandt.

"No Surrender" is a statement—maybe an overstatement—of youthful defiance with allusions to blood brotherhood and forced warlike metaphors ("Like soldiers in the winter's night with a vow to defend/No retreat no surrender") and its oft-quoted insistence that "We learned more from a three minute record than we ever learned in school." Springsteen admitted later that even he finds the song to be a bit simplistic in its anthemic affirmation: "It was a song I was uncomfortable with. You don't hold out and triumph all the time in life. You compromise, you suffer defeat; you slip into life's gray areas." But Van Zandt persuaded Springsteen that the song's depiction of friendship and of the "inspirational power of rock music" was integral to the new album's message, and Springsteen eventually added the song to *Born in the U.S.A.* in the eleventh hour.[13]

"Bobby Jean" is more overtly a statement of good luck and good-bye. The song came along late in the sessions as Springsteen, Landau, and co-producer Chuck Plotkin were struggling to agree upon a selection of songs. As Marsh records, "The song was a breakthrough for Bruce in several ways. . . . This simple, spacious music was the essence of rock and roll: effortless, joyous, deeply grieved. It was the sound they'd spent the summer searching for."[14]

Although the title character's name is vaguely feminine, her/his name could stand in for the name of any close friend that the singer has known "ever since we were sixteen." (Also note that the compounded first-and-middle name adds yet another rustic, inland touch to the album.)

In *The Mansion on the Hill*, Fred Goodman suggests that Van Zandt's departure from E Street also had something to do with tensions between himself and Jon Landau. As Columbia A&R man Pete Philbin remembers, "Steve and Jon clashed constantly." Goodman writes that Van Zandt was the person the band and crew members turned to as a mediator. His friendship with Springsteen predated his involvement in the band, and he had his ear. That role only served to heighten the tension between him and Landau. Having fought to carve out his own niche as a producer when Mike Appel was the manager, Landau now appeared cool to having Van Zandt as a collaborator, reportedly fighting with him over royalties and production credits.[15]

Born in the U.S.A. might have been the album on which Landau cemented his role within the Springsteen camp. Indeed, he would have arguably his biggest influence on Springsteen's career toward the end of the *U.S.A.* sessions. Most important was Landau's role in getting two songs onto the album that would turn into the first two singles and effectively launch the *Born in the U.S.A.* machine.

The people for disco queen Donna Summer had asked Springsteen to write a song for her, and despite the apparent mismatch in genres, Springsteen agreed. Springsteen later alluded to his distaste for what he identified as the "veiled racism" behind the antidisco movement;[16] and no doubt, writing for Summer offered him the opportunity to reach an R&B audience from which he had been steadily drifting. One song he initially offered to Summer was "Cover Me," which evolved out of an earlier song, "Drop On Down and Cover Me." With its references to the rain and driving snow and the search for a lover's cover, "Cover Me," is a revved up, sexual answer to Dylan's "Shelter from the Storm." It might have worked for Summer, but Landau liked it so much that he persuaded Springsteen to keep it for his own. Instead, Springsteen gave Summer "Protection"—the opposite of "Cover Me," with the singer confessing to the object of his obsession that he needs to be protected from her love. Summer ended up recording the song, with Springsteen himself providing a strong guitar track.

The version of "Protection" recorded by the E Street Band is one of many noteworthy nonalbum tracks to emerge from the *U.S.A.* sessions, for which Springsteen reportedly wrote anywhere from 50 to 70 songs. These include:

- "My Love Will Not Let You Down"—a rousing pick-up line of a song with some not-so-subtle coercion ("Well hold still darling, hold still for God's sake")

- "County Fair"—a melodic slice of bucolic life
- "Brothers Under the Bridge"—a strong-muscled anthem that combines the sentiment of "No Surrender" with echoes of "Born in the U.S.A."
- "None but the Brave"—a variation on the aphoristic sentiment "only the strong survive," with a soaring sax solo from Clarence
- "This Hard Land"—a Guthriesque tune with an "electric *Nebraska*" sound
- "TV Movie" and "Stand on It"—two fast-paced, rockabilly-style numbers.
- "Shut Out the Light"—a wistful, harmonic song about the return of a man (most likely a veteran, though the song could just as well be about a parolee) welcomed home by his lover and his family
- "Janey Don't You Lose Heart"—a slower, more subtle, and more melodic venture into the territory of "Be True," and the first song the E Street Band recorded with new guitarist Nils Lofgren and resident violinist Soozie Tyrell
- "Johnny Bye Bye"—the "I'm on Fire" B-side that borrows its two opening lines from Chuck Berry's "Bye Bye Johnny" (Berry got cowriting credits on the song) and serves as an ode to Elvis, with the image of Hank Williams's white Cadillac death car thrown in for good measure
- "Lion's Den"—a horn-infused R&B number in which the singer announces his triumph over a recent heartbreak
- "Pink Cadillac"—a down-tempo, rockabilly rewrite of the Garden of Eden myth and a sustained sexual metaphor; the song nearly made the cut for *Born in the U.S.A.*
- "Wages of Sin"—the song of a man resigned to keep paying for having wronged his lover

In the summer of 1983, Springsteen began thinking of a lineup for the album and had Chuck Plotkin do a rough mix of "Born in the U.S.A.," "Glory Days," "My Hometown," "Downbound Train," "Follow That Dream," "Shut Out the Light," "My Love Will Not Let You Down," and "Sugarland." After Springsteen and the band recorded "No Surrender" and "Brothers Under the Bridge" that fall, he polled people on which songs to include.

According to Himes's history of the album, four songs—"U.S.A.," "Glory Days," "Downbound Train" and "This Hard Land"—made everyone's ballot. Springsteen leaned toward a lineup of "U.S.A.," "Murder Incorporated," "Downbound Train," "Glory Days," "This Hard Land," "My Love Will Not Let You Down," "Johnny Bye Bye," "Frankie," "I'm Goin' Down," "Working on the Highway," and "I'm on Fire"; B-sides were to include "Don't Back Down," "Sugarland," "Little Girl Like You," and "Follow That Dream." By the following March, the team was looking at a revised list that was very close to the final lineup, save for the inclusion of "Murder Incorporated," "Frankie," "This Hard Land," and "Pink Cadillac"—and with one song still missing.[17]

The sessions had been enormously prolific, and in them, Springsteen had shown an increasing pop sensibility. Yet Landau felt they still had not produced the hit single that could effectively launch the album. He told Dave Marsh:

> The type of single I was talking about was a single that would truly represent what was going on. And I was also searching for a way to express the idea that I wanted something that was more direct than any one thing that was on the record. As I said to Bruce, a song where a person who is a Bruce fan, who stayed with you on *Nebraska*, even if it was mysterious to him, a song where that guy's gonna say, "Yeah, that's Bruce; that's what he's all about, right now, today."[18]

Now, telling Springsteen at this point that he still lacked a good hit record was incendiary stuff. They argued the point, and Springsteen reportedly left the studio, telling Landau: "I've written seventy songs. You want another one, *you* write it."[19]

But Springsteen settled down and went back to his hotel suite in search of just such a song. In fact, he began to write *about* this search. The chorus, a statement of creative frustration, came to him: "You can't start a fire without a spark/This gun's for hire, even if we're just dancin' in the dark." And thus was born "Dancing in the Dark," the song that would introduce Springsteen to a whole new generation of listeners in 1984.

The song is one of the more frank examinations of the creative process. It shows the songwriter struggling not just with writer's block but also with the very nature of being a public performer. The singer is bored with himself, he can't stand the sight of himself in the mirror, and he feels confined by the walls around him. He bids a nearby love to help provide the creative "spark" he needs. "I'm sick of sitting 'round here trying to write this book," he says. He's "dying for some action . . . a love reaction."

The admission that he is a "gun for hire" no doubt carries sexual innuendo (the song *is* called "Dancing in the Dark," after all) but it also comments on the reason the song was written in the first place. Some might see it as a sardonic look at the argument that he'd had that day with the manager who demanded a commercial hit. The gun-for-hire image also casts Springsteen in the tradition of the freelance troubadour, ever in search of an audience.

As Bob Clearmountain, an engineer who culled the Rolling Stones' bestselling 1981 album *Tattoo You* from unreleased outtakes, completed mixing the rest of the album, "Dancing in the Dark" was released as an advance single in May 1984, with "Pink Cadillac" as a B-side that received radio play in its own right. Soaked in synthesizer, "Dancing in the Dark" was an instant radio hit, rising to Number 2 on the Billboard chart, held out of the top spot by Prince's "When Doves Cry," a crossover hit that appealed to both black and white audiences.

The *Born in the U.S.A.* tour touched off on June 29 in St. Paul, Minnesota, opening with "Thunder Road" before a sold-out crowd at the Civic Centre. The night's setlist included eight songs from the new album, along with five from *Nebraska* (which hadn't had a supporting tour). After the intermission, the band performed "Dancing in the Dark" with the houselights on. Then, Springsteen announced that they were making a "movie" and that they were going to perform the song again. (At least one of these performances must have been lip-synced for the benefit of the video—something he would choose not to repeat for the video to "Born in the U.S.A.") The night before, film director Brian DePalma (*Scarface, Body Double*) had shot close-ups with the band, local extras, and a young actor named Courtney Cox, who played a fan pulled onstage by Springsteen to dance with him. DePalma's video, the first true music video to feature Springsteen, introduced a suddenly buff Springsteen to the MTV generation. For some long-time fans, synthesizer tracks and a music video smacked of a sellout, but these things were very much within the musical zeitgeist of the early-to-mid-1980s, and they helped

Springsteen reach the audience he had sought ever since first signing his contract with Mike Appel. As Springsteen says in the liner notes of his *Greatest Hits* collection, "A bunch of autograph seeking Catholic school-girls came rushing up to me on the streets of N.Y.C. screaming they'd seen the video." Bobbie Ann Mason's novel *In Country,* which includes many references to *Born in the U.S.A.*–era Springsteen, has Sam, the teen-girl narrator, dreaming that "somewhere, out there on the road, in some big city, she would find a Bruce Springsteen concert. And he would pull her out of the crowd and dance with her in the dark."[20]

Born in the U.S.A. would top even Michael Jackson's *Thriller* as a gold-mine for singles, and as with the two singles released during *The River,* Springsteen established a pattern of B-sides of previously unreleased songs. A second single, "Cover Me," reached into the Top 10 at number 7. The flipside was a live recording of Tom Waits's "Jersey Girl" from the Meadowlands in 1981, a performance so convincing that the song sounds as if it were written for, if not *by,* Springsteen. These were followed by "Born in the U.S.A."/"Shut Out the Light" (#9), "I'm on Fire"/"Johnny Bye Bye" (#6), "Glory Days"/"Stand on It" (#5), "I'm Goin' Down"/"Janey Don't You Lose Heart" (#9), and "My Hometown"/"Santa Claus Is Comin' to Town," a live recording from C.W. Post College way back in 1975 that has since become a holiday classic (#6).

As the hits mounted, the tour continued to gain momentum. The band played arenas throughout the United States in 1985. At the end of January, they played their first outdoor full-stadium shows, in consecutive nights at the Carrier Dome in Syracuse. Then, the band took some time off before launching a world tour at the end of March. They played eight dates in Australia, then seven in Japan. In June, they played Slane Castle in Ireland and toured Europe through July, ending with dates at Wembley Stadium in London and Roudhay Park in Leeds, before returning home for a full-out tour of America that was tacked on to answer ticket demand. A year before, the Brendan Byrne Arena was a typical E Street Band concert venue. This time, Springsteen and the E Street Band were selling out football stadiums like Washington's RFK Stadium, Philadelphia's Veterans Stadium, Detroit's Silverdome, Miami's Orange Bowl, the Cotton Bowl in Dallas, and, of course, Giants Stadium. The tour came to an end on October 2, with a 33-song show at the Los Angeles

Coliseum. Fittingly, the encore for that show included covers of "Travellin' Band" and "Rockin' All over the World."

Born in the U.S.A. was recognized as an instant classic. In her initial *Rolling Stone* review, Bull gave the album five stars and praised its "indomitable spirit": "He's set songs as well drawn as those on his bleak acoustic album, *Nebraska*, to music that incorporates new electronic textures while keeping as its heart all of the American rock & roll from the early Sixties."[21] At year's end, the magazine's readers gave Artist of the Year, Band of the Year, Album of the Year, Single of the Year ("Dancing in the Dark") and Music Video of the Year (ditto) honors to Springsteen and the E Street Band. The cornucopia of hit singles and the mammoth world tour created a phenomenon around *Born in the U.S.A.* that endured over a year and a half. In 1985, that magazine's readers again named him Artist of the Year despite his not having a new album (an unprecedented feat), as well as Best Songwriter, Best Male Singer, and Best Live Performance and ranked "Glory Days" the third-best Single of the Year.

The Springsteen/*Born in the U.S.A.* machine helped proliferate a pop-culture emergence of American heartland rock, and artists such as John Mellencamp, Tom Petty, and Bob Seger would all reap benefits. Madison Avenue sought to exploit the trend, and Lee Iacocca reportedly offered Springsteen $12 million to transform "Born in the U.S.A." into a commercial jingle for Chrysler. Springsteen turned down the offer, and Chrysler turned to Plan B with a generic "Made in the U.S.A." slogan.

While Springsteen was able to prevent Madison Avenue from co-opting his songs, he couldn't prevent politicians from doing the same. At a campaign stop in Hammonton, New Jersey, in September 1984, Ronald Reagan told a cheering crowd, "America's future rests in a thousand dreams inside your hearts; it rests in the message of hope in songs so many young Americans admire: New Jersey's own Bruce Springsteen. And helping you make those dreams come true is what this job of mine is all about." Later, when asked what his favorite Bruce Springsteen song was, the 73-year-old Reagan implausibly responded "Born to Run." Democratic nominee Walter Mondale answered that Springsteen "may have been 'born to run,' but he wasn't born yesterday."

Larry David Smith argues that "Reagan—in no way—co-opted Springsteen's view or implied any type of association" but merely "did what all public speakers do when visiting a particular area: He mentioned a local hero's name as an applause line."[22] Smith's rationalization might well illustrate how Reagan earned his nickname as the "Teflon president," as Reagan's allusion is a textbook example of a candidate attempting to co-opt a celebrity's popularity for a political sound byte— which is exactly what it became on the evening news that night. Surely, the famously jingoistic Reagan summoned Springsteen not just because he was a "local hero" but because he was a pop culture icon who transcended localities—and voting-age demographics. The implied message was that Springsteen's songs are about hope and Reagan would fulfill that hope. Reagan was telling the American public: Springsteen and I are working for the same thing.

Performing onstage at Pittsburgh's Civic Arena on September 22, Springsteen said, "The President mentioned my name the other day, and I kinda got to wondering what his favorite album must have been. I don't think it was the *Nebraska* album. I don't think he's been listening to this one." And then he played "Johnny 99."[23]

The mass media began to take notice of the growing phenomenon of the *Born in the U.S.A.* tour. On September 12, 1984, Bernard Goldberg had profiled Springsteen on the CBS *Evening News,* saying, "His shows are like old-time revivals with the same old-time message: If they work hard enough and long enough, like Springsteen himself, they can also make it to the promised land."[24] For anyone who had been paying attention, Springsteen's lyrics carried none of the "Be like me and you can make it, too!" message that Goldberg saw. It would be easy to write off Goldberg's analysis if not for the column that George Will published the following day, titled "Yankee Doodle Springsteen." Will, a conservative syndicated columnist, took in the Springsteen concert at the Capitol Centre in Landover, Maryland, and reported that Springsteen "is no whiner, and the recitation of closed factories and other problems always seems punctuated by a grand, cheerful affirmation: 'Born in the U.S.A.!'" Will then went off on a tangent, arguing that "If all Americans—in labor and management, who make steel or cars or shoes or textiles—made their products with as much energy and confidence as Springsteen and his merry band make music, there would be no need for Congress to be thinking about protectionism."

Granted, Will admitted, "I have not got a clue about Springsteen's politics," and surely Will's column said more about his *own* politics than Springsteen's. The off-point observation that Springsteen is "no whiner" plainly bespeaks a certain conservative mind-set, one that would label any questioning of the economic status quo as unmanly. At the 2004 Republican Convention, Arnold Schwarzenegger—who followed in Reagan's footsteps as a questionable actor-turned-even more questionable governor of California—drew the same insulting comparison when he called those who would complain about a struggling economy "girly men." Back in 1984, Will had prefaced his column by saying, "There is not a smidgen of androgyny in Springsteen."[25]

Will's observation placed Springsteen firmly within the 1980s political-cultural zeitgeist. Reagan had attempted to co-opt Springsteen's popularity, just as he had similarly done in alluding to popular 1980s movie characters such as Clint Eastwood's Dirty Harry ("make my day") and Sylvester Stallone's Rambo. Stallone's character, a muscular Vietnam vet who spoke in the equivalent of sound bytes, was especially symbolic of everything with which the jingoistic Reagan attempted to identify himself. Susan Jeffords argues in *Hard Bodies: Hollywood Masculinity in the Reagan Era,* the "distinction between 'soft bodies' and 'hard bodies' was an important one in Reagan's ideology." As Bryan Garman puts it, "Reagan's combination of masculinity and nationalism shaped and was reinforced by a popular culture that 'remasculinized' the country's image of itself."[26]

> Whereas the stereotypically "soft," languid bodies of "lazy" welfare mothers, drug addicts, the unemployed, and gay men were represented and perceived as being either female or African American, the determined, individualistic, patriotic, and authoritative "hard body" was associated with white men such as Reagan and Rambo.[27]

Garman further notes, "Even though Springsteen questioned the moral and political motives and ramifications of the war, his masculinity, patriotism, and identification with the working class were enough to attach him to the Reagan-Rambo bandwagon."[28]

Indeed, for those who did not look beneath the message of the chorus to "Born in the U.S.A.," Springsteen must have resembled John Rambo more than Johnny 99. The character of Rambo was an Italian-American

Vietnam vet who wore a headband in battle. On the *Born in the U.S.A.* tour, Springsteen, an Italian-American, sang about Vietnam vets, sported a muscular frame, and occasionally wore a bandana around his forehead (an apparent nod to the Vietnam soldier). For many—especially his new fans—Springsteen *was* the Rambo of rock, and his "Born in the U.S.A." anthem was a "celebration of a resurgent American militarism."[29]

To be fair, Springsteen himself knew the risks he was taking in soliciting a wider audience, and (as he himself would admit in retrospect) he was not entirely innocent in how his music was perceived. As Garman points out:

> With the Summer Olympic Games being held in Los Angeles and a presidential election slated for November, 1984 was a year of patriotic rhetoric and the flag, a "powerful image" that Springsteen certainly used to his advantage. Although he would try to clarify his cultural politics during the tour, he personally benefited from and helped create the patriotic fervor that swept the nation. The flag appeared on his album cover and hung behind his concert stage, and when he sang the chorus of "Born in the U.S.A." in his performances, he and his audience rhythmically and triumphantly pumped their fists in the air.[30]

In 1975, Springsteen had landed on the rock 'n' roll map with his release of *Born to Run.* Ten years down the road, he had rewritten that map. *Born in the U.S.A.* brought Springsteen unimaginable success as a recording and performing artist. Yet Springsteen's on-the-record ambiguousness hints at the doubled-edged nature of the album's success. "I put a lot of pressure on myself over a long period of time to reproduce the intensity of *Nebraska* on *Born in the U.S.A.* I never got it. But 'Born in the U.S.A.' is probably one of my five or six best songs, and there was something about the grab-bag nature of the rest of the album that probably made it one of my purest pop records."[31]

Today, the album remains a litmus test among fans. Several songs, including "Dancing in the Dark," "Glory Days," and (despite its awkward transition to stadium settings) "My Hometown" draw rousing ovation from concert audiences. Still, the album is often shrugged off by hardcore fans who remember with a touch of embarrassment the muscular patriotism—real or perceived—of the title song, the fashion faux pas (bandana headbands, jean vest over leather jacket), the 18 months of nonstop airplay on Top 40 radio that had pastel-wearing girls singing Springsteen in school hallways. In many ways, the album is very much a time capsule of the 1980s music scene that favored jingly pop songs, and in which a "grab-bag" album like *Born in the U.S.A.* would become a blockbuster success. But regardless of one's viewpoint, the album became the proverbial lion in the road—one that Springsteen himself would have to confront as he planned the next step in his career.

* 8 *

Bruced Out

Live/1975-85 (1986)

In December 1986, Columbia released *Live/1975–85*, the first official release of concert recordings of Bruce Springsteen and the E Street Band. Following in the wake of *Born in the U.S.A.*, the album was a fittingly blockbuster event: a five-LP boxed set that included performances of songs from all seven studio albums. Reviewing the set's release on the campus of Rutgers University in Springsteen's home state, I said something about the set not being enough (citing the many favorites left off the collection). I was right and wrong; *Live/1975–85* was both not enough and too much.

Two decades later, Springsteen's boxed set stands very much as a record (*record* in the sense of *document*) of the *Born in the U.S.A.* era. Springsteen had decided not to go the traditional route of releasing an album of performances taken exclusively from the preceding tour, something that the Rolling Stones, for one, have done with live tour albums such as *Love You Live* and *Still Life*. Nevertheless, with 17 of the box's 40 songs taken from *U.S.A.* concerts at the Los Angeles Coliseum or the

Meadowlands Arena/Giants Stadium complex, the album struck many as being the audio equivalent of a 1984–85 tour program.

More puzzlingly, the set offered next to nothing in the way of performances from the early years, when Springsteen and the E Street Band had performed in intimate venues and established their reputation as live performers. *Live/1975–85* included no tracks from, say, the band's historic Bottom Line dates. Only *one* song, an October 1975 performance of "Thunder Road" at the Roxy, even dates from before 1978. Rather than chronicling the best performances from throughout the band's career, the boxed set presents a virtual concert framed within the arena-and-stadium setting from the *Darkness, River,* and *U.S.A.* tours. Performances from different years and venues were mixed with audience noise fading one into the next in an attempt to re-create a single concert experience. Thus, a November 1980 performance of "Badlands" from Tempe flowed into a December 1980 performance of "Because the Night" from Nassau, which flowed into a July 1981 performance of "Candy's Room" from East Rutherford, as if they were all from the same show.

The selection of songs raised some eyebrows among long-time fans. Did the instrumental "Paradise by the 'C'" or the tongue-in-cheek performance of "Fire" need to be included—especially when they came at the expense of such omissions as "Incident on 57th Street" or (most glaringly) "Jungleland"? Did fans need Springsteen's monotone performance of Woody Guthrie's "This Land Is Your Land" (from December 1980) when many still awaited the release of "The Promise"? Did they really need live versions of two-thirds of the *Born in the U.S.A.* record?

Still, the boxed set was not without a number of highlights that came as blessings to die-hard fans. "Thunder Road" was a nice relic from the *Born to Run* tour, during which Springsteen would open with the song on piano before the band joined him on stage. Both "Growin' Up" and "The River" included effective monologues from Springsteen. "Growin' Up," from the 1978 performance at the Roxy with his parents in the crowd, has Springsteen playfully triumphant. He tells the crowd how unpopular he was in his house as a youth, how unsightly he looked and how his own lawyer (for a traffic accident lawsuit) was repulsed by his looks, and how he defied his parents' wishes and became a rock 'n' roll star. In the introduction to "The River," he tells a 1985 L.A. Coliseum crowd a less defiant, more heartwarming story. He remembers his father repeatedly saying that the army would "make a man" out of him; but when Springsteen goes for his draft physical, he fails. The Coliseum audience cheers his failing the physical, but while the rock 'n' roll punk of 1978 might have let them, the 1985 populist rocker chides them, saying, "It's nothing to cheer about." He closes in recounting how he went home to tell his father, "They didn't take me," and his father says, "That's good." It's a great moment, one that cuts across politics and speaks of the power of familial ties.

Other highlights include "Adam Raised a Cain" and "Because the Night," which both stand out as relentless, hard rock numbers. "Nebraska" and "Johnny 99" worked surprisingly well as sung to tens of thousands of New Jersey faithful. A September 1985 performance of Edwin Starr's "War" was powerful, as was a blistering version of "Born in the U.S.A." from that same night in Los Angeles. In the end, what made *Live/1975–85* work was the same thing that had made *Born in the U.S.A.* such a hit: it was a grab bag with something for nearly everyone.

Live/1975–85 not only became the first boxed set to reach number one—debuting at the top of the Billboard charts despite a hefty price tag—but it opened the door for future boxed set releases. Bob Dylan's *Biograph* predated *Live/1975–85*, but the latter was much more successful and much more influential in establishing the boxed set as a commercial model. But it also set the stage for the inevitable reaction of "Enough, already!" from the media and the listening public. Ever since the hype heyday of *Born to Run*, Springsteen had been viewed skeptically by hipsters who viewed his—or anybody's—meteoric rise with cynicism. Ten years later, with the one-time rock 'n' roll future having become pop music's present, even those who had heralded his coming began to turn against Springsteen. Years after his brilliant piece on *Born to Run*, Lester Bangs used his drug-addled prose to rail against Springsteen's omnipresence in the popular culture:

> if I see Bruce Springsteen or REO Speedwagon release new LPs, I know they'll be in [the Top 10]. . . . And as Tom [Petty] himself steps into Them Boots of Next Springsteen (some people still think the world never needed the first one) you have practically committed a patriotic act by going out and buying not just Rolling Advertisement but also that worthless album where it all sounds like recycled Byrds/Stones and the omnipresent SPRINGSTEEN.[1]

Even among average listeners, it became fashionable in some circles to declare that one was not a Springsteen fan. For such music fans, Springsteen's omnipresence equated him with the status quo, and denouncing Springsteen gave one credentials as an *independent thinker*. Never mind that many such listeners might in the same breath express enthusiasm for a vapid pop crooner (Phil Collins), a jazz-light dabbler (Sting), a computer-nerd power trio (Rush) or any number of disposable hair metal bands (Motley Crüe, Poison, etc.); declaring an anti-Springsteen platform made one sound *alternative*.

Marsh remembers that his book *Glory Days: Bruce Springsteen in the 1980s*, which hit stores in the spring of 1987, was "published straight into the teeth of the so-called 'Boss backlash' ... with program directors talking of 'Bruce burnout.' "[2] While the first single from the boxed set, "War," charted, the follow-up, "Fire," died out quickly. The media, which regularly enjoys tearing down that which they once built up, reported the "Fire" flop as a chink in the Springsteen armor. "News" stories reported returns of the *Live* box set, despite the fact that returns are not only a frequent but an expected occurrence among record trade retail.

Born in the U.S.A. had been the sonic equivalent of Dr. Frankenstein's monster—a creation that threatened to eclipse its creator. Just as successive generations would come to attribute the name *Frankenstein* to the monster and not the doctor himself, a new generation of music fans would equate Springsteen with the Top 40 pop of *Born in the U.S.A.*, unaware of the landmark achievements of *Wild* or *Born to Run* or *Darkness*. With its heavy emphasis on the *U.S.A.* tour, the *Live* box had only reinforced this image. Looking back in a 1992 *Rolling Stone* interview, Springsteen himself admitted: "I really enjoyed the success of *Born in the U.S.A.*, but by the end of that whole thing, I just kind of felt 'Bruced' out. I was like 'Whoa, enough of that.'[3] You end up creating this sort of icon, and eventually it oppresses you." Biographer Christopher Sandford quotes an unnamed "ex-colleague" (a band member? roadie? ticket taker?) as saying, "I, for one, knew we were fucked. That box should really have been a coffin." A quote offered from Springsteen himself is perhaps more insightful: "We all sat there listening to [the boxed set] and sensed that it was the end of something ... next time would be different."[4]

Different, indeed. One important thing that had happened during the *U.S.A.* tour was Springsteen meeting Julianne Phillips, a pretty, young, blond actor. They met in October 1984, and after a brief courtship, they got married on May 13, 1985, at a ceremony in Lake Oswego, Oregon.

The Springsteens moved into a house in Rumson, an upper-class neighborhood in New Jersey. He had everything he could have hoped for in life: the house, the girl, and gold records many times over. Springsteen now had to confront a crucial question: What happens when you achieve all your goals . . . but you still aren't fulfilled?

Tunnel of Love (1987)

Examining the musical landscape and reexamining the reasons behind his chosen career, Springsteen considered his next move carefully. History had shown him that trying to top *Born in the U.S.A.* would have been a "losing game."[5] What's more, releasing a *Son of Born in the U.S.A.* would have sold well, but it also would have been a strategic mistake in the face of a public still showing signs of a Bruce backlash.

Springsteen returned to a more personal, introspective mode of writing. "I decided to reintroduce myself to my fans as a songwriter," he explained later.[6] He began to work on new material in 1986, splitting time between studios in New York and Los Angeles, working with session musicians—an early sign that he was headed in a new direction. Unsatisfied with the results, he holed up in the personal 24-track recording studio he'd created at his Rumson home and worked through some new material on his own. Then he headed into the studio (multiple studios, really, on the East and West Coasts) and recorded the basic tracks alone; only then did he call in members of the E Street Band to overdub their individual parts. Max Weinberg was the only one to appear consistently throughout the album; Clarence Clemons appeared only once—to provide backing vocals.

On October 6, 1987, Springsteen released *Tunnel of Love*, his eighth studio album. It had been more than three years since his last album of new material, but thanks to the long-lasting *U.S.A.* tour, the flood of singles along the way, and the release of the boxed set, the new album seemed to follow quickly upon the last. In truth, the album showed a great deal of musical growth since *Born in the U.S.A.*

The new album caught everybody off guard. For an artist who had recently been married, many might have expected a record (especially one titled *Tunnel of Love*) that indulged in romantic clichés. Some fans doubtless worried that Springsteen, now rich, famous, and (it seemed) in love would lose his creative edge. On the contrary, the album was marked by an unseen commitment to both melody and musical subtlety; it also offered lyrical themes that hinted at the dangerous undercurrents of doubt and fear that lie beneath the surface of love.

The opening song, "Ain't Got You," frames the rest of the album, practically serving as a prologue to introduce the theme of love as that which is desired to complete one's life. The title comes from Bill Boy Arnold's R&B hit "I Ain't Got You," but with its a cappella opening and hoedown rhythms, Springsteen's song is quite different. "Ain't Got You" plays with the I'm-nothing-without-you cliché, throwing out a laundry list of riches that prove unsatisfying without the unnamed object of desire: diamonds, gold, bonds, houses, fame, adoring "little girls," a "house full of Rembrandts," caviar, and a "fancy foreign car," as well as journeys across the "seven seas." Interestingly, most of Springsteen's listeners probably didn't own many of these items, and it's doubtful that Bruce himself was keeping a pound of caviar on ice and a string of Rembrandt paintings in his house in Rumson. Clearly, the listener is supposed to recognize that these things are signifiers of wealth, but they themselves are clichés that create a joking mood that ends up treating the theme of desired lover from a distance.

But prologues don't necessarily begin the story as much as they do tease the audience with what is to come. If "Ain't Got You" is the prologue for the album, the next song, "Tougher than the Rest," is chapter one. Musically, the song introduces a melodic and layered synthesizer sound, and despite a too-heavy drum beat from Max Weinberg, it's suddenly clear that we've moved past the in-your-face anthems of *Born in the U.S.A.* "Tougher than the Rest," an earnest love song, shows Springsteen venturing into new territory as a songwriter. The singer sings to a girl in blue on a Saturday night, and we know that he, she, or both of them are on the rebound: "somebody ran out" and "left somebody's heart in a mess." The singer makes his pitch in the second verse, admitting that he isn't a "handsome Dan" or a "sweet-talkin' Romeo" but that he's "tougher than the rest." We're reminded of the pitch in "Thunder Road," in which the singer stands outside Mary's screen door and tells her, "You ain't a beauty but hey you're all right." The singer in "Tougher" admits he's "been around a time or two" and wonders, "maybe you've been around, too." But unlike Mary's suitor, who wants to take her away and trade in their wings for wheels, here the singer just wants to ask his girl to dance. The contrast is meaningful; whereas the single Springsteen had established his reputation with songs about the mythic romance, the married Springsteen was now writing about a sphere or romance that was smaller yet more realistic.

"All That Heaven Will Allow" completes the first stage of *Tunnel of Love*. Here, the singer has the girl and all is right with the world. He's got money in his pocket and a locket with a picture of his girl inside, and there isn't a cloud in the sky. He's so happy that he even seems to enjoy arguing with the bouncer who won't let him into the club to meet his date. Nothing can stop him—not "dark skies" or "Mister Trouble." In the end, he restates his joy at having something to live for. He ponders those who might want to die "young and gloriously" and says, "that ain't me"— he wants all the time that heaven will allow.

What's interesting, though, is despite its positive message, the song also makes reference to a number of obstacles: the other guys whom he tells not to bother noticing his girl now that he's with her, the bouncer who doesn't want to let him into the club to meet her, the bad weather (literally or figuratively), Mister Trouble, dying young. The affirmation of love and its redeeming qualities is subtly undercut by the mention of the many things that could get in the way.

Lest the reader think we're overanalyzing the matter and that *Tunnel of Love* really is an album of hearts and flowers, the next song on the record disrupts any comfort level that may have set in. The first line of "Spare Parts," a rare X-rated moment for Springsteen, is immediately jarring: "Bobby said he'd pull out, Bobby stayed in." Suddenly, and very purposefully, the focus is on the actual love act rather than on love as an abstraction. The second line, "Janey had a baby, it wasn't any sin," establishes the moral center of the song. Yes, what the couple did might have been a sin according to the Catholic Church, but her having a baby wasn't a sin of morality; instead, Janey is a victim of Bobby's act. Bryan Garman states:

> In these lines, Springsteen rewrites more than thirty years of male rock and roll fantasies that celebrate the liberating effects of sexual expression but do not examine the power relations in which they are embed-

ded. Bobby's power play begins when he fails to "pull out." His promise to do so indicates that he and Janey had negotiated the terms of their encounter, but he betrays her confidence, asserting his strength and sexuality in a stereotypically masculine manner that establishes control over both his and Janey's body. Social constructs permit him to remain narrowly focused on his own immediate pleasure rather than on the possible long-term effects of his actions.[7]

(As Chuck Berry once said, Hail, hail, rock 'n' roll . . .)

Now, after Bobby leaves her at the altar and flees town, Janey does contemplate committing a sinful act. She takes her baby down to the river with the plan to let it wash away, an obvious allusion to the Moses myth from the Old Testament, though here we assume that Janey's baby would encounter a much less miraculous fate. But she reconsiders her act and brings her baby home, then she hocks her wedding ring and dress for money to help get started in her new life as a single mother.

With "Spare Parts" establishing the theme of love as a lie, *Tunnel of Love* moves on to a cluster of five songs that deal with the problematic nature of love and relationships. "Cautious Man," "Walk Like a Man," "Tunnel of Love," "Two Faces," and "Brilliant Disguise" form the thematic core of the album.

In "Cautious Man," Springsteen again borrows from a Robert Mitchum movie. The protagonist, Bill Horton, has the word *love* tattooed on one hand, the word *fear* on the other, much like the Mitchum character in *Night of the Hunter*. And much like Springsteen himself, Horton is a "cautious man of the road" who suddenly finds himself married after a speedy engagement—and after letting his "cautiousness slip away." But here, the obstacle comes from within; Horton prays at night for "steadiness" of heart, for he knows that "in a restless heart the seed of betrayal lay."

"Walk Like a Man" is one of the most touching songs Springsteen has written. The singer recalls his wedding day and his feelings as he watched his bride walk down the aisle. But the song is as much about the singer's relationship with his father as it is about his own marriage. The touch of his father's hand at the wedding makes the singer reminisce about his childhood, tracing his father's footsteps at the beach. Now, as his father steps away from the singer at the altar, the singer is conscious of his new role in life. When he prays for the strength to walk like a man, it's with the

growing realization of the "many steps" he'd have to make on his own. After seeing his father have his "best steps stolen away" from him by a rough
life (symbolized by the father's "rough" hands in the opening line), the
singer vows to do what he can to "walk like a man." It's a promise he makes
to his father, his bride, and ultimately, to himself. But in the end, all he can
promise is to do what he can because what follows is a "mystery ride."

"Tunnel of Love" takes us on another mystery ride. With sound effects
from an amusement park ride in Point Pleasant, New Jersey, the album's
title song returns us to familiar territory on the Jersey shore. But the
whole idea of the song is that unfamiliar territory of love, and though the
beat-box rhythm and "sha na na na" hooks create a playful atmosphere,
the lyrics and Nils Lofgren's eerie guitar bridge offer a darker dimension.
Obviously, the tunnel here is a metaphor for love itself, and through this
tunnel the singer and his date travel into a scary land. Their images are
distorted by a funhouse mirror, and a "room of shadows" encloses them
in darkness. Within this darkness lie hints of sinister sexuality. The image
of the tunnel carries sexual tones, of course, and in the darkness the singer
recognizes "it's just the three of us"—either a joke on sexual arousal or,
more abstractly, a reference to "all that stuff we're so scared of." No late-
1980s public service announcement for AIDS awareness, the terrors found
within this figurative amusement ride are outlined in the final verse: When
a man and woman fall in love, the ride can get "rough" and the tunnel can
become "haunted." It's easy, he says, for lovers to "lose each other" in the
tunnel of love.

"Two Faces" and "Brilliant Disguise" complete the album's core with ruminations of the psychological complexities of love and commitment.
While "Brilliant Disguise," the first single released from *Tunnel of Love,* was
described by Springsteen as the "center" of the album,[8] Larry David Smith
contends (and I agree) that "Two Faces" provides the "narrative foundation" for the album as a song about a man "at war with himself." Springsteen strums a restrained pizzicato chord progression on guitar, providing
a gentle background for the singer's contemplation of his schizophrenic
personality within relationships. He met a girl and ran away with her, and
like the singer in "Walk Like a Man," he made a vow to make her happy. But
now he's left to confront a dual nature that he's unable to control. One
"face" allows him to be happy; the other is self-destructive, threatens to
take his love away, and makes him do things he can't understand. We hear

that his two faces make him "feel like half a man"; the whole is less than the sum of the parts. The song closes with a nostalgic roller-rink organ that echoes the song's inspiration, Lou Christie's "Two Faces Have I," adding a texture that is more wistful than playful.

"Brilliant Disguise" begins playfully, with the singer dancing with his girl. In "Tougher Than the Rest," the singer's goal in life was to dance with the object of his affection. But "Brilliant Disguise" shows us the next day and afterward. Here, the singer struggles with his inner doubts. In the first two verses, he directs his doubts at her. What did she whisper when she turned away? What was she doing last night on the edge of town? What's really in her mind? When he looks in her eyes—at *her* face(s)—does he see her, or "just a brilliant disguise"? What is a woman like her doing with him?

That last question hints at the singer's underlying insecurities that fuel his doubts and suspicions. Indeed, as we get deeper into the song, we encounter someone like the singer of "Two Faces," someone struggling with inner demons. With the singer's admission that "I want to know if it's you I don't trust/'cause I damn sure don't trust myself," the song emerges as a textbook example of projection. In an album filled with relational vows, the singer promises to "play" the role of the "faithful man" if she'll be his "loving woman." Nevertheless, the song ends on a down note, with the singer in a passionless bed. "God have mercy on the man," he says, in a great line, "Who doubts what he's sure of."

Having explored the tenuous ground of love, the album moves on to two songs dealing with scenarios at love's end. "One Step Up" is, ironically, the album's most beautiful song musically, a well-crafted duo between Springsteen and vocalist Patti Scialfa, a veteran of the Jersey shore music scene who had joined the E Street Band for the *Born in the U.S.A.* tour. The vocal interaction between Springsteen and Scialfa, with eerie guitar chords that slice through their harmonizing, frame this story of a couple falling apart. They fight, they don't learn from their mistakes, and they keep taking "One step up and two steps back." As in "Brilliant Disguise," the singer turns his examination inward and finds himself lacking. When he looks in the mirror, he doesn't see the "man I wanted to be," and when he spots a "girl across the bar" and tells himself, "Mmm she ain't lookin' to marry," we get the picture that the singer's infidelity might be the reason that the couple keeps taking two steps back.

"When You're Alone" completes the breakup cycle, giving us a glimpse of a relationship's aftermath. Abandoned by his lover, Johnny is left to ponder that, "When you're alone, you're alone." It's a seemingly redundant statement, but not so; it shows the onset of painful realization of the solitude (the second "alone") when your relationship falls apart and you're no longer part of a couple (the first "alone"). What adds complexity to the song is that Johnny is speaking to his departed love in the second stanza, telling her that being alone (the second type) will "knock you down" and send her "crawling . . . back home." In the final stanza, we find out he's right; she has come back to him, but he doesn't take her back—not out of "hard feelings," but simply because the love is gone.

"When You're Alone," described by Guterman as "one of the most hard-hearted songs in the Springsteen catalogue,"[9] could have been the final song on the album, but it would have left too fatalistic a message. The final song, "Valentine's Day," is a lover's denouement to the album, a slow, waltz-like number in three/four time. One of the few "car songs" on the album—Tunnel of Love told stories about a "man in the house," not a "man on the road," Springsteen explains in Songs[10]—the singer drives down the highway thinking of an absent lover. The singer recounts a nightmare, dipping once again into river imagery (of "the cold river bottom" he felt "rushing over") and even an allusion to "The River" ("the bitterness of a dream come true"). Haunted by the sensation that he'd felt her "rushing through his arms," he closes the song and the album with a standard lover's plea: "say you're forever mine . . . my lonely valentine."

Without this final song and final plea, the album's fatalism would be the only message that one could take from Tunnel of Love. But with this closing waltz, the album comes full circle, returning to the eternal search for love. Love fails, love is lost, but the search for love continues. The road gets rough, but you'd better keep driving.

With more sex but less sax, Tunnel of Love was nowhere near the blockbuster that Born in the U.S.A. had been, but it did reach number one in its third week, making Springsteen the only artist with four chart-topping albums in the 1980s. It spawned two Top 10 singles ("Brilliant Disguise" and "Tunnel of Love") and a third that just missed ("One Step Up"). The "Brilliant Disguise" video featured Springsteen alone with his guitar, singing a live version of the song specifically for the video (rather than lip-syncing to the album's track) with the camera slowly panning in to a close-up of the singer's face. The minimalist video, shot by Meiert Avis, was a breath of fresh air to those still suffering from a *U.S.A.* hangover.

As usual, the flipsides of the singles gave Springsteen a chance to release outtakes from the album. The flipside of "Tunnel of Love" was "Two for the Road," a song that is strictly B-side material. Springsteen sings it well, and the melodies are sweet, but like another *Tunnel* outtake called "When You Need Me" (found on *Tracks*), "Two for the Road" is too straightforward and simplistic for Springsteen. "The Honeymooners," another *Tunnel* to *Tracks* outtake, is a throwaway musically, the equivalent of the plastic bride and groom on the top of a wedding cake. The "Brilliant Disguise" B-side was "Lucky Man," musically minimalist but hard-driving and with hard-edged vocals on top. The singer states his motto: "I don't miss no girl, I don't miss no home/He who travels fastest travels alone." Springsteen dubbed a fading, lonesome cry at the song's end, caught somewhere between Jimmie Rodgers' blue yodel and Robert Johnson's hell-bound wail.

Springsteen has denied that the *Tunnel of Love* collection was entirely autobiographical. Nevertheless, anyone who listened closely to the album's lyrics couldn't have been completely surprised when Springsteen and Phillips's marriage fell apart. Springsteen had given Patti Scialfa a prominent role in the *Tunnel of Love* shows, and many commented on the chemistry that the two shared during the tour. "They can't be acting," people said. They weren't.

Those who paid attention during the *Tunnel of Love* world tour were not all that surprised when an Italian paparazzo caught Springsteen and Scialfa during intimate moments on a balcony in Rome in June 1988. Springsteen began a relationship with Scialfa on the tour, and he and Phillips separated soon after he admitted to the affair. Phillips filed for divorce at the end of August 1988, and the couple went their separate ways. Springsteen and Scialfa stayed together.

During the tour, Springsteen regularly performed a never-released song titled "I'm a Coward." (I've never heard it, but Guterman says the song was put together from pieces of "Gino Is a Coward," an early 1960s sock-hop rocker.)[11] In "I'm a Coward," Springsteen would dub himself brave enough to take down Hulk Hogan, "King Kong" Bundy, or Mike Tyson but "a coward when it comes to love." The idea of the song bears a slight resemblance to another tongue-in-cheek song, "On the Prowl," that Springsteen had performed years earlier at the legendary Stone Pony in New Jersey, and which he gave to the group Cats on a Smooth Surface. In that song, Springsteen had described his lothario self as a monster in the same league with Dracula and "Frankenstein's son." But personifying one's libido in a small New Jersey club is one thing; singing of romantic cowardice night after night while making the transition from Wife No. 1 to eventual Wife No. 2 is another.

It's tempting to use lyrics as a lens through which we can examine the songwriter. More interesting is examining how the life of the artist manifests in his lyrics. With *Tunnel of Love* and its tour, Springsteen had cast his public self in the role of a self-fulfilling prophet: someone who failed yet was committed to trying again despite his fears.

* 9 *

Snake Eyes

Human Touch and Lucky Town (1992)

One of the more annoyingly enduring clichés tossed around by the popular media is that whenever a performer undergoes some sort of artistic transformation, someone invariably says that the artist has "reinvented" himself or herself "like Madonna." It's as if Madonna was the first—let's use the term loosely here—artist to ever switch music or fashion styles in mid-career. Never mind that we've seen a group such as The Rolling Stones flirt with psychedelia in the late 1960s, disco in the 1970s, synth-pop in the 1980s, and Dust Brothers arrangements in the 1990s. No performer has *ever* been so praised for following cultural bandwagons as has Madonna.

Back before Madonna began to speak with a British accent (and when she was more than like a virgin) Bruce Springsteen had reinvented his career several times over. In the 15 years spanning the releases of *Greetings from Asbury Park, N.J.* and *Tunnel of Love,* he had gone from writing folk-jazz hybrids to street-punk epics to hard-rock guitar riffs to country-tinged ballads to middle-America anthems to romantic ruminations. To the cynic for whom everything is about money and nothing about sincerity, Springsteen's evolving styles might be confused as Madonna-like attempts calculated for commercial appeal—except Springsteen's directions have almost always gone against the grain. Signed by Columbia to fit into the popular mold of the singer-songwriter, Springsteen had reinvented not himself but the singer-songwriter mold itself by incorporating elements of jazz, R&B, even classical music in his first three albums. Once he had broken through with *Born to Run*, he shifted gears with *Darkness*. As the musical landscape embraced British punk and new wave, Springsteen turned toward the music of American populism. And once he had achieved monstrous success with *Born in the U.S.A.*, he purposefully avoided expanding upon that success and, rather, turned inward for a much more subtle, introspective sound. Thus, as Bruce and Madonna stood among a handful of 1980s artists identifiable by their first names alone, Springsteen was more an anti-Madonna than one of her peers.

As the decade came to an end, Springsteen pondered reinvention in many phases of his life.

Like Jack Burden in Robert Penn Warren's *All the King's Men*, Springsteen headed west during a time of confusion. In Warren's Pulitzer Prize–winning novel, the protagonist observes,

> West is where we all plan to go some day. It is where you go when the land gives out and the old-field pines encroach. It is where you go when you get the letter saying: *Flee, all is discovered.* It is where you go when you look down at the blade in your hand and see the blood on it. It is where you go when you are told that you are a bubble on the tide of empire. It is where you go when you hear that that's gold in them-that hills. It is where you go to grow up with the country. It is where you go to spend your old age. Or it is just where you go.[1]

In the fall of 1989, Springsteen took a road trip across the country on his Harley. "What he thought about as he rode down I-70, or got up to in the unbuttoned privacy of Hyatts and Super 8s, isn't known," Christopher Sandford records. "What is known is that he told a casual friend, Woody Lock, at work in a mill in St. Louis: 'You know, you can always get off the wheel . . . it really *is* your land." He ended up at Matt's Saloon, a desert inn in Prescott, Arizona, and performed versions of "Glory Days" and "I'm on Fire," backed by a surprised house band.[2]

In October 1989, Springsteen called the members of the E Street Band and disbanded the group for the foreseeable future. In New Jersey, meanwhile, Springsteen had begun to feel (as he would later describe) like Santa Claus at the North Pole.[3] A forthcoming song, "Local Hero," was based on the time he passed by a local storefront window and saw a black velvet painting that portrayed Springsteen playing poker with Bruce Lee and a Doberman. When the local artists are writing you into the same role that Elvis has traditionally held in kitsch Americana, it might well be time to move.

And Springsteen did. First, he and Scialfa moved to an apartment in New York City for a brief period. Feeling hemmed in—try to imagine the king of the late-twentieth-century car song living in a city where everyone travels by foot, subway, taxi, or limo—the couple bought an estate in Beverly Hills, California, and moved westward. "People always came west to refind themselves or to re-create themselves in some fashion," he explained. "This is the town of recreation, mostly in some distorted way, but the raw material is here, it's just what you make of it."[4] So he had moved west like his parents before him. And on July 25, 1990, Springsteen himself became a parent when Scialfa gave birth to their son, Evan James. The couple was married on June 8, 1991, and on December 30 of that year, they had a second child, Jessica Rae.

After the comparatively subdued *Tunnel of Love* tour, he had spent the next year and a half playing benefits and appearing with fellow musicians on the New Jersey bar scene. In the fall of 1988, he joined a lineup of Sting, Peter Gabriel, Tracy Chapman, and Youssou N'Dour on the Human Rights Now! tour that celebrated the fortieth anniversary of the Declaration of Human Rights.

On the tour, Springsteen's setlist resembled that of the *Tunnel of Love* tour months earlier. Highlights included covers of Bob Dylan's "Chimes of Freedom" and Bob Marley's "Get Up, Stand Up," the latter becoming an unofficial anthem for Human Rights Now! Springsteen had also begun to perform an acoustic version of "Born to Run," which he would preface with a meditation upon how the meaning of the song had changed over the past 13 years, and he spoke of the notion that anyone running away from something must be running *to* something else.

This was all most people heard from Springsteen for a while. He told Anthony DeCurtis that he tried to write new material in 1988 and 1989, but as he described, "every time I sat down to write, I was just sort of rehashing. I didn't have a new song to sing. I just ended up rehashing *Tunnel of Love*, except not as good."[5]

In November 1990, Springsteen joined Jackson Browne and Bonnie Raitt for two concerts at Los Angeles's Shrine Auditorium to benefit the Christic Institute. The Christic Institute was a nonprofit activist group founded in 1980. The institute had helped to organize a suit on behalf of the late Karen Silkwood against the Kerr-McGee Nuclear Corporation, leading to the 1984 U.S. Supreme Court decision for $1.3 million against Kerr-McGee. More recently, Christic was raising funds for a lawsuit against the CIA for its involvement in the Iran-contra scandals under Reagan-Bush.

In the long run, Christic was about as successful as the MUSE initiative. But the Christic performances gave Springsteen a chance to perform acoustically as a solo act for the first time. He also debuted some new material, including "Red Headed Woman," an ode to strawberry blondes and to performing a particular act on them: "Your life's been wasted/Until you've got down on your knees and tasted/A red headed woman." It's a fun song that works so simply that it seems like it must be a cover of an old-time barrelhouse number. Guterman jokes, "Springsteen may be the first rock'n' roller who had to settle down before he could write a good song about sex."[6]

At the Christic shows, Springsteen also debuted the songs "57 Channels," "Real World," "Soul Driver," and "When the Lights Go Out." He also showed a side of himself that few fans had seen. Reports describe him looking nervous at times. "If you're moved to clap along, don't," he told the audience. "It'll fuck me up." More tellingly, when one fan yelled out "We love you, Bruce," he responded, "But you don't really *know* me."[7] In the two-plus years Springsteen spent largely out of the spotlight, he began to question the nature of stardom and even his very reasons for writing and performing.

Earlier that spring of 1990, Springsteen had picked up his guitar again and begun to work on new material in his Thrill Hill Recording Studio. Roy Bittan visited and played a couple of pieces for Springsteen. These evolved into two songs, "Roll of the Dice" and "Real World," both up-tempo R&B-flavored numbers. Springsteen tried to keep the momentum going with Bittan. Together they recorded a demo in Springsteen's garage apartment and then went into the studio to record as a "two-man band."[8] Springsteen experimented with elements of pop, rock, R&B and soul, and he brought in studio musicians as he searched for a groove that was long in coming. He recruited leading soul men such as Sam Moore (from Sam and Dave), Bobby Hatfield (from the Righteous Brothers), and Bobby King to provide background vocals on a number of tracks. Ironically, his new direction seemed to be taking him back to the soul-infused pop that sang out of transistor radios up and down the shore during Springsteen's Asbury Park days. He even hooked up with fellow Upstage (and E Street) alum David Sancious for a couple of new songs.

Springsteen also made connections with Southside Johnny Lyon and Little Steven Van Zandt. Southside Johnny and the Asbury Jukes were back in the studio for a comeback album, *Better Days*, which Van Zandt produced. Springsteen wrote a song for the group, "All the Way Home," and he also provided vocals (along with Van Zandt and fellow New Jersey native Jon Bon Jovi) on the album's single, "It's Been a Long Time."

Springsteen had been away from the game for years, and the sessions for his own album came slowly. Historically, studio sessions had been arduous experiences for Springsteen, but he had nevertheless been enduringly prolific as a songwriter. Yet as he looked to rediscover himself as a writer and musician, inspiration gave way to the process of craft. For the first time in his career, he did most of his writing during the day; music was now his day job. Springsteen even admitted that working on the new material "was definitely something that I struggled to put together. It was like a job. I'd work at it every day."[9]

Finally, by the fall of 1991, Springsteen thought he had completed an album's worth of material—almost. He felt he still needed one more strong song to complete the collection. Then, after hearing a song called "Series of Dreams" on the first *Bob Dylan Bootleg Series* release, he was inspired to write a song called "Living Proof," a revelatory song about fatherhood. (The two songs aren't very much alike, save perhaps in their pacing.) He remembers:

Then I wrote the song, "Living Proof," and when I wrote that, I said: "Yeah, that's what I'm trying to say. That's how I feel." And that was a big moment, because I landed hard in the present, and that's where I wanted to be. I'd spent a lot of my life writing about my past, real and imagined, in some fashion. But with *Lucky Town*, I felt like that's where I am. . . . This is what's important in my life right now.[10]

Suddenly, he discovered a well of creativity, and another album's worth of material came flowing out over the next three weeks.

On the whole, "Living Proof" and the rest of the songs that followed it were better than the previous material, which Springsteen acknowledged later was somewhat "generic."[11] Springsteen still felt connected to the earlier songs, and he also wanted to have a healthy selection of songs that he could play on a planned tour. Rather than release another double album, he copied Guns 'N Roses, who had released two separate albums, *Use Your Illusion I* and *Use Your Illusion II,* on the same day just months earlier in 1991. On March 31, 1992, Columbia released two new Springsteen albums, *Human Touch* and *Lucky Town. Human Touch* collected the material that had come slowly over nearly two years; *Lucky Town* was the album that "had the ease that came with the relaxed writing and recording of its songs" in that three-week creative burst.[12]

The albums debuted at numbers two and three on the charts, respectively. After a live radio broadcast of a "dress rehearsal" on June 5, Springsteen hit the road with a new lineup consisting of Shayne Fontayne on guitar, Tommy Sims on bass, Zachary Alford on drums, Crystal Taliefero on vocals/percussion/guitar/saxophone, and backing singers Gia Ciambotti, Carolyn Dennis, Cleopatra Kennedy, Bobby King, and Angel Rogers. The 1992–93 tour showcased the more party-friendly R&B sound that Springsteen and the E Street Band had abandoned in the 1980s. To help support his new material, Springsteen agreed to his first-ever live television performance and appeared on *Saturday Night Live* in May. In September, he appeared on MTV's *Unplugged,* though he apparently surprised the network after performing just one acoustic song, "Red Headed Woman," by having his band plug in and join him onstage.

By then, however, sales of the albums had fallen off, and though both albums would sell more than one million copies each, neither would approach even the success of *Tunnel of Love,* much less *Born in the U.S.A.* Today, both albums have been all but discounted by many fans as the products of an ill-thought vacation in the California sun, away from the

E Street Band. Speaking at his induction into the Rock and roll Hall of Fame in 1999, Springsteen himself admitted he'd tried writing "happy songs . . . in the early '90s and it didn't work; the public didn't like it." Guterman writes: "Rock 'n' roll is not music about being satisfied; it's music about shouting that you can't get no satisfaction."[13]

Human Touch is indeed an inferior Springsteen release, yet there are some rubies among the rocks. *Lucky Town* is an underrated album, one that has merited reevaluation as a strong release that would be remembered as a stronger one if it had been released by anyone else.

The highlights on *Human Touch* include the title song (the first single from the twin releases) and the two songs cowritten with Bittan, "Roll of the Dice" and "Real World." While none of those songs break any new ground lyrically, they take refreshing steps away from the drier moments of his country flirtations in the 1980s. "Human Touch" might be just as good a pop song as "Dancing in the Dark," minus Courtney Cox's two-step. The song is a solicitation for closeness couched within statements of what *isn't*: There's no kindness in the face of strangers, no mercy to be found on the street, no miracles to be found; he's not looking for praise, pity, or a crutch. "You can't shut off the risk and the pain/Without losin' the love that remains." Springsteen had said the same thing with "The Ties That Bind," and he had discounted romantic salvation back in "Thunder Road." But here the voice is more world-weary. He admits he himself is "nobody's bargain," but, he hints that with a "little touchup/and a little paint . . ." The song revolves around an almost-chorus that begins with different lines in each verse but returns to thoughts of "human touch," and new wife Patti Scialfa blankets her husband's rough-hewn vocals in a sweet harmony.

Alterman writes "To the degree that *Human Touch* swings at all, it swings as sixties soul,"[14] and both "Roll of the Dice" and "Real World" dip back into the classic soul and R&B that had blared up and down the New Jersey Shore three decades prior. Like "Human Touch," "Real World" speaks of the heartbreak, hurt, and self-pity of the singer's past while affirming a lover's commitment to face the realities of love. "Ain't no church bells ringing/Ain't no flags unfurled," Springsteen sings, both dismissing mythic romance while perhaps subtly commenting on his own flag-draped days of the mid-1980s. Sam Moore's wonderful background vocals add a dimension that (to be fair) would have been improbable with the E Street Band in their 1980s stadium-rock days.

"Roll of the Dice" emerged as a surprising centerpiece during Springsteen's ensuing concert tour. Again, the lyrics are nothing new, and they verge on clichés more often than not. The singer casts himself as a "losing gambler" repeatedly throwing "snake eyes," but he tells his newfound love that he wants to gamble on her. Clichéd though it is, the song is undeniably uplifting, and Bobby King's vocal work defies anyone not to sing along.

While the musical directions in these songs hinted at promising things, the misses outnumber the hits on *Human Touch*. Although Springsteen spoke at the time of his belief in the new material, in retrospect he seems to have downgraded *Human Touch*. (He doesn't even discuss many of the album's songs in his commentary for *Songs*.)

It's not easy to say why one song works and another doesn't, and to a certain extent, a number of songs on the album just don't work—or more accurately, they *sound* like work. The sheer time that it took Springsteen to record the *Human Touch* tracks might indicate a lack of inspiration, if not for the fact that almost all of Springsteen's albums had been painstakingly crafted in the past. But this time, the lyrics show Springsteen relying too heavily on stock phrases: from the king on a white horse in "Gloria's Eyes" to the nothing-new sentiments of "All or Nothin' At All," "Man's Job" ("Lovin' you's a man's job"), "Real Man" ("Your love's got me feelin' like a real man") and "The Long Goodbye." Springsteen falls back on self-references, bringing back "Mr. Trouble" in "Real World," a muted trumpet straight out of "Meeting Across the River" in "With Every Wish," even quoting "Born to Run" ("I got to know if your love is real") in "Real Man."

Tellingly, the religious imagery that had once added spiritual depth to his songs now seems forced. "Soul Driver" begins with descriptions of enduring "forty nights of the gospel's rain" and plagues of snakes and frogs, before veering awkwardly into an allusion to Robert Johnson's "Love in Vain." In "With Every Wish," we have an "angel of the lake" appearing to a fisherman in search of a mythical catfish—not quite an Arthurian moment. The "blessed name of Elvis" and the disturbance of the "almighty piece" are cited in "57 Channels," a protosong built around a bass line (played by Springsteen) and a true-but-tired complaint: "57 channels and nothin' on." This song, which barely would have distinguished itself as an outtake from previous album sessions, was actually released as a *single;* it became even more un-fortunate when Springsteen attempted to turn it into a performance piece on tour, spinning it into in-your-face social commentary—his ver-sion of U2's "Zoo TV."

Performing on *Saturday Night Live*—his first-ever live television performance—on May 9, 1992, Springsteen and his new band performed an overblown version of "57 Channels" and then they went straight into "Living Proof." (Earlier in the program, Springsteen had performed an-other new song, "Lucky Town," putting him on an elite list of artists who have performed more than the customary two songs on *SNL*.) "Living Proof" is one of the strongest songs from the twin albums, describing the salvation of a father by the birth of his son.

The power of the song comes from the singer's descriptions of his state before becoming a father. Like the author of the hymn "Amazing Grace," the singer looks back on a wretched state. Before fatherhood, the singer had been separated from his heart and soul and had lost his faith in him-self. He had "crawled deep into some kind of darkness" and lived in a "prison" of his own making. But the birth of his son conveys a salvation that is described in explicitly religious terms, bringing "God's mercy" and the "Lord's undying light." It's not unusual for a parent to describe the birth of a child as being a miracle, but "Living Proof" reclaims the birth-miracle from secular clichés and recasts it as an act of spiritual salvation. As the child cries in his mother's arms, the singer is nearly overcome with its beauty, and he equates the crying to "the missing words to some prayer that I could never make." The song makes references to Springsteen's own motorcycle journey across the southwest in 1989. When the singer of "Living Proof" goes down to the "desert city" to "shed my skin," images of death and (not implausibly) Original Sin abound. In one of Springsteen's most Catholic songs, the child is, literally, a gift from God, conveying God's grace as an act of salvation and rebirth.

"Living Proof" is one of the best "happy songs" in rock. Two other happy songs from *Lucky Town* are the title song and "Better Days." "Lucky Town" is instantly catchy, a 16-bar declaration that the singer will "lose these blues I've found" in "Lucky Town"—and perhaps a roundabout public rationalization for his move to Los Angeles. (The song "Local Hero," also found on this album, seems to hint at the reasons why he needed to move away.)

Not to be confused with the title song of Southside Johnny's album, Springsteen's "Better Days," the first track on *Lucky Town,* is a joyous statement of having lost those blues and found happiness and rebirth. While "Living Proof" is an expression of wonderment, "Better Days" is an announcement of triumph over past inner struggles.

For Springsteen, both songs carry strong autobiographical ties. But "Better Days" is especially interesting for its undeniable commentary on Springsteen's own career. The song declares it both sad and funny to end up "pretending/A rich man in a poor man's shirt." Later, the singer admits that a life of leisure and a "pirate's treasure/Don't make much for tragedy." Springsteen has spoken about having sessions with a therapist at the turn of the decade, with one of the issues explored being Springsteen's own motivations as an artist. These lines in "Better Days" show a sophisticated self-awareness of his own role as the so-called blue-collar rocker, the latter-day voice of the Common Man, the latter-day Woody Guthrie ... who struck it rich and moved to the Hollywood Hills. Although the woman to whom "Better Days" is sung is the rescuing vehicle, the deeper triumph seems to be the singer's self-acceptance. He's no longer the "sad man ... who's livin' in his own skin/And can't stand the company."

One can easily recognize a redheaded Patti Scialfa in the "pretty red rose" mentioned in "Better Days." As Bob Dylan did on *Blood on the Tracks,* Springsteen writes a number of songs in this period referring to the virtues of red hair. "Leap of Faith" is not quite as overtly sexual as "Red Headed Woman," but with a line like "you were the Red Sea, I was Moses," the double entendre is clear. The singer slips into a "bed of roses," the "waters" part and "love" rushes inside. Borrowing a phrase from Lou Reed's "Heroin," the singer sanctifies himself as "Jesus' son." This sexual leap of faith develops the tried and true connection of sex and spirituality, with the singer's lover's body likened to an altar, heaven, and the holy land. In her love, he sings, he's born again.

Two melodic folk-country songs, "If I Should Fall Behind" and "Book of Dreams," are dedicated to marriage. The first considers it in anticipation, but with a realistic sense of the uncertainty that lay past the exchange of vows. In this song, the lovers have sworn to travel "side by side" and to "help each other stay in stride," but this is followed by the recognition that "each lover's steps fall so differently" and of "what this world can do." The affirmation of the song lies in the recognition that the lovers can still have control over their fates. In the closing verse, the singer looks ahead to their wedding ceremony beneath the bough of an oak tree, and the natural setting becomes a metaphor for the struggles they will face. Should they "lose each" other in the shadows, he vows to wait for her and calls for her to likewise wait for him.

"Book of Dreams" carries us through a wedding ceremony, from the preparations (with the singer's betrothed showing off her dress to her friends) to the wedding "ritual" to the dance floor afterward, "alive with beauty/Mystery and danger." Counting "The Honeymooners," this makes three wedding songs to come from Springsteen within just a few years, collectively showing the before, during, and after.

"The Big Muddy" and "Souls of the Departed" peer into the "mystery and danger" at which "If I Should Fall Behind" and "Book of Dreams" only hint. Both "Muddy" and "Departed" are constructed with a similar structure as "Reason to Believe," with verses showing glimpses of new situations to illustrate the overall point of the song. The title and chorus of "The Big Muddy" come from Pete Seeger's "Waist Deep in the Big Muddy," a song about military maneuvers in Louisiana. Springsteen uses Seeger's phrase like the core image of Caddy with muddy drawers in William Faulkner's *Sound and the Fury,* evoking a base and sinful sexuality. The first verse tells of Billy and his mistress. She lives on A and 12th (Belmar? Alphabet City?), and in the afternoon the two go "wadin." It could be that simply they're headed out to Greasy Lake—or these muddy waters could be metaphorical. "You start out standing but end up crawlin," the song says, and there's even a borrowed line from Pete Dexter's *Paris Trout* that warns, "Poison snake bites you and you're poison too." *Lucky Town* is one of Springsteen's happiest albums, but "Big Muddy" is one of his most ominous songs. The singer dismissively notes how nice the river flows and the birds sing, but he notes "you and I we're messier things." Notions of Original Sin are nothing new in a Springsteen song, but here they seem unredeemable. No one leaves this world, we're told, without getting dirty or bloody.

"Souls of the Departed" is drenched in blood. We meet a young American soldier in the Gulf War whose task is to go through the clothes of his dead comrades. At night, he's plagued by nightmares of their souls rising into the sky. We also meet a seven-year-old boy in East Compton,

California, shot down in the schoolyard by *cholos*. Finally, the singer takes us into his own world as he tucks his son in bed. He worries about his own ability to protect his son from the threats outside the walls of his house. "I want to build me a wall so high nothing can burn it down," he says. In the final verse, he ponders working in the "land of king dollar/Where you get paid and your silence passes as honor." Specifically, it could be a reference to Oliver North, but the connections to Iraq and Compton of the early 1990s would be vague at best. The general implications against George Bush Senior's America, though, are all too clear.

The final song of *Lucky Town* is also the most mysterious. Springsteen described the singer of "My Beautiful Reward" as "searching for something unnamable."[15] The unnamed singer seeks riches and ease from pain, moving from mountain to valley, then, in the second verse, through the hallways of an empty house on a hill. In the third verse, the singer addresses an unnamed love. The sun shining in her hair makes him high— but then sends him "crashing down like a drunk." In the final verse, the singer becomes a southwestern shape-shifter of sorts, transformed into a bird with long, black feathers soaring over the river's edge in the search for the proverbial beautiful reward.

What are we to make of this beautiful yet haunting song? Though many songs on *Lucky Town* speak of having won a battle over the dark night of the soul, the lingering image is one of an unending search. For Springsteen the songwriter, the search for artistic relevance as a middle-aged adult, and within the New World Order, would define his work through the end of the decade and into the new century.

* 10 *

At the Movies

The Ghost of Tom Joad (1995)

Who's Tom Joad?" the young sales clerk at Strawberries had asked me when I handed her the jewel case for the latest Springsteen compact disc in 1996.

"He's a character in *The Grapes of Wrath*," I explained.

"Oh," she said with a shrug. "I never saw that movie."

I suppose this would make a good story to illustrate the dumbing down of American culture, except Springsteen himself seems to have been inspired more by John Ford's film adaptation than John Steinbeck's novel. Whether on his own or through Landau, Springsteen had acquired an interest in Ford's work as far back as *Darkness on the Edge of Town,* and Ford's adaptation of Steinbeck's classic Exoduster tale left a mark on Springsteen the film buff. As his career progressed into the mid-1990s, his music would take on a growing connection with the silver screen.

Springsteen had first written for the screen as a payback to director Paul Schrader for appropriating the phrase *Born in the U.S.A.* He wrote the song "Just Around the Corner to the Light of Day" and gave it to

Schrader for his 1987 film *Light of Day*, which starred Michael J. Fox and rocker Joan Jett as a brother and sister in a Cleveland rock band. Jett performed the song for the film's soundtrack; Springsteen included it in his own setlist for the *Human Touch/Lucky Town* tour and performed it on his *MTV Plugged* performance in 1992. Lyrically, the song is vague, sung by a character down on his luck and headed to Galveston; he's a "little down under" and "a little lost," but he feels okay and senses he's "just around the corner to the light of day." (One could say this is the message that George Will had read into the Springsteen concert he attended back in 1985.)

Although willing to write for the silver screen as a way of paying a debt, Springsteen didn't take up any other offers until the early 1990s. Jonathan Demme had first approached Neil Young to write a song for his forthcoming film, *Philadelphia*, the story of an AIDS-stricken lawyer (played by Tom Hanks) who sues his company for unlawful termination. The subject of the movie threatened to make it unpalatable to Middle American taste, so Demme wanted a song sung by an artist with strong heartland credentials. When things didn't work out with Young, Demme turned to Springsteen, who wrote the song "Streets of Philadelphia" for the film. Springsteen recorded the song by himself, making use of a hip-hop-light drum track and a mournful synthesizer to balance an urban setting with an introspective atmosphere befitting the topic. Shrewdly, the song makes no overt mention of AIDS; the narrator is "bruised and battered" and "wasting away" so that his clothing doesn't fit. He bids his "brother" to receive him with a "faithless kiss," the only phrase even remotely referring to homosexuality.

Demme uses the song effectively in the film: Hanks stands on the city sidewalk, dejected, and "Streets of Philadelphia" begins to play, providing a correlative to his character's emotions. Some gay rights advocates would criticize Springsteen's lyrical vagueness as being a moral cop-out, but it nevertheless ensured that the song would receive wide airplay and, thus, spread the message of the film (albeit indirectly) and help *Philadelphia* to play in Kansas. It also won Springsteen an Oscar for Best Song.

Actor/director Sean Penn, who had drawn inspiration from Springsteen's "Highway Patrolman" for the film *Indian Runner*, approached Springsteen for a song for the forthcoming film *Crossing Guard* (1995). Springsteen played him "Missing," a song built around a jungle-rhythm drum track. The song's narrator bemoans an absent loved one. She might be a lover, as the song seems to be a lyrical cousin to "Downbound Train," right down to its cold-sweat-inspiring dream. "Missing" helped the film tell the story of a couple, played by Jack Nicholson and Anjelica Huston, coping with the death of their daughter in a car accident.

Springsteen's title song for the film *Dead Man Walking* (1996) also shares a nod to "Downbound Train." "Once I had a job, I had a girl," the doomed narrator sings on the eve of his execution. The narrator also shares a kinship with Johnny 99, as he looks back on his life and wonders where it went wrong. His conclusion is vaguely philosophical: "between our dreams and actions/Lies this world." Although he begins the song by describing himself as the biblical pale rider about to ride the Apocalyptic pale horse, he deems himself beyond redemption and says he won't ask for forgiveness. "My sins are all I have," he says, a clichéd line but nevertheless a fitting sentiment for the assignment at hand. The song was the title track for the film, which stars Sean Penn as convicted murderer Matthew Poncelet and Susan Sarandon as Helen Prejean, the nun-turned-author upon whose book the film is based.

"Secret Garden" is a song now well known for its use in the 1996 film *Jerry Maguire*, and the ensuing radio mix of the song interspersed with saccharine lines from Tom Cruise and Renee Zellwegger in the film became a hit for adult contemporary radio. But Springsteen wrote the song while working on a rumored album in 1994 and recorded it during a sudden reunion with the E Street Band in early 1995. He'd assembled his old bandmates at The Hit Factory in New York City for the purpose of recording new material for a forthcoming "greatest hits" album. The brief reunion produced "Blood Brothers" (a sort of "No Surrender" 10 years down the road), the hip-hop-inspired "High Hopes," and the party-flavored "Without You."

Although it was left off his first *Greatest Hits* album, "Secret Garden" would be the song to make the most noise from the 1995 Hit Factory sessions. With a synthesizer track as syrupy as the one on "Streets of Philadelphia" is mournful, the song was perfect for *Jerry Maguire*'s date-movie atmospherics. But the opening verse is surprisingly NC-17 rated: "She'll let you in her mouth . . . If you pay the price." Now, this doesn't necessarily have to be about oral sex, and we already know that when

Springsteen sings about paying a price, it's not necessarily about money. Nevertheless, Springsteen entered his own "blue period" of sorts in the 1990s. In addition to "Red Headed Woman" and "Secret Garden," there were two new songs that Springsteen performed live but has yet to record: "Pilgrim in the Temple of Love" and "In Freehold." "Pilgrim" tells the story of a visit to a strip club during Christmastime. "In Freehold," an ode to his hometown that he performed during a performance at his alma mater St. Rose of Lima in 1996, has joking references to a gait-impairing erection (after his first kiss with Maria Espinoza, mentioned by name) and to masturbation.

The film *Blood Brothers*, director Ernie Fritz's documentary of the temporary E Street reunion, features a performance of "Back In Your Arms." Available on record only on disc four of *Tracks*, the song is a hidden gem, perhaps Springsteen's most emotional of the decade. The song's story is a simple one: the narrator has loved and lost, and he wants her back again. The lines are straightforward, but Springsteen had not sung this powerfully or passionately in years. It had been even longer since he'd written a song that featured Clarence Clemons in so prominent a role. The song builds to an emotional crescendo, and after Springsteen sings the final line, "Now darlin' I just wanna be back in your arms again," Clemons takes the baton and brings the song to the finish line with a powerful solo.

During the E Street reunion, the band worked on a new Springsteen composition inspired by *The Grapes of Wrath*, "The Ghost of Tom Joad." In both novel and film, *The Grapes of Wrath* is a strong indictment of the social and economic forces of capitalism. The archetypal tale of the Joad family's migration is presented as a latter-day Exodus, a microcosm of the plight of Okie sharecroppers as they fled the Dust Bowl and headed west based on false rumors of California as a promised land of milk and honey.

Woody Guthrie, another influential figure in Springsteen's career, had been inspired by the *Grapes* story. He named his song, "Tom Joad," after the story's main protagonist, a parolee who had been imprisoned for a killing that was just as much self-defense as it was manslaughter. Searching for his family after his parole, he finds that they've lost their home and have moved in with their uncle, himself struggling to make ends meet. As the Joad family moves west, Tom undergoes a transformation from isolated bitterness to a resolve to fight for humankind's collective soul:

> I'll be all around in the dark—I'll be everywhere. Wherever you can look—wherever there's a fight, so hungry people can eat, I'll be there. Wherever there's a cop beatin' up a guy, I'll be there. I'll be there in the way guys yell when they're mad. I'll be there in the way kids laugh when they're hungry and they know supper's ready, and when people are eatin' the stuff they raise and livin' in the houses they built—I'll be there, too.

Given Springsteen's interest in Guthrie after reading Joe Klein's biography of the folk singer, the ballad of Tom Joad came to Springsteen collectively, as the result of movie, book, and song. Springsteen had paid homage to Guthrie on the *Folkways: A Vision Shared* CD (1989), which gathered artists for cover songs of classic tunes from Woody Guthrie and Leadbelly. Springsteen performed two Guthrie compositions, "I Ain't Got No Home" and "Vigilante Man." "I Ain't Got No Home" is both beautiful and mournful, sung delicately in the mode of *Tunnel of Love*. "Vigilante Man" is one of the best little-known Springsteen songs, a fierce song with a steely edge that's only hinted at in Guthrie's original.

In the fall of 1996, Springsteen participated in an all-star tribute to Guthrie, held at Severance Hall in Cleveland and sponsored by the nearby Rock and Roll Hall of Fame. He performed two songs solo that night, "Riding in My Car" and "Wreck at Los Gatos (Deportee)." The first song is more of a playful castoff, a children's song with a "Let's go ridin' in my car, car" line and car-engine-rumbling vocal effects, and Springsteen has fun with it. "I'm going through this Guthrie song book, and I was kind of excited," he recounted that night. "I said, 'Hmmm, automobiles, that's *my* business, Mr. Guthrie. No disrespect, but that's *my* business.'" "Wreck at Los Gatos" was originally a poem by Guthrie (later set to music by Martin Hoffman) inspired by a 1948 plane crash in which 28 Mexican farm workers slated for deportation were killed. Springsteen's version is haunting, one of his best unreleased performances from the 1990s. (The two songs are available on the *'Till We Outnumber 'Em* import-only CD.)

Springsteen's "The Ghost of Tom Joad," the title track for his eleventh studio album, arose out of the sessions with the reunited E Street Band

members. But as with the eventual *Nebraska* material, Springsteen decided an electric "Joad" didn't work with the full band treatment and ultimately reworked it as an acoustic song and then recorded it with a
five-piece group.

Whereas Guthrie's "Tom Joad" is essentially the story of *Grapes of
Wrath* set to music, Springsteen's "Ghost of Tom Joad" examines the lives
of latter-day inhabitants of life on the fringe. He had visited this territory
with the song "Seeds," performed during the *U.S.A.* tour and captured
on *Live/1975–85*. That song tells a Joadlike story of a man and his family
lured to Houston for a job in the oil fields, only to find no work and end
up sleeping in a car by the railroad tracks. ("Parked in the lumberyard
freezin' our asses off/My kids in the back seat got a graveyard cough.")

The opening verse of "Ghost" presents a snapshot of railroad tran-
sients, homeless people sitting around a fire under a bridge, a line at a
shelter, families sleeping in their cars in the very American Southwest to
which the Joads migrate. Whereas Springsteen had removed references
to *Wrath*'s Reverend Casy from Guthrie's "Vigilante Man," the connection
to Steinbeck's characters in "The Ghost of Tom Joad" is made plain. The
second verse introduces a preacher reminiscent of Casy in *Grapes*, living
in a cardboard box beneath an underpass. In the final verse, Springsteen
summons the spirit of Tom Joad with some poetic license applied to his
"I'll be there" speech: "Wherever somebody's strugglin' to be free/Look
in their eyes Mom you'll see me."

In the song, Springsteen balances references to both past and present.
In addition to the *Grapes* allusions, he references his own past work. "The
highway is alive tonight," he sings, seemingly summoning the spirit of *Born
to Run,* but we're quickly told, "nobody's kiddin' nobody about where it
goes." Gone are the endless, romantic possibilities of that earlier album.
Likewise, a reference to *Darkness* is found in the line about a "one-way
ticket to the promised land," but while that album's "Promised Land" puts
forth a belief in such a mythical destination, "The Ghost of Tom Joad"
shows that myth to be as hollow as the one that Steinbeck's Joads sought
at the end of Route 66. Springsteen's song depicts a world of homeless
people sleeping in their cars and bathing beneath an aqueduct. "Welcome
to the new world order," the singer grimly concludes.

The ghost of *Nebraska* haunts Springsteen's *Ghost of Tom Joad* album
on such songs as "Highway 29" and "Straight Time." "Highway 29" pre-

sents a road-bound couple that harkens back to the couple of "Nebraska," though their meeting at the shoe store where he works reminds one of Sharon Stone's up-skirt scene in *Basic Instinct:* he tells her there's no smoking allowed, she crosses her legs. And like *Basic Instinct*, "Highway 29" is latter-day noir with the woman as a femme fatale; when they meet later at a roadhouse, we're told, "My hand slipped up her skirt, everything slipped my mind." The couple robs a bank and heads toward the Sierra Madres, but they come to an end in a fatal crash. The fatal verse is one of Springsteen's most skillful in his use of selective detail. We're told the road is "filled with broken glass and gasoline," that she's beside him "sayin' nothing," that the wind is coming through the windshield, and all he can see is "snow and sky and pines." He closes his eyes, imagines himself running, as if in a "dream," and then he's "flyin'" off to unconsciousness and (probably) death.

The protagonist of "Straight Time" is an ex-con who works at a rendering plant and tries to stay clean. At night, though, he has intrusive thoughts about "tripping across that thin line." In an echo of *Nebraska* outtake "James Lincoln Deere," the singer is tempted by the life of his uncle, who deals in stolen cars. Looking back on his eight years in jail, he remembers feeling beaten but then, more tragically, getting used to a life of imprisonment. He goes into his basement and saws off the end of his hunting rifle, apparently committed to committing an unspecified crime. The enduring line of the song is the singer's confession of being unable to live outside of jail: "I'm sick of doin' straight time."

The songs Springsteen wrote for *Joad* fed one into one another. "The ex-con of 'Straight Time' became the shoe salesman of 'Highway 29,'" he explained. Likewise, the "unemployed steelworker of 'Youngstown' left the Monongahela Valley and became [the narrator of] 'New Timer.'"[1]

Like *The Grapes of Wrath*, *The Ghost of Tom Joad* focuses on the life of those on society's borders and on the "economic division of the '80s and '90s."[2] "Youngstown" speaks of the economic woes in the northeastern Ohio city that had prospered for decades while making weapons and ammunition as far back as the Civil War. The lyrics to the song were included in Howard Zinn's *Voices from a People's History of the United States*, and the song is more than a fitting entry for the book, for Springsteen's song describes the city of Youngstown as having been used up by the American military-industrial complex and then forgotten. In the Civil

War, the listener is told, Youngstown's blast furnaces made the cannon balls "That helped the Union win the war." In World War II, Youngstown steel works built "the tanks and bombs/That won this country's wars." In the Korean and Vietnam wars, the boys of the (predominantly lower class) families of Youngstown fought and died for their country, and those left behind wonder "what they were dyin' for."

Toward the end of the song, we're reminded that this is not just the story of one dying steel-belt city. Rather, just as the struggle of the Joad family in *Grapes* symbolizes the plight of an entire cross-section of society, "Youngstown" stands as an example of the economic slash-and-burn conducted by corporate America from the Monongahela Valley to the Mesabi iron range to the Appalachian coal mines. "The story's always the same," we're reminded. As this denizen of Youngstown, a Vietnam vet (Springsteen had not yet moved past his Vietnam fetish) sings, "Once I made you rich enough/Rich enough to forget my name." He is so resigned to his fate as an outcast that in imagining his own death, he is unable to picture himself doing "heaven's work" and prays that the devil will take him "To stand in the fiery furnaces of hell."

Having left the northeast, the narrator of "The New Timer" travels the American countryside by rail looking for work. He meets "Frank," a transient laborer with boxcar hobo credentials dating back to the Depression. Frank becomes a mentor of sorts to the narrator, showing him "the ropes" as they travel from east Texas to New Mexico to Colorado to California, hoeing sugar beets and (in a nod to Steinbeck's Joads) picking peaches. Frank's advice is "don't cross nobody/You'll be all right out here kid"— except the following summer, Frank is found dead in Stockton, California, the victim of a motiveless crime. The narrator becomes consumed with anger and paranoia, and with thoughts of the family he left behind.

Much like Steinbeck's novel had been based on his own nonfiction writing regarding displaced Dust Bowl farmers, Springsteen accessed a number of nonfiction sources in writing *Joad*. During one spell of insomnia, he picked *Journey to Nowhere: The Saga of the New Underclass* (a book he'd bought back in the mid-1980s) off his shelf. Dale Maharidge and photographer Michael Williamson's chronicle of Rust Belt poverty inspired "Youngstown" and "The New Timer." (Springsteen authored an introduction for the 1996 reprint of the book, which also included lyrics for the two songs.) Two *Los Angeles Times* articles, Sebastian Rotella's

"Children of the Border" from April 1993 and Mark Arax and Tom Gordon's "California's Illicit Farm Belt Export" from March 1995, also proved influential. Rotella's article on Mexican border children near San Diego inspired "Balboa Park." Arax and Gordon's article on methamphetamine kitchens inspired "Sinaloa Cowboys." Arax remembers:

> I got a call. It was [Springsteen's assistant] Terry Magovern saying, in effect, "Bruce liked it. He wants me to ask you some questions." I gave him a few colloquial phrases and local color. Apparently Springsteen wanted some, quote, evocative images, such as what type of trees grow in the valley. Eucalyptus, I told him. Later, I got a second call. This one was for "cheat notes," mainly Spanish-language terms. Eventually, I worked up a memo called "Images From the Meth Fields" and sent it on. [3]

The Ghost of Tom Joad is primarily concerned with the economically disenfranchised—nothing new for Springsteen. Yet the album is also Springsteen's first sustained consideration of the ethnically disenfranchised. "Sinaloa Cowboys," "The Line," "Balboa Park" and "Across the Border" trace what Springsteen describes as the "lineage of my earlier characters to the Mexican migrant experience in the New West."[4]

"Sinaloa Cowboys" is a song about two brothers from a small Mexican town who cross the border and find work on a San Joaquin orchard. The brothers discover that they can either "spend a year in the orchards/Or make half as much in one ten hour shift" working in a methamphetamine kitchen. Such kitchens are notoriously hazardous due to inflammable chemicals, and indeed, Louis dies when the kitchen shack explodes. Miguel digs up the ten thousand dollars he and his brother had been saving, and he lays the lifeless body of his brother there in the ground, an act that symbolizes the exchange of money for life and recalls their father's words to them: "for everything the north gives, it exacts a price in return."

The cost of living in the promised land of the New West is also the subject of "Balboa Park," a grim tale of drug mules in underground San Diego. Little Spider and his fellow hustlers X-Man and Cochise smuggle cocaine-filled balloons in from Mexico. In the process, the boys are pawns in a game between the drug dealers "in their Mercedes" and the men of the border patrol. At the end, Spider is hit by a border patrolman's car during a raid and limps bleeding to his "home" beneath the underpass.

In "The Line," Springsteen gives us the perspective of one of those patrolmen. The narrator is a California border patrolman who, like Joe Roberts in "Highway Patrolman," must choose between official duty and personal ties. An ex-soldier and a widower, he is "good at doin' what I was told," though inside he admits to feeling less than "whole." The notion of doing what one is told is a virtue in neither rock nor populist music, and indeed, the song questions the value of his job; his partner (a Mexican by descent) explains that the illegal immigrants they arrest and send back to Mexico will only keep trying to come back, driven by poverty and hunger at home.

The border agent meets Louisa, an illegal Mexican, in the border patrol holding pen. He falls for Louisa, who reminds him of his late wife—or more profoundly, of "what I'd lost." Later, as the agent and his partner drink at a Tijuana bar alongside the same people they'd sent back the day before, Louisa convinces him to help her, her child, and her brother cross the border into California. The night comes to carry out their plan, and as he picks them up in his truck and drives away, Louisa's brother's shirt comes open to reveal that he's carrying a wire. His partner drives up, and the two patrolmen stare at each other in a standoff while Louisa runs off.

The song leaves us with the image of the singer, having left his job, drifting along the central valley and searching local bars and migrant towns for Louisa. Guterman describes, "Like a character from a dark fairy tale, all he does now is search for her. Like most of the characters here, he'll never find anything."[5]

"Across the Border" is a lover's prayer for two Mexicans on the eve of their attempt to cross illegally onto American soil. The singer describes his dreams for their future, presented in a series of three-line stanzas. "Where the sky grows grey and white/We'll meet on the other side/There across the border," he assures her. The phrase "across the border" is repeated eight times, stressing both the idealized image and the single-minded desperation of their dream. The closing lines, in which the singer ponders love and fortune and "eating the fruit from the vine," resonate with the false hopes of Okies who sought a land of milk and honey in California, and there is a hint that the dream is already disintegrating in the singer's mind. He's lost the clarity of a specific destination ("There across the border") and vaguely dreams of love and fortune "Somewhere across the border."

"Galveston Bay" is the one song on the album to present a dual perspective—that of Le Bing Son, a Vietnamese ex-soldier who has fled to America after the fall of Saigon, and Billy Sutter, a fisherman and Vietnam veteran. Sutter, inspired by hatred for the foreigners he and his friends see taking jobs in east Texas, allies himself with local Klan members. Son kills two locals in self-defense, and Sutter threatens revenge. But when the time comes, Sutter can't do it; he sheathes his knife and returns to his wife.

In *Songs*, Springsteen explains that the purpose of "Galveston Bay" was to take the ideas only dreamed of in "Across the Border" and to make them "feel attainable." This seems a forced interpretation, given the disparity of settings and ethnic groups between the two songs, but it might serve to explain why Springsteen altered the original ending of the song, which had a "bloody" climax before Springsteen rewrote it with a peaceful ending.[6] Still, the last-minute triumph of tolerance over hate in "Galveston Bay" can't come close to redeeming the patterns of ethnic and economic division that are observed throughout the album.

Joad can be hard listening. Reviewing the album for the *Philadelphia Inquirer*, Tom Moon notes Springsteen's "downcast narratives that ramble down one blue highway, then another, spitting out the usual road-as-wisdom, road-as-escape tropes like spent chewing tobacco on the median strip."[7] As Guterman aptly observes, despite its lyrical accomplishments, the album is "musically quite samey [*sic*] and will likely suffer the fate of being one of those records everyone agrees is terrific, but no one actually listens to . . . for more than a song or two at a time."[8]

Guterman's observation is right on mark. Four years after *Human Touch/Lucky Town* had fallen flat for many critics, the lyrical achievements on *Joad* were applauded, and Springsteen won the Grammy for Best Folk Album of 1996. *Stereo Review* said, "Springsteen's map of the U.S. shows the paths of twelve disenfranchised characters walking the backroads and pot-holed streets of America" and called the album a "deeply affecting narrative about men and women driven to desperate deeds in desperate times."[9] With its concern for the downtrodden, *Joad* was also embraced by left-leaning fans. (When I told a girlfriend in grad school that I preferred the *Human Touch/Lucky Town* material to *Joad*, she looked at me as if I'd just admitted that *Birth of a Nation* was my favorite film.) Yet there definitely is something to be said for the campfire-music "sameyness" of the album. Whereas *Nebraska*'s acoustic sound was sparse, Springsteen's guitar playing often had a feverishness that's missing on much of *Joad*. On songs such as "Dry Lightning," with its great image of a rainless thunderstorm serving as a metaphor for the memory of a relationship's lost passion, Springsteen purposely underplays, giving primary focus to the narratives. "Dry Lightning" is a microcosm for much of the album: haunting lyrical brilliance that burns and dies on its own. Thinking back on the time with his stripper girlfriend, her "appaloosa's/Kickin' in the corral smelling rain," the narrator is left in a state of barren dryness: "there's just dry lightning on the horizon line . . . and you on my mind."

Joad ends on a dry note, with the sardonic "My Best Was Never Good Enough." The narrator strings together a number of clichés ("A quitter never wins and a winner never quits"/"The sun don't shine on a sleepin' dog's ass," etc.), an allusion to the sheriff in Jim Thompson's *The Killer Inside Me*. Springsteen called the song his "parting joke and shot at the way pop culture trivializes complicated moral issues, how the nightly news 'sound bytes' and packages like to strip away the dignity of human events."[10] It's an undeniably accurate sentiment, yet "My Best" is about as effective in conveying that message as "57 Channels" is in critiquing mass communication. *Joad* lacks something that almost every other Springsteen album has—a strong closing song.

Despite its dryness and "sameyness," *Joad* gave Springsteen a new direction in work. He cowrote two songs with Pittsburgh musician Joe Grushecky for Grushecky's 1995 album, *American Babylon*. "The Dark and Bloody Ground" is a tale of Native Americans in the Kentucky territories. "Homestead" is the Pennsylvania suburban correspondent to "Youngstown." Springsteen also cowrote four songs for Grushecky's next album, *Coming Home*, including "Idiot's Delight," a song of St. Peter and purgatory, which Springsteen performed a number of times during his *Devils and Dust* tour in 2005.

Springsteen's final soundtrack song of the decade was "Lift Me Up," which appeared as credits-rolling music for John Sayles's *Limbo* (1999). Yet while songs that play with the rolling of the credits are usually there to provide music for the audience as they leave the theater, "Lift Me Up" is used strategically. (SPOILER ALERT!) Stranded in the Alaskan wilderness, David Strathairn, Mary Elizabeth Mastrantonio, and Vanessa Martinez wave to the pilot of a search plane, unsure as to whether the pilot has been sent to rescue them or to kill them; before the audience learns their fate, the screen fades to black and Springsteen's song plays as the credits roll. The song features Springsteen's first falsetto performance on record, as his vocal dance among a high register serves to illustrate the ascendancy to which the narrator aspires: "Lift me and I'll fall with you . . . . Let your love lift me up."

"Lift Me Up," available on the bonus third disc for *The Essential Bruce Springsteen*, was Springsteen's last song to appear in any forum during the millennium. Soon after the new millennium had begun, he would turn back to the theme of the ascendant at a time when many looked to American popular culture to help lift the nation's spirits again after a period of sudden darkness and anger. At the same time, songs such as the *Joad* cycle and "Dead Man Walkin'" made it impossible for the more politically conservative percentage of Springsteen's fan base to ignore his movement toward a Liberal world view. In the twenty-first century, Springsteen would exist within an artistic dichotomy, held up as the voice of the nation's collective spirit while at the same time expressing political views that would be rejected at the polls in a bitterly divisive presidential election.

* 11 *

September and Everything After

Live in New York City (2001) and
The Rising (2002)

Was *The Rising* a "9/11" concept album? Not exactly—a number of songs on the album can be seen as "9/11 songs" in only the broadest of interpretations. Nor, certainly, was it even popular music's first response to the terrorist attacks upon the Twin Towers and Pentagon. Other artists had recorded songs responding to the attacks, ranging from the overly reverent (Alan Jackson) to the comically irreverent (Eminem). What *The Rising* was, though, is a good, possibly great, and undeniably well-timed comeback album with roots in Springsteen's 1999–2000 Reunion Tour with the E Street Band.

A month after Springsteen was inducted into the Rock and Roll Hall of Fame in March 1999, Springsteen and the E Street Band touched off a European tour with two dates in Barcelona, Spain. Long-lost brother Steve Van Zandt, now perhaps known better to millions as a cast member of *The Sopranos*, rejoined the E Street fold as a second guitarist. The band began an American wing of the tour with eight dates at the Meadowlands in July, played dates through the end of November, and then went back out on the road again at the end of February 2000—culminating with 10 dates at Madison Square Garden in June and July.

It was very much a reunion tour, and the focus was on the band's collective work from the past two and a half decades. The most recent Springsteen record release had been *Tracks*, the four-disc set that collected previously unreleased material dating from 1972 to 1995.

New material did begin to pop up: songs like "Land of Hope and Dreams," and another song penned with Joe Grushecky, "Code of Silence," a desperate plea for open communication within a failing relationship. Another one debuting famously (or infamously, depending on your perspective) on the Reunion Tour was "American Skin (41 Shots)," written in response to the February 19, 1999 slaying of New York City street vendor Amadou Diallo. The incident raised racial tensions in Gotham: Diallo, a black immigrant from Guinea, was killed when four white NYPD officers fired a combined 41 bullets when he reached into his pocket for a wallet. (The policemen said they thought he was reaching for a gun; they were subsequently acquitted of any charges.)

On June 4, 2000, in Atlanta, Georgia, Springsteen and the E Street Band debuted "Further On (Up the Road)" a hard-driving though somewhat generic rock number. Later on in the show, they played "American Skin," a song that begins with band members taking turns in reciting the phrase "41 Shots"—at once summoning the tragedy while highlighting the seeming unlikelihood that the police had needed to fire 10 rounds each at an unarmed man.

The song quickly joined the band's nightly rotation. The *New York Times* printed the lyrics, and the song drew disproportionate notice as the tour inched toward summer, overshadowing an historic stay at Madison Square Garden. Patrick Lynch, president of the Policemen's Benevolent Association, accused Springsteen of exploiting the incident for financial motives (though the concerts were already sold out and the song was not released on any recording until the *Essential Bruce Springsteen* package three years later). "The title seems to suggest that the shooting of Amadou Diallo was a case of racial profiling," Lynch wrote in a letter to PBA members, urging them to boycott Springsteen's concert. "I consider it an outrage that he would be trying to fatten his wallet by re-opening the wounds of this tragic case at a time when police officers and community members are in a healing period." Police lieutenant George Molé attacked Springsteen in an Op-Ed piece for the *New York Times*, and commissioner Howard Safir told the *New York Daily News*, "I personally don't care for Springsteen's music or his song." Most extreme was the re-action of Bob Lucente, the president of the New York chapter of the Fra-ternal Order of Police, who called Springsteen a "fucking dirt bag" and a "floating fag" and said, "He goes on the boycott list."[1]

With its repeated focus on the "41 shots" and its observations that "You can get killed just for living/In your American skin," it's hard to ar-gue that the song does not convey a certain perspective on the Diallo shooting. Yet as Springsteen has done time and again in his songs, the song explores multiple perspectives—not just that of a mother telling her son to "always be polite [and] keep your hands in sight" but also of cops who must make split-second, life-or-death decisions: "Is it a gun, is it a knife/Is it a wallet, this is your life." The song presents both sides of the equation, and with the verse depicting Lena giving street-survival advice to son Charles, Springsteen expands the reach of the song beyond this one tragic incident.

"American Skin" is more statement than song. "Land of Hope and Dreams" is a rock song through and through, as if the band had revved-up "This Hard Land," set it atop 18 wheels, and let it loose on the open road. From the opening guitar chords, the song has great momentum and is tailor-made for the arena setting. The song's metaphorical "train" is borrowed from Curtis Mayfield's "People Get Ready" and the tradi-tional folk song "This Train (Bound for Glory)" by way of Big Bill Broonzy and Woody Guthrie. Broonzy's and Guthrie's train carries no whores or gamblers; Springsteen's is an all-inclusive joyride with universal invites to saints and sinners, losers and winners, whores and gamblers, lost souls and thieves, fools and kings. The power chords and ringing organ of "Land of Hope and Dreams," along with its images of "big wheels roll[ing]," "steel wheels singing," and "Bells of freedom ringin'," make this one of Springsteen's most uplifting. (As I sit here listening to it again, I realize it might be one of the band's best songs from the second half of Springsteen's career.)

The Reunion Tour culminated in dates at Madison Square Garden on

June 29 and July 1 in the summer of 2000. HBO would broadcast a special 13 performances from the two shows, and a two-CD, 20-song companion set would follow in the spring of 2001. Highlights include the Pentecostal-inspired "rock and roll exorcism" of "Tenth Avenue Freeze-Out," a fiery version of "Murder Incorporated," a dusting off of "Lost in the Flood," a bluesy, bottleneck reinterpretation of "Born in the U.S.A.," and an astonishing "Jungleland." And there is the soulful performance of "If I Should Fall Behind," with Bruce, Clarence, Patti, Nils, and Steven all stepping up to take turns on the mic. Sung in this fashion, the song becomes a pledge of brotherhood among the reunited band.

Hoping to continue the momentum of the very successful reunion tour, Springsteen and the group had gone into the studio in the fall of 2000. But the sessions weren't satisfying to him. He felt "something was missing," and he told the *New York Times* that he was having a hard time finding his "rock voice."[2]

Sessions for the album stalled, but Springsteen continued to work on new material. He worked on new material ranging from the joyous ("Waitin' on a Sunny Day") to the meditative ("Nothing Man").[3] There was also a song called "My City of Ruins." Originally, "My City of Ruins" was about the continuing decline of Asbury Park. But in the wake of 9/11, the song took on a different life.

Springsteen was invited to perform a song for the televised *America: A Tribute to Heroes* benefit for the September 11th Telethon Fund. Springsteen went to work on a song expressly for the benefit concert, a tribute to firemen lost that day called "Into the Fire," inspired by a 40-minute phone conversation that Springsteen had with Stacey Farrelly, the wife of fallen fireman Joe Farrelly from Manhattan Engine Co. 4.[4] But he didn't finish the song in time and ended up playing a slightly reworked version of "My City of Ruins," backed by Scialfa, Clemons, Van Zandt, Soozie Tyrell, Lisa Lowell, and Dee and Layonne Holmes. It was a stirring performance, with the notion of ruins obviously taking on a different meaning, and its ascending and transcendent call to "rise up" provided an inspirational message. (Television commercials for the *America: A Tribute to Heroes* soundtrack CD sampled this part of the song in the background.)

The terrible events of September 2001 and the aftermath left an impression on Springsteen. The town of Rumson, New Jersey, where he lived was one of several Monmouth County towns and cities to lose residents in the attacks on the Twin Towers. Springsteen read obituaries that listed WTC victims among his dedicated fans. He spoke to the families of victims on the phone, and he sent a tape of him singing "Thunder Road" to be played at the funeral of one late fan.

As fellow Rumson native Edwin Sutphin recalled on the *Today* show, he was driving through a Sea Bright, New Jersey, parking lot when he spotted New Jersey's most famous resident passing by in his car. "I rolled down the window, and I yelled as loud and as hard as I could, 'We need you now!' "[5]

Springsteen began to write again.

He and the band had been out of the studio game for the better part of two decades. On the advice of a friend, Springsteen met producer Brendan O'Brien. O'Brien, who'd produced albums for such 1990s alternative rock artists as Pete Drooge, Stone Temple Pilots, Pearl Jam, Matthew Sweet, Rage Against the Machine, Korn, and Limp Bizkit, seemed an unlikely fit for Springsteen, who by then seemed to some to be a holdover from 1970s and 1980s classic rock. But O'Brien provided not just a new set of ears but a sense of vision that Springsteen and the group needed as they recorded their first album of the millennium.

First O'Brien came to Springsteen's home studio to listen to demos. Then Springsteen and the E Street Band went into the studio with O'Brien. The sessions went surprisingly well—and quickly. The songs for the next album were recorded in the span of just four months. Thanks in part to the publicity surrounding Springsteen's first studio album with the band in nearly two decades, *The Rising* debuted at number one upon its release on July 30, 2002.

The advance reviews billing *The Rising* as Springsteen's commentary on September 11 no doubt also helped. Always in search of pithy labels, the media framed it as the album that would heal America. *Time* declared "*The Rising* is about September 11, and it is the first significant piece of pop art to respond to the events of that day." More fairly, the *New York Times* called it a "song cycle about duty, love, death, mourning and resurrection."[6] In *Slate*, A. O. Scott grandiosely dubbed Springsteen "The Poet Laureate of 9/11."[7]

Such labels both oversold and undersold the album. No album in and of itself can heal an entire nation, and the relationship of some songs to 9/11 was either dependent upon context ("Waitin' on a Sunny Day" and

"Mary's Place") or simply nonexistent ("Let's Be Friends" and "Further On)." And while the album was almost uniformly praised for its message of resilience and rebirth, some felt the songs didn't live up to their billing. In his review, Tom Laskin criticized Springsteen's use of "the forced [religious] language of *Saved*-era Bob Dylan" and for delivering "big, mystical statements, chains of symbolism" instead of the "plain language, a touch of journalistic detail, [and] artfully penned re-creations of vernacular expression."[8] Nevertheless, *The Rising* provided what many considered to be American popular culture's most poignant and most uplifting response to the events of September 11.

The album also signaled Springsteen's return to rock music while introducing subtle but new musical textures to the E Street Band. Wisely, O'Brien didn't try to fit Springsteen into the alternative/grunge mold. Instead, from the opening songs "Lonesome Day," "Into the Fire," "Waitin' on a Sunny Day" and "Nothing Man," the listener encounters a fresh new sound. Soozie Tyrell steps up to take a more prominent role, much like Lisa Germano does with her fiddle work on John Mellencamp's *Lonesome Jubilee*. Synthesizers and acoustic guitars provide layered subtleties, and Springsteen sings perhaps more artfully than he ever has. On "Into the Fire," for one, the steel guitar, violin phrasing, and Springsteen's controlled falsetto provide a rustic and melodic texture that would have been unattainable on E Street circa 1985. The textured retro-soul choir of "Let's Be Friends (Skin to Skin)," the violin that weaves in and out of "You're Missing," the slow beat-box track on "The Fuse" and of course the Middle Eastern vocals and instrumentation on "Worlds Apart" provide surprising dimensions to Springsteen and the E Street Band's repertoire. Meanwhile, one point often missed is that with the focus on those left behind (for example, the widows of two firemen and one Pentagon employee) Springsteen's *Rising* songs delve into the female point of view more than he ever had before.

The "9/11" core of the album derives mostly from its lonely-hurt-song core: "Lonesome Day," "Into the Fire," "Countin' on a Miracle," "Empty Sky," and "You're Missing." In "Lonesome Day," the narrator copes with unbearable loneliness. "It's gonna be okay/If I can just get through this lonesome day." "Into the Fire" is a prayer to the soul of the departed: The narrator is the wife of a perished firefighter or rescue worker, to whom she prays that his strength, faith, hope, and love will endow her with the same. "Countin' on a Miracle" depicts a "sleeping beauty" waking from a dream of her "lover's kiss." "Your kiss was taken from me/Now all I have is this," she says, meaning the dream, which is musically signified by synthesizer and violin. The singer in "Empty Sky" wakes up next to an impression on the bed next to her (or him). "You're Missing" considers the loss of a family left behind: "Coffee cups on the counter, jackets on the chair/Papers on the doorstep, you're not there." To these songs we can add two songs about survivor's guilt: "Nothing Man," which (according to A. O. Scott) was rewritten to be about a Twin Towers rescue worker (his life is "forever changed/In a misty cloud of pink vapor") and "The Fuse," a strange song that shows two lovers attempting intimacy while, across town, the courthouse flag hangs at half-mast for a funeral.

"Waitin' on a Sunny Day" and "Mary's Place" are only tangentially related to the overall context. ("Sunny Day" is about wanting to be happy again and "Mary's Place" is where everybody is going to get happy again.) Both songs reach back to 1960s soul: Despite its cryptic religious allusions (with its "seven pictures of Buddha" and "eleven angels of mercy") "Mary's Place" bears a close relationship to Sam Cooke's "Havin' a Party," while Springsteen described "Sunny Day" on *VH1 Storytellers* as "a good example of pop songwriting" and the type of song he tends to "want to throw out . . . directly into the trash can" until "Mr. Landau usually steps in there and says, 'No! Not that one!'" Springsteen said the song was meant to be sung back at him, a pure pop song in the style of Smokey Robinson. He even sang (or attempted to sing) in the style of Robinson in the *Storytellers* performance. Both "Sunny Day" and "Mary's Place" served as centerpieces of the live set on the *Rising* tour, when he would go down along the front row and play to the crowd.

The two songs that most encapsulate the album's message of rebirth, though, are the title song and the full-band version of "My City of Ruins." "The Rising," a companion piece to "Into the Fire," takes us straight onto Ground Zero with a fireman (carrying a "sixty pound stone" on his back and a "half mile line" on his shoulder) charging into the holocaust. Beginning in what Springsteen called a spiritual "nether world"—"Can't see nothin' in front of me/Can't see nothin' coming up behind"—the fireman's act of bravery is depicted as a religious act. Beginning with the church-like bells of the fire station, the fireman wears the "cross of his calling" and has spirits above and behind him as he wanders amidst the wreckage, where the "precious blood" of victims has been spilled. Even the fire is described as the "fiery light" of the "Lord." He thinks back on the image of his wife (*Mary*) in the *garden*, and of "holy pictures" of their children. The firefighter is practically a preacher, bidding his rescuees with a Pentecostal fervor. In Springsteen's solo performances of the song (*VH1 Storytellers*, the *Devils and Dust* tour) even the song's *li li lis* take on a gospel feel; it's almost as if Springsteen is speaking in tongues. "These are the songs that you wait for," Springsteen said when discussing his inspiration in writing "The Rising." "And so you pray to the gods of creativity and aliveness that you remain awake and alert and in command of your senses, so that when the moments arrive, you are ready."[9]

"My City of Ruins" didn't start out as a 9/11 song. The men on the corner "Like scattered leaves" and the "boarded up windows" are images of Asbury Park in its faded glory. And with the images of the "blood red circle" on the ground and the doors of an empty church blowing open with organ song, it sometimes takes on a postapocalyptic feel like "Lost in the Flood" from three decades before. As the last song on the album, though, "My City of Ruins" functions as "The Rising" Part Two. In the third stanza, a lover left behind ponders the pillow next to her, and the "city" in ruins becomes a metaphor for her emotional and spiritual state. Musically, the song occupies a spiritual space between gospel and secular soul, and with the song's prayerful crescendo in search of faith, love, and strength, the call to (once again) rise up is all-encompassing. At the time of its recording, New York City had begun to rise back up, and the album version of "My City of Ruins"—much more melodic with its full-band instrumentation and soulful vocals—hints at a sense of resolution not evoked by Springsteen's earlier performance, when notions of resolution were nowhere to be found.

Back then, revenge was the order of the day for many, and Springsteen even alludes to this once or twice. "I want an eye for an eye," we're told in "Empty Sky." In "Lonesome Day," we're told, "A little revenge and this too shall pass." But Springsteen subverts that message with songs like "Paradise" and "Worlds Apart," two songs that fly in the face of any jingoism that could have been perceived. "Paradise" opens with lines from a suicide bomber making his or her way through a crowded marketplace, then switches to a woman in the Virginia hills, remembering a husband lost in the attacks. (This part of the song was inspired by a conversation Springsteen had with a widow of a Pentagon worker who died on September 11.) "Worlds Apart" could be parenthetically titled "Middle-East Side Story," with guest Pakistani singer Asif Ali Khan and his group introducing the story of forbidden love between an American GI and a Muslim woman.

When Springsteen performed "Worlds Apart"—one of the best songs on *The Rising*—at the July 26 show (one of 10 sold-out dates that summer) a good portion of the crowd took the chance to head for the concession stands. *The Rising* posed many of the same political and ideological paradoxes that arose out of *Born in the U.S.A.* two decades earlier. For some, this well-timed album of rebuilding and resilience gave Americans a very positive—and thus pro-American—message. In concert, a song like "The Rising" served as a communal anthem that could even get drunken frat boys to stand and sing with raised arms to the song's prayer-like chorus. On the other hand, preaching sympathy with our enemies is the type of thing that got Richard Gere booed offstage in New York the year before, and songs sung from the perspective of a suicide bomber, or even with melodies from the Middle East, were clearly not aimed at the neo–George Will contingent.

During the 2002–2003 *Rising* tour, Springsteen prefaced "Land of Hope and Dreams" (a regular part of the encore) with what he self-mockingly called a "public service announcement":

> People come to my shows with many different kinds of political beliefs; I like that, we welcome all. There have been a lot of questions raised recently about the forthrightness of our government. This playing with the truth has been a part of both the Republican and Democratic administrations in the past and it is always wrong, never more so than when real lives are at stake. The question of whether we were misled into the war in Iraq isn't a liberal or conservative or republican or democratic question, it's an American one. Protecting the democracy that we ask our sons and daughters to die for is our responsibility and our trust. Demanding accountability from our leaders is our job as citizens. It's the American way. So may the truth will out.[10]

Despite the nonpartisan disclaimer, the target of the message was undoubtedly the Bush administration and Republican congress pushing a war despite clear evidence of a connection between Saddam Hussein and Osama bin Laden. When he performed the song on July 26 at Giants Stadium, one fan in the bleachers yelled out (with no hope of being heard onstage) that he hadn't paid to hear Springsteen's political platform. "Face it, Bruce, you're a liberal!" he shouted, to the amusement of his friends. (Hey, pal, no one paid to hear your platform, either.)

Despite the political messages and songs of rebirth, more than anything else the 2002–2003 tour was about the band's return to rock 'n' roll. Night after night, the shows offered classic E Street performances: a blistering version of "Because the Night" leading into a triumphant "Badlands," the obligatory "Born to Run" leading directly into a rollicking version of Moon Mullican's "Seven Nights to Rock," and the return of "Rosalita," performed every night during the encore, leading into a send-'em-home-happy version of "Dancing in the Dark." Highlights from the final weeks of the tour included:

- On August 31, the tenth Giants Stadium gig, the band welcoming back "Kitty" and Tom Waits making an appearance for "Jersey Girl."
- September 10, 2003, in Toronto—a performance of Warren Zevon's "My Ride's Here" in tribute to Zevon, who'd passed away three days earlier. In the final year of his life, Zevon had knowingly recorded his swan song, *The Wind.* Springsteen made cameos for two tracks: atmospheric vocals on "Prison Grove" and raucous guitar and vocal work on "Disorder in the House," perhaps his best performance on another artist's album.
- September 18 in Hartford, Connecticut—a solo-piano performance of "Incident on 57th Street" buffeted by the winds of Hurricane Isabel; as Springsteen played the song's ending, Bittan came onstage and took over like the middle man of a relay team, while Springsteen stepped back to the mic and strapped in for a seamless transition into "Thunder Road."
- September 20 in Buffalo, New York—the first live performance of *U.S.A.* outtake "County Fair."
- October 4 at New York's Shea Stadium—Bob Dylan joined the band onstage for a version of his classic "Highway 61 Revisited" on the final night of the tour.

When all was sung and done, *The Rising* had returned Bruce Spring-steen to the rock stage. While he was no longer rock 'n' roll's future, he was no longer its past—he was now its senior statesmen. And even as he worked on new material backstage on tour, he began to consider how old songs, and even older traditions, could point him toward new directions down the road.

* 12 *

Dust Devils and Dixieland

Devils & Dust (2005)

In August of 2004, Springsteen announced that he would participate in the Vote for Change tour, in which artists as varied as Pearl Jam, Dave Matthews, R.E.M., John Fogerty, Jurassic 5, Bonnie Raitt, Bright Eyes, and Babyface played 28 cities in "swing states" to support John Kerry's bid to unseat George W. Bush. "I felt like I couldn't have written the music I've written and been onstage singing about the things I've sung about for the last 25 years and not take part in this particular election," Springsteen explained.

In an Op-Ed letter to the *New York Times* on August 5, he gave his print endorsement to Kerry/Edwards. Admitting that he didn't think Kerry and Edwards "have all the answers," he cited the Iraq war as the prime reason for the country needing a change at the top. "I supported the decision to enter Afghanistan and I hoped that the seriousness of the times would bring forth strength, humility and wisdom in our leaders," he wrote. "Instead, we dived headlong into an unnecessary war in Iraq, offering up the lives of our young men and women under circumstances that are now discredited."

Performing mostly to the converted, Springsteen performed a string of his greatest hits on the VFC tour dates. A video of Springsteen and his cohorts singing an everyone-onstage version of Patti Smith's "People Have the Power" appeared on MTV in the days leading up to the election.

As a political initiative, Vote for Change was about as successful as No Nukes and Christic had been. Bush/Cheney defeated Kerry/Edwards, and at the time of this writing, American forces remain in Iraq.

During a sound check before a show in Vancouver on the *Rising* tour in April 2003, Springsteen and the E Street Band tried out a new song called "Devils & Dust," his first musical statement on the Iraq war. At first he envisioned it as a possibility for an angry, martial rock song (perhaps in the same vein as "Born in the U.S.A.") and intended it for his next album with the E Street Band. But as he had done with "The Ghost of Tom Joad," Springsteen decided the song worked better as an acoustic song, and it eventually became the title track for an acoustic-based album.

"Devils & Dust" begins with a soldier standing on duty in a far-off land with his finger on the trigger of his weapon. While Springsteen had made his views on Iraq publicly clear, the song effects its message of protest not by damning the government but, more subtly, by creating sympathy for those following the government's orders. The songwriter puts the listener in the shoes of a soldier, much as he had put us in the shoes of a Vietnam vet in "Born in the U.S.A." or a New York City policeman in "American Skin." "What moved me the most was the idea of a young kid stationed at a checkpoint," Springsteen told Renée Montagne of NPR. "You've got a very, very short period of time where you have to decide about the car that's driving toward you, whether it's an innocent family, or whether it's your death coming at you."[1]

The narrator's reminders to himself and to "Bobbie" back home that "We've got God on our side" echo the evangelist rhetoric of Bush the Lesser. Yet as he has often done ("Streets of Philadelphia," "My City of Ruins," etc.) Springsteen strips the song of any too-specific language that would anchor it to a specific time and place. The terms *Iraq*, *WMD*, or even *war* do not appear in the song, and according to Christopher Phillips in *Backstreets* magazine, an early line referring to "a world of earth and oil" was scratched.[2] As a result, the song becomes less grounded in a particular time or issue, allowing listeners who don't happen to be (in this case) soldiers in Iraq to still relate to universal questions ("What if what you do to survive/Kills the things you love") and messages ("Fear's a powerful thing/It can turn your heart black").

Released in April 2005, *Devils & Dust* continued Springsteen's partnership with producer Brendan O'Brien while providing another "side project" from the E Street Band. O'Brien also figures prominently as a musician on the album, playing bass guitar on half of the twelve songs, and contributing instrumental work on the sitar, the tambora, the hurdy-gurdy, and an electric sarangi. The Nashville String Machine (which had provided string arrangements for "Countin' on a Miracle" and "You're Missing") also appears on six tracks. Soozie Tyrell and Patti Scialfa figure prominently, as does drummer Steven Jordan, who played on Scialfa's solo album from 2004, *23rd Street Lullaby*.

Although the album displays the twenty-first-century textures that O'Brien had brought to *The Rising*, it reaches as far back as 1991 in its material. Springsteen first wrote the song "All the Way Home" for Southside Johnny's *Better Days* album (see chapter 9). In Johnny Lyon's hands, this musical come-on to a divorcée with "the shadow of that ring" on her finger receives the standard, bar-band-ballad treatment. Springsteen's *Devils & Dust* version, almost unrecognizable from Lyon's, is a genre-defying song that sets the musical tone for much of the album: not quite acoustic yet not quite rock; rustic yet not quite country; pop music for adults yet lacking the saccharine sap of the adult contemporary format.

At least two other songs, "Long Time Coming" and "The Hitter," date back to the *Tom Joad* tour. Another song, "Black Cowboys," is based on a 1995 journalistic study, Jonathan Kozol's *Amazing Grace: Lives of Children and the Conscience of a Nation*. Another, "Matamoros Banks," is a sequel to *Tom Joad*'s "Across the Border." Meanwhile, the Southwestern and Border Culture settings throughout *Devil & Dust* hearken back to those on *Tom Joad*: There's "Reno," in which a man is distracted during sex with a prostitute by his memories of riding with *vaqueros* in Mexico; the red Oklahoman sun at the end of "Black Cowboys"; the mesquite wind in "Long Time Comin'"; the Louisiana tent-boxing circuit in "The Hitter"; the west Texas *mustaneros* in "Silver Palomino"; and the failed crossing of the Rio Grande in "Matamoros Banks."

But it would be wrong to portray *Devils & Dust* as *The Ghost of Tom Joad*

Part 2. With all the social consciousness of *Tom Joad,* the songs on *Devils & Dust* feel more engaged with their characters; Jon Pareles observed in his piece for the *New York Times* that where *Tom Joad* is "full of reportorial detail, the songs on 'Devils & Dust' dissolve into memories and visionary images."[3] And while *Tom Joad* deals with those marginalized from society, the characters we meet on *Devils & Dust* are marginalized from themselves. Springsteen described the album as being a collection of "individual stories of people wrestling with their demons." Most of these wrestling matches take place within two arenas—the dynamics of family ("Long Time Comin'," "Black Cowboys," "Silver Palomino," "Jesus Was an Only Son," and "The Hitter") and male-female relationships ("All the Way Home," "Reno," "Maria's Bed," "Leah," and "All I'm Thinkin' About").

"Long Time Comin'" and "The Hitter" both debuted during Springsteen's solo *Tom Joad* tour. Christopher Phillips calls "Long Time Comin'" a "spiritual sequel" to "Adam Raised a Cain," but it could just as well be a response to Harry Chapin's "Cat's in the Cradle."[4] While Chapin's song depicts a cycle of neglect in three generations of males, Springsteen's is about a father committed to overcoming his own past and dancing on the grave of his "old soul." Looking back on his own absent father, he tells his children, "if I had one wish in this god forsaken world, kids/It'd be that your mistakes would be your own." As he and his pregnant wife lie next to a campfire, with their two children sleeping nearby, he feels his third child kicking in his mother's womb and vows "I ain't gonna fuck it up this time." (Springsteen and Scialfa had had a third child, Samuel Ryan, in 1994.) In a May 1997 performance Springsteen told a Paris crowd, "This is a song mainly about sort of not doing unto others as was done unto you, which is a pretty good lesson to learn. Our kids come along, and you have the chance to sort of do it differently. To correct or change some of the things about the way that you were brought up."

"The Hitter," which Springsteen had performed on the *Joad* tour in November 1996, is told from the perspective of a boxer at the end of his rope, talking to his mother from outside her front door. He recounts a life of boxing in tents throughout Louisiana, and in a world-weary voice he asks only that his mother let him inside to rest for a little while. That the boxer has been estranged from his mother is all too clear: he says that if she doesn't recognize his voice, she need only open the door and see her own "dark eyes" in his face. Despite their separation over the months, maybe years, the mother's downtrodden spirit lives on in her son.

The relationship between mothers and sons is the central one of the album. In "Black Cowboys," Rainey Williams's dreams of the West are based on the drugstore novels about the African-American cowboys and Seminole scouts on the Oklahoma range—novels that his mother has brought home for him. The song is set in Mott Haven, the South Bronx neighborhood that Kozol studies in *Amazing Grace*. When Rainey's mother Lynette takes up with a crack dealer, the mother's smile on which Rainey depended is "dusted away." He takes a train and leaves the city, traveling westward through Pennsylvania, Ohio, and eventually Oklahoma. Even though he leaves behind the mother who betrays his love, his route of escape nevertheless can be traced directly to signs of his mother's love.

"Silver Palomino" is Springsteen's *in memoriam* message to his son's two best friends, whose mother had passed away at a young age. It introduces a 13-year-old boy in west Texas who believes his late mother returns in the form of the palomino horse that comes down to him from the mountains at night. Musically, the song drags: Phillips calls Springsteen's singing "sloppy [and] twangy," and the singer himself said, "There's a lot of bars missing and things in the music. It's sort of in free time." But as Springsteen explained to Montagne, the idea was to evoke the "instability" experienced by a child during the loss of a parent.

The moment of supreme loss is depicted in the metaphor of "Jesus Was an Only Son," which approaches the story of the crucifixion from the more secular concern of a mother's loss. While the biblical Jesus has siblings, the notion of Jesus as an only son underscores his sense of loneliness while carrying his cross up Calvary Hill (his "proving ground . . . his darkness on the edge of town," as Springsteen described on *VH1 Storytellers*). The song even goes back to the night of Jesus' capture in Gethsemane— the point at which his isolation from all family and friends begins. But this is no passion play and Mel Gibson is nowhere to be found. The final image is one of reassurance: Jesus tells Mary, "still your tears/For remember the soul of the universe/Willed a world and it appeared."

"Maria's Bed" takes a secular look at salvation. Springsteen sings, "I was burned by the angels, sold wings of lead/Then I fell in the roses and sweet salvation of Maria's Bed." Soon after leaving Maria, we eventually hop into bed with "Leah." Like "Maria's Bed," "Leah" is a low-key, melodic song that looks forward to happiness at the end of the road with a woman, though here the goal is less to bed her than to share a house and bed with her. "All I'm Thinkin' About" is similarly lighthearted. In a quick-footed falsetto akin to Canned Heat's "Going Up to the Country," Springsteen sings of a single-minded obsession for a girl with "sweet brown legs." "Ain't no one understand," he sings, "this sweet thing we do."

While "All I'm Thinkin' About" may treat sexual desire comically, "Reno" shows it to us explicitly. (The song earned the *Devils & Dust* album a warning label for explicit lyrics, a Springsteen first.) The song takes us "south of the border" both physically—the song describes an afternoon visit with a prostitute—and geographically, as the narrator remembers being with an ex-lover, Maria, near the Amatitlan (not a river in central Mexico, as the liner notes say, but a lake in Central America). In its frank presentation of sexuality, the song takes things further than Springsteen has ever gone—the prostitute quotes prices for both vaginal and anal sex, performs fellatio on the narrator, and then masturbates herself before mounting him. But beneath the explicit sex, the real story of the song is that the narrator seems unable to enjoy the moment because he is haunted by memories of Maria. Although there are just two references to her, the whole song is sung to her—an inner conversation that the narrator has with her while bedding someone else. "She had your ankles," he tells Maria, describing the prostitute. In the end, when the prostitute makes a laughable toast to the best he ever had, he confesses to Maria, "It wasn't the best I ever had/Not even close"—and it's pretty clear to the listener who *was* the best he'd ever had. Although the song may be Springsteen's most explicitly sexual, it's also one of his most wistful and bittersweet. In introducing the song to an audience in Chicago in May 2005, Springsteen explained, "This is a song about not being able to handle real love, so you try something else"—or as he told Jon Pareles, "He's in this room with this proxy because he couldn't handle the real thing."[5]

This song cycle of family and relationships is bookended by "Devils & Dust" in the beginning and, in the end, "Matamoros Banks." *Joad*'s "Across the Border" was a lover's prayer on the eve of an attempted border crossing; "Matamoros Banks" shows an attempted crossing's fatal end, beginning with the image of a body on the bottom of the Rio Grande and then floating to the surface, where "turtles eat the skin from your eyes, so they lay open to the stars." From this ghastly image in the opening verse, Springsteen takes us back to a picture of the man walking across the desert, dreaming of holding his beloved in his arms across the border in Brownsville. The effect of the song's reverse chronology is that the descriptions of the protagonist's dreams are rendered tragic by the prior knowledge of his ultimate end.

In the liner notes, Springsteen notes that, "Each year many die crossing the deserts, mountains, and rivers of our southern border in search of a better life." During his solo world tour in 2005, Springsteen introduced the song with the *Devils & Dust* version of a public service announcement, in which he discussed the need for a "humane immigration policy." (The issue would come front and center in April 2006 in California during protests of the United States policy.)

The *Devils & Dust* tour focused on the newly released material along with solo versions of older songs such as "Lost in the Flood," "Incident on 57th Street," "The Promise," "Wreck on the Highway," a Jerry Lee Lewis–like version of "You Can Look (But You Better Not Touch)" on piano, "Reason to Believe," and "The Rising." The occasional song made an awkward transition to the solo-with-guitar treatment (e.g. *The River's* "Two Hearts"). "Part Man, Part Monkey" became an unlikely showpiece; the song was perhaps not as entertaining as Springsteen's own introduction of the song, a commentary on how the Kansas Board of Education and George W. Bush seemed to have forgotten that the Scopes Monkey Trial had already been tried—78 years earlier. (In European dates on the tour, he made joking references to the "United States of Amnesia.")

Although Springsteen performed solo, the tour featured a long cast of instruments: a piano, open-tuned acoustic guitars (for a "folky, countrified [and] resonant"), Gretsch guitars with heavy reverb and a Bigsby tremolo bar (for a "spooky 'surf-noir' sound" *a la* power-chord pioneer Link Wray, who passed away that November), an electric piano, a tremolo harmonica (with two sets of reeds to create a "dense, saturated sound") and even a "banjitar" (a six-string banjo with a "bluesy" sound).[6] Springsteen also utilized a bullet microphone when singing songs such as "Idiot's Delight," which lent his words an echoing effect but left them largely unintelligible.

Also prominent was the pump organ, on which Springsteen would "hold single chords for long stretches, eschewing the dramatic flourishes and arpeggios that color his piano playing." Springsteen played the pump organ while performing the surprising set closer on the tour: an eight-minutes-plus cover version of "Dream Baby Dream." The song first appeared on an album by Suicide (the band that had inspired *Nebraska*'s "State Trooper"), but it sounds like it could just as well have been an old Roy Orbison tune. "I happened to hear that song recently," he told Nick Hornby during the tour. "I came across a compilation that it was on and it's very different at the end of the night. It's just those few phrases repeated, very mantra-like."[7] Coming at the end of the night, "Dream Baby Dream" had an ethereal quality that stayed with you in the parking lot and on the ride home.

We Shall Overcome: The Seeger Sessions (2006)

Nearly a year to the day after the release of *Devils & Dust*, Springsteen put out *We Shall Overcome: The Seeger Sessions*. Like *Devils & Dust*, *The Seeger Sessions* album had roots in the mid-1990s. After the *Devils & Dust* tour ended, Springsteen had planned to take a year off, compile some never-released material for a follow-up to the 1998 *Tracks* collection, and then go back into the studio with the E Street Band. When he revisited his archives, he focused at first on the album of songs with tape loops he'd been working on in the early 1990s (in the same style as "Secret Garden" and "Streets of Philadelphia"). But then he rediscovered tapes of the four songs he'd recorded one day in 1997 with an eclectic group of musicians. He'd been asked to record a song for the tribute album *Where Have All the Flowers Gone: The Songs of Pete Seeger*. Along with "We Shall Overcome" (the song he contributed to the tribute album), he and his fellow musicians recorded three other folk songs during the first "Seeger session": "Jesse James," "My Oklahoma Home," and "Pretty Boy Floyd." When he listened to these tapes again, he liked this material so much that he scrapped plans for *Tracks II* and recalled the musicians from the first session.[8]

It was a singularly eclectic group that Springsteen had met mostly through Soozie Tyrell. Along with Tyrell and Scialfa, there were vocalist

Lisa Lowell, guitarist Frank Bruno, bassist Jeremy Chatzky, violinist Sam Bardfield, banjo player Mark Clifford, percussionist Larry Eagle, Charles Giordano on accordion, organ, and piano, tuba player Art Baron, saxophone player Ed Manion, trumpet player Mark Pender, and trombonist Richie "La Bamba" Rosenberg. They gathered at Springsteen's farm in New Jersey and played more of the traditional songs that Seeger himself had once recorded (hence the name of the album). *The Seeger Sessions* collects the performances from three separate days—one in 1997, a second in 2005, and a third in early 2006. The album tracks are not studio constructions but unrehearsed live performances preserved on a Dual-Disc release.

These semi-impromptu sessions allowed Springsteen to rediscover the music that Seeger and others had popularized during the hootenanny craze of the early 1960s. "People were looking for songs that addressed the concerns of the day. Pop music hadn't evolved to that yet. That was when I started playing. [But] I only lasted on the folk thing three or four months, then I learned how to play 'Twist and Shout.'"[9] The selection of instruments gathered also allowed Springsteen to revisit the genre experimentation of his earlier recordings. "My second album had an accordion, a tuba, jazz sounds, circus sounds. When we streamlined E Street into more of a rock band, we did less of that. So it's an area I like getting back to."[10] The *Seeger Sessions* songs span 400 years of musical history, ranging back to broadside ballads from the British Isles. "Froggie Went a-Courtin'," the oldest song on the record, was originally a Scottish shepherding ballad that appears in a songbook from 1549. "Mrs. Mc-Grath," meanwhile, was an Irish broadside with an anti-English, anti-recruiting message during the Napoleonic Wars in the early nineteenth century. Songs like these were transported to America by settlers of the New World and became the source material for Appalachian folk ballads and early country music.

The rest of the songs on the album originated within American culture. "Shenandoah," described in the liner notes as an "American pioneer's homesick and lovelorn lament," was a popular shanty in the 1830s. "Old Dan Tucker" originated as a fiddle tune popularized by a blackface minstrel in the 1840s. "Jacob's Ladder" and "Oh, Mary Don't You Weep" were Negro spirituals based on Old Testament stories. "How Can I Keep from Singing?" was a Quaker abolitionist hymn. "John Henry" was based

on the story of a steel-driver on the railroads. "Buffalo Gals" immortal-
izes the prostitutes of Buffalo, New York, in the mid-nineteenth century.
A minstrel named Billy Gashade wrote "Jesse James" soon after Robert
Ford shot down James in 1882. "Pay Me My Money Down" is a shanty that
originated among black dock workers in Georgia and South Carolina,
with a message to ship captains who might try to stiff them of their hard-
earned pay.

From the twentieth century come "Erie Canal," a nostalgic song of
canal life written by Thomas Allen in 1905; "My Oklahoma Home," a
dust-bowl ballad by Bill and "Sis" Cunningham; "Eyes on the Prize," originally a pre–World War I hymn but updated by Alice Wine in 1956 for the
civil rights movement; and "We Shall Overcome," the anthem of union
strikes and civil rights marches.[11]

Springsteen has made a career of albums that have often surprised
his audience, and along with *Nebraska* and *Tom Joad,* the release of *The
Seeger Sessions* was yet another anticommercial release that fans could
not have foreseen. Not only was this the first collection of song *arrangements* that the nation's most famous singer-songwriter had ever released,
but it dusted off songs associated with a folkie who was decades removed
from pop-culture relevance. But what for some was a self-serving exercise
in musicology was for others a tasty serving of roots-based raucousness.

"The folk thing has always been a mixture of social consciousness,
outlaw ballads, tall tales and love songs," Springsteen said. "It's a broad
mixture of almost all of the human experience."[12] The *Seeger Sessions* rev-
els in the atmosphere of songs intended to be sung within groups—
music made more for communal hand clapping and foot stomping than
fascistic fist raising. "There's jazz in there. Swing. Sam brings this Eastern
European thing; Soozie's a totally down-home country sound. 'Jacob's
Ladder' has this Kansas City-Dixieland horn thing on top of the gospel.
There's no straight two-and-four, no rock tempos. This band rolls,"
Springsteen said.[13] The brass section rings out with Dixieland phrasings
on "Oh, Mary Don't You Weep," "Erie Canal," "Jacob's Ladder," even on
the slow and seething take on "Eyes on the Prize" and the otherwise
country-bluegrass interpretation of "Oklahoma Home," while Giordano's
accordion lends a taste of zydeco to "Pay Me My Money Down." Other
songs harken back to folk traditions: the banjo-driven "Old Dan Tucker,"
the violin jig "Mrs. McGrath," the front-porch fiddle stylings on "John

Henry," the Old Country melodies of "Shenandoah," and the gospel feel of the backup vocals on several of the renditions.

The *Seeger Sessions* tour took these new-old songs worldwide, along with a sampling of Springsteen tunes like "Johnny 99," "Open All Night" and "You Can Look (But You Better Not Touch)." Added to these were surprises like "Daring Young Man on the Flying Trapeze" (reminiscent of "Wild Billy's Circus Story" from *The Wild, the Innocent & the E Street Shuffle*) and the oft-interpreted "Long Black Veil," a traditional song most famously performed by The Band on *Music from Big Pink*. Two semipermanent titles on the setlist were "When the Saints Go Marching In" and the Blind Alfred Reed song "How Can a Poor Man Stand Such Times and Live?"

Reed wrote "How Can a Poor Man" during the Great Depression, but Springsteen updated the lyrics to comment on the plight of New Orleans residents whose city was literally washed away when Hurricane Katrina floodwaters overpowered four of the city's levees in late August 2005. Springsteen arranged a group of musicians who brought a decidedly Dixieland feel to many of these traditional standards. Just as "My City of Ruins" became a song for 9/11, the Seeger Session Band version of "How Can a Poor Man" proved timely at the New Orleans Jazz Fest in April 2006. As evidenced by a tour rehearsal soundboard recording of the song that was made available on Springsteen's Web site, Marty Rifkin's pedal steel guitar slices through the song's core while the horn section and a flute resemble Van Morrison in his early "Caledonia soul" phase. Springsteen sings it powerfully, recalling his impassioned performance of "Johnny 99" on the *Live/1975–85* box. The first added verse shows an unnamed visitor giving an ineffectual "pep talk" to the "poor black folk"— a not-too-subtle allusion to the president's visit to the disaster area after Katrina. The second verse describes the lawlessness left in the wake of the flood: "There's bodies floatin' on Canal and the levee's gone to Hell/Martha, get me my sixteen gauge and some dry shells/Them who's got out of town/And them who ain't got left to drown." Springsteen's final verse borrows a line from Woody Guthrie's "I Ain't Got No Home" to describe the plight of those dispossessed, and then reaches back to the Negro spirituals and notions of an impending Judgment Day.

The Crescent City has played a pivotal part in the history of American music. European, African-American, and Latin American cultures came together in New Orleans like ingredients in a musical gumbo pot. Modern jazz, blues, R&B, and rock 'n' roll all trace their lineages back to the mouth of the Mississippi Delta. It seems fitting, then, that we come to an end of our exploration with Springsteen dedicating a genre-blending song to the people of New Orleans.

Springsteen said, "Once we put [*The Seeger Sessions*] together, it was like, 'Wow. I can make records and I don't have to write anything.'" Although it sounds like a throwaway line, one can imagine him, nearly 35 years after signing his first record deal, suddenly considering the wealth of material left to him by his musical forebears. "There are thousands of great songs sitting out there waiting to be heard," he said, "and I know a way to act as an interpreter on these things."[14]

Yet even as *The Seeger Sessions* tour began, Springsteen looked ahead to his next project with the E Street Band. "I love playing with E Street. I always will," he told the *New York Daily News*. "I have a bookful of new songs sitting there to play with E Street," he said,[15] though he told *USA Today* that he hoped to delve further into American and international folk music, and that he also had a roots music solo project on the back burner.[16] Even though Springsteen would turn 57 later that year, it seemed likely that he would continue to forge his singer-songwriter legacy for a long time coming.

✻ Afterword ✻

Back to the Future with
Hammersmith Odeon, London '75

Since 2001, Springsteen has embraced the DVD format to release a number of concert performances to fans. *Live in New York City* (2001) chronicled performances from the band's final two Reunion Tour shows at Madison Square Garden in the summer of 2000. *Live in Barcelona* (2003) was the first release, in any official format, of a Springsteen concert in its entirety. The band is captured in the early stages of its *Rising* world tour, at an October 16, 2002 date at the Palau Sant Jordi in Barcelona, Spain. The *Bruce Springsteen: VH1 Storytellers* DVD (2005) was more clinic than concert. Filmed at the Two River Theater in Red Bank, New Jersey on April 4, 2005, Springsteen performed eight songs, providing commentary along the way (sometimes line-by-line) for songs ranging from "Blinded by the Light" to "Devils & Dust."

The biggest DVD treat came in November 2005, when Columbia released a 30th Anniversary Edition boxed set of *Born to Run*. The box includes a (slightly) remastered version of the landmark album, along with two DVDs: *Wings for Wheels: The Making of Born to Run,* directed by Thom Zimny, and *Hammersmith Odeon, London '75,* a complete recording of Springsteen's first European performance from 30 years before the release of the box.

It's an understatement to say that most fans had not seen anything like the *London '75* DVD before. It isn't just that none of the Hammersmith performances ever appeared on any television (aside from some precious seconds of clips here and there); an entire generation of fans had grown up with the stadium-filling, fist-pumping version of Springsteen, having never seen what the E Street concert experience was like when the shows were about magic and romance in small settings and on an intimate scale. For fans that had only heard stories of these days, *Hammersmith Odeon, London '75* was manna from rock 'n' roll heaven.

For years, prevailing wisdom held that Springsteen had an off night for his first-ever European gig, on November 18 at London's 3,000-seat Hammersmith Odeon. In his book on Springsteen, Eric Alterman (despite not having been at the show) reports that Springsteen delivered "a near comatose performance, probably his worst ever."[1] In the liner notes to the audio CD of the concert (released months after the DVD), Springsteen remembers, "For me, the set went by like a freight train. Later, all I remember is an awkward record company party, that 'what just happened?' feeling, and thinking we hadn't played that well."

He'd begun the night in a foul mood. Having just come off the *Time/ Newsweek* cover controversy, Springsteen had a low threshold for record-company hype. When he and the band got to the Hammersmith Odeon that day, they were met by a large sign on the marquee that boasted, "Finally. London is ready for Bruce Springsteen" (which Springsteen tore down). Inside the theater, buttons that read "I have seen the future of rock 'n' roll at the Hammersmith Odeon" had been placed on every seat. It was the band's first performance in Europe, and in Springsteen's mind, that was pressure enough—the occasion didn't need any added hype.

We don't see much of the audience on the *Hammersmith Odeon* DVD, but we can imagine the young Londoners maintaining dubious façades as they witnessed for the first time America's Great White Hype. Modern rock music had been *invented* on their side of the Atlantic. After all, no one had ripped off American R&B like The Beatles, Rolling Stones, Who, and Led Zeppelin. Back in 1966, an audience at London's Royal Albert Hall had practically booed another American popular music icon, Bob Dylan, off the stage as he and his backing band, The Hawks (who later changed their name to The Band) plugged in and played rock. So we can imagine the skepticism surrounding Springsteen and the E Street Band's first date in the motherland. The "future of rock 'n' roll"? So typical of these Americans.

Reviewing the show, the UK magazine *Melody Maker* wrote that Springsteen was "cast down by a response that was less magnanimous than he usually receives." Steve Van Zandt later said of Springsteen that night, "I've never seen him so subdued." In the *Guardian*, Robin Denslow wrote, "I think he might really be the genius his publicists and managers claim, but they've made it hard to show it. We certainly didn't quite see it last night."[2]

Springsteen has undoubtedly had a "worst" show at some point in his career, but as the *London '75* DVD shows, this one wasn't it. The setlist is strong, the performances tight, and (it must be said) the crowd sounds like they're having a pretty good time.

The performance begins with Springsteen singing "Thunder Road," accompanied only by Roy Bittan on piano. Bathed in blue stage lighting, the 26-year-old Springsteen looks like a psychedelic gypsy—bearded, wearing a leather jacket, a big hoop earring, and a floppy knitted cap. As he sings about the song that would become a classic, he looks upward as if summoning inspiration for the evening.

At the song's conclusion, Springsteen and Bittan are joined by the rest of the band. Springsteen bows to "Big Man" Clemons, smiles approvingly at Bittan, and hugs Van Zandt. The visual dynamics of the band are instantly fascinating. Clemons and Van Zandt look like rival pimps, with Clemons wearing a white suit with a red flower on the lapel, Van Zandt wearing a red suit with a white flower on the lapel. Gary Tallent looks like he's headed to the prom on a budget dressed in a brown tuxedo. Bittan is dressed down in a plaid shirt. All four wear fedoras, joining Springsteen in the Silly Hat Club. Then there's Danny Federici, looking West-Coast casual in a tan blazer and open-collar shirt. In the back, Max Weinberg dons a tank top and looks ready for business. And there's Springsteen, dressed as though he's just stumbled in from Piccadilly Circus and waving his arms like a big band conductor at the Tropicana as he leads the E Street Band into "Tenth Avenue Freeze-Out."

Toward the end of that song, Springsteen starts to loosen up, breaking into spastic dance steps and into a well-received version of "Spirit in the Night." He has some fun with the crowd as he enacts the line about Hazy Davey crawling in Greasy Lake, crawling off the side of the stage and then poking his head up to sing about making love with Crazy Janey in the dirt.

Then comes the band's first performance of "Lost in the Flood" in nearly a year. The leather jacket's off now...Springsteen's found his groove. Next, Springsteen's bouncing intro on harmonica leads into the Bo Diddley rhythms of "She's the One." The band's rendition of the song is a revelation: tight and inspired, one of the best performances of "She's the One" you're likely to hear. Springsteen and Van Zandt feed off each other's energy as they share the same mic and sing about the desperate liar with the angel in her eyes, and the thunder in her heart that makes you never want to leave her.

The lights go dark for a moment, and then you hear Weinberg's drum roll announce the beginning of "Born to Run." The song has been out for just a few months and is still fresh (only years later would it become the overblown, obligatory concert closer). It's not as good as their version at the Bottom Line three months earlier, but the E Street Band delights the crowd as it rips through its newfound anthem.

After "Born to Run," Springsteen addresses the crowd for the first time in the evening and asks the wonderfully tacky question: "How's things goin' over here in England and stuff?" The band then eases into a sauntering, melodic version of the song "E Street Shuffle." Van Zandt weaves a lyrical guitar line from Manfred Mann's "Pretty Flamingo" in and out of the song, Clemons draws some hoots when he pumps his arms to demonstrate "east coast muscle," and Springsteen creates a whimsical moment as the song winds down and he apes the "boy prophet" trying on sunglasses in a store window. As far as Springsteen's audience monologues go, it's not one of his most fascinating—he seems unsure of himself without the crowd interaction he's used to—and it only hints at the gritty theatricality that Springsteen and band often achieved in these early years.

After "E Street Shuffle," the band regroups for a high-energy version of "It's Hard to Be a Saint in the City." At song's end, they spin a tight jam that builds to the climax that is missing from the vinyl version on *Greetings* (which merely fades out on). This takes us into the meaty portion of the set: an epic sequence featuring "Backstreets," "Kitty's Back," "Jungle-land" and "Rosalita."

"Backstreets" is a treat, with the various available camera views edit-ing effectively to heighten the already heightened emotions of the song. Springsteen's guitar solo (which is nicely captured on an isolated track on the *Wings for Wheels* documentary) is fervent as he leads the song into a powerful crescendo. If you had to pick one song during which Spring-steen announces himself to the far side of the ocean, you might have to pick this one. This is Bob Marley singing "No Woman, No Cry" at the Lyceum. It's Bob Dylan at the Royal Albert Hall telling The Hawks to crank up "Like a Rolling Stone" *really loud.*

"Kitty's Back," though, might be the centerpiece of the night. On record, the song is a barely contained jazz-rock exploration. Live, it be-comes a furious jam session that, all told, eclipses 17 minutes. Solos from, respectively, Federici on organ, Bittan (who breaks off into an in-terlude of Van Morrison's "Moondance") on piano, Clemons on sax, and Springsteen on guitar lead into a cacophonous symphony before the band takes us to the bridge.

Then comes "Jungleland." Just as the evening had opened with "Thunder Road," Bittan introduces the song while Springsteen stands poised at the mic. Bittan takes a trip up and down the scales for the song's famous melodies, and the Hammersmith crowd cheers in anticipa-tion. *This* is really the climax of the night. As Clemons drifts into his fa-mous solo, Springsteen faces away from the stage with his head angled back and his eyes closed. If not for his reputation as being famously square when it comes to drugs, one would suspect he's enjoying an arti-ficial high; instead, he seems to have simply drifted away, lost in the mu-sic around him. When the time comes for him to return to earth and deliver the song's closing lines, he grips his cap and sings into it almost as if he's praying.

Finally, "Rosalita" is introduced to the English crowd. We don't get the crazed energy that we see in the Arizona State footage from three years later, and as Springsteen uses it as a chance to take roll call for the mem-bers of the band, we perhaps get an early hint of what would lead this war-horse to be temporarily retired from setlists 10 years down the road. But this *is* Rosie, and as Springsteen breaks into spontaneous bugaloo steps while playing guitar during the instrumental break, the hall is definitely in celebration mode. One would have to search the bootlegs far and wide for a stronger four-pack from Springsteen and the E Street Band.

After Rosie says good-bye, we say hello to Sandy. "4th of July, Asbury Park" returns the mood to the sense of intimacy with which the band had made its name in small venues during the early 1970s. "Detroit Medley" is not as frenzied as the *No Nukes* version that would hit the radio years later. The song starts a bit slowly, almost like an antique car that has to be cranked up, but when it gets going the band hits cruise control for some classic rock 'n' roll. In the middle of it all, Springsteen breaks off into a countrified riff that leads into some roadhouse pounding from Bittan, and then they travel back north to Detroit and the famous come-on to Jenny.

The band takes its bows. Springsteen comes back for an encore and takes a seat at the piano for a solo version of "For You." The rest of the band returns one last time to play "Quarter to Three," and then they bid London good-bye.

Simon Frith later wrote in *Creem* that when he first saw Springsteen take the stage that night, he thought, "This is the future of rock 'n' roll?" But as he watched him play, Frith was won over:

> I thought maybe and then yes. At the end of one of the encores . . . his band had to carry him off, two by the ankles, two by the armpits, and Bruce had a smile of great joy which you rarely see on a rock star these days. I had seen why you have to see him. The Springsteen stage show is a jumpy, nervous, desperately dramatic affair; not carefully constructed like The Stones', not floppily spontaneous like The Who's, but lived. Bruce Springsteen has seen a future without rock 'n' roll and he's hanging on to what he's got.[3]

Springsteen would be back six days later for a return engagement at the Hammersmith Odeon. Most accounts rate the November 24 show as superior to the November 18 one, and it's a shame that (for now) we can't see footage of *that* night. But first introductions happen only once, and as *London '75* shows us, Springsteen and the E Street Band had nothing to apologize for.

Now, here's wishing for *Red Bank '75, Phoenix '78, Uniondale New Year's Eve '80* . . .

* Update *
That Old-Time Magic

Live in Dublin (2007) and Magic (2007)

This book was originally published in hardcover format under a different title at the end of 2006, just months after the release of the *Seeger Sessions* album. It didn't seem fitting that the last release to be discussed in a book on one of the classic American singer-songwriters was a collection of cover songs from another singer—and not even a collection of tunes penned by that particular artist, but songs that he was known for having covered himself. In essence, the *Seeger Sessions* album was a collection of *covered* cover songs, twice removed from the original source of inspiration. As well received as the Seeger tribute disc was, for an artist who—as Hugo Lindgren observed in *New York* magazine—recorded the archetypal rock album of both the 1970s and 1980s, it was a somewhat anticlimactic endpoint to a discussion of Springsteen's body of work. So while this paperback version allows the book to see new life on the bookshelves, it also allows me the opportunity to put a more fitting end to this look at Springsteen's music.

The year 2007 saw the release of two albums from Springsteen beginning with the 2-CD/DVD *Live in Dublin* package, which documented performances from Springsteen and the seventeen-piece Sessions Band over three days in November 2006. With the album attributed to Springsteen "with the Sessions Band" and the Seeger name no longer weighing down the project with its folkie-tribute trappings, the collection casts Springsteen's roots-music side jaunt in a new light, and the Old Country seems an especially fitting locale—as Harry Browne observed in *Counterpunch*, "Springsteen's last project started with a tribute to Pete Seeger and ended up sounding like the Pogues."[1]

The *Seeger Sessions* material was well represented on the live package— Dan Tucker, Jesse James, Mary and Mrs. McGrath all came to the party, and Springsteen's traveling troupe sailed the Erie Canal, bemoaned their Oklahoma Home and climbed Jacob's Ladder—but *Live in Dublin* was most valuable for the reinterpretations of Springsteen originals: the vagabond pennywhistle of "Further On (Up the Road)," Gypsy violin and Latin rhythms of "Blinded by the Light," "If I Should Fall Behind" as western waltz, "Highway Patrolman" transformed into a country ballad, "Open All Night" as 1950s roadhouse rock accented with World War II–era Andrews Sisters scat from the gals and then joined in a call-and-response by the guys—"like something from Pump Boys at the Dinette," said Thom Jurek in his *AllMusic* review[2]—and "Growin' Up" sounding like country skiffle. The traditional rapture call of "When the Saints Go Marching In" sounds surprisingly like "If I Should Fall Behind" on *Live in New York City* with its contemplative, rotating vocals, but then gives way to the communal sing-along gospel of "This Little Light of Mine," which is closer to the fun and raucousness one might have expected from "Saints."

Most surprising is "Love of the Common People," a song first recorded by Waylon Jennings in 1967. Springsteen's vocals sound practically reedy on this one, and the brassy bounce of the Sessions crew seems to borrow a page from Jamaican artist Nicky Thomas, who reinterpreted the song as a reggae number in the seventies. There's also a new Springsteen original, "American Land," one of five bonus tracks (along with "Buffalo Gals," "How Can I Keep from Singing," "How Can a Poor Man Stand Such Times and Live?" and "Bring 'em Home") on the "American Land Edition" of the *Sessions* disc released later in 2006. In this ode to hardworking immigrants who crossed the Atlantic to Ellis Island in search of the American dream, the protagonist can hardly control his enthusiasm as he describes to his family (for whom he will later send) his planned journey to the land where legends speak of gold that "comes rushing out of the rivers straight into your hands...Diamonds in the sidewalk," the gutters "lined in song." One is reminded of the plight of the Dust Bowl Okies, but there's something more fun at heart here: "Dear I hear that beef flows through the faucets all night long." (Imagine!) The song was inspired by Seeger's translation of a poem by a Slovakian immigrant steelworker,[3] and Springsteen stretches out the lyrics to include the Irish, Poles, English, blacks, Italians (by mention of the "Zerillis," alluding to his mother's Italian family), and Jews, expanding the song to represent the American melting pot.

As the *Dublin* collection was released, the finishing touches were being put on Springsteen's first album with the E Street Band since *The Rising*. "I wrote most of this [new] album on tour with the Sessions band," he told *Rolling Stone*. "I wrote some of it the minute I came off *The Rising*. My idea was to pick up with the political and social results of what came out of the tragedy of 9/11. 'Livin' in the Future' I've had since then, and I might have had 'Radio Nowhere.' I had a few things, but I didn't have enough. So I set it aside.'"[4] One song, "Long Walk Home," had been played at the end of the Sessions tour. Late in 2006, Springsteen invited producer Brendan O'Brien to his home in New Jersey, played the new material for him, and let him pick which songs they should work on in the studio. Then in March 2007 they headed back into the Southern Tracks Recording Studio, where they cut the vocal tracks and overdubs. Bittan, Tallent, and Weinberg flew in each weekend to record their instrumental tracks, and the rest of the band came in to record with O'Brien as called for. Springsteen made sure to be in the studio when Clemons recorded his parts. "There's a whole dynamic there that spans decades," O'Brien explained. "I don't even get in the middle of it."[5]

Released in October 2007, *Magic* makes for a fitting end to this musical biography given the ways in which the album—his fifteenth full-length album of new material—pays tribute to his own storied career. In the *Rolling Stone* interview that coincided with the release, Springsteen alluded to being "in the middle of a very long conversation with my audience." When interviewer Joe Levy asked what he was hearing from his fans, Springsteen responded, "A lot of different things," and then added with a laugh: "I like the old Bruce better . . ."[6]

It's a creative territory not unfamiliar to most long-surviving bands, those whose setlists can often be divided into two categories: the classic songs and the new stuff they play while you head to the restroom. The *Rolling Stone* interview calls to mind the scene from Woody Allen's *Stardust Memories*, in which the director character played by Allen is told his best movies are his "early, funny ones." In Dave Marsh's *Glory Days*, we read the story of when Springsteen saw Allen's film in a Denver theater in 1980. Referring then to the endless cavalcade of sycophants that demand attention from Allen's character in the film, a fan in the theater that night asked Springsteen, "Is this the way it is? Is this how you feel?"[7] Now, nearly three decades later, Springsteen has had a rebirth with *The Rising* and *Devils & Dust*, yet there were still longtime listeners who were saying, "We love your music, Bruce . . . especially your early, romantic ones."

And all this is just fine with Springsteen, who's found himself revisiting the work of his younger days. "Lately, I've had a little romance with my oldest stuff," he told Levy. "There was a lot of freeness in it." It's no coincidence, then, that *Magic* is, as David Fricke wrote in his *Rolling Stone* review, "the most openly nostalgic record Springsteen has ever made."[8]

The echoes of earlier songs are heard throughout *Magic*. It's not quite as straightforward as Lindgren outlined in his *New York* review, who draws the following equations:

> You'll Be Comin' Down = Lucky Town
> Livin' in the Future = Tenth Avenue Freeze-Out
> Gypsy Biker = The River
> I'll Work for Your Love = Thunder Road
> Last to Die = Roulette[9]

Admittedly, the chorus of "You'll Be Comin' Down" has a similar chord progression to that of "Lucky Town." "Livin' in the Future" shares the soulful bounce like "Tenth Avenue Freeze-Out" (and more conspicuously, the roller-rink melody held over from the cutting-room floor of "Hungry Heart"). "Gypsy Biker" opens with a harmonica solo, as does "The River."

"I'll Work for Your Love" begins with a classic, *Born to Run*–style Roy Bittan piano line. And "Last to Die," like "Roulette," is a hard-driving story of distrust and paranoia. Added to that are the "burn this town down" sentiment of "Girls in Their Summer Clothes" that harkens back to "Rosalita" and "Born to Run," and "Long Walk Home," a song that reprises the father-son conversation of "My Hometown" even as it summons the mood and feel of the *Rising* sessions. For Lindgren, the album had a "rote familiarity"; for Amy Linden in the *Village Voice*, it was "a maddeningly uneven record that often sounds like legends coasting . . . Springsteen 101."[10] But while the album unquestionably relies on a musical past, it does so as a return to form. As Fricke keenly described, "After wrapping himself in a thousand fiddles on *The Seeger Sessions*, Springsteen has rediscovered the boardwalk-dance-party power of *Born to Run* and the Mitch Ryder and Jackie DeShannon encore covers in his 1975 and '78 shows."[11]

With material that began coming just after *The Rising*, *Magic* is its sequel of sorts. It's also the third in a Springsteen-O'Brien trilogy, and as a review posted online by *Sputnik Music* said, "it could be argued the sound of Bruce's music was becoming dated and perhaps a bit too obvious . . . O'Brien has refined and refreshed the E Street sound, bringing textures, instrumentation, and arrangement to the group which were absent on past efforts."[12] Gone are any of the plodding dynamics of "Racing in the Street," "Drive All Night," or even "My Hometown," replaced by layered textures of "Your Own Worst Enemy" and "Long Walk Home," along with the atmospherics of "Devil's Arcade" that more closely resemble the sound of the Smashing Pumpkins' *Ava Adore* than any past Springsteen release.

Lyrically, it's one of the most vivid of his recent albums. Descriptions of the natural world are infused with more descriptions of colors—one counts hues of red, white, blue, green, gray, and black—than on any other Springsteen cycle, as if the drivers on *Born to Run* finally pulled in to watch a drive-in movie in all its Technicolor glory. The language of *Magic* is also consistently fresh and active, with its gerund parade of clickin', sparklin', spinnin', rollin', sinkin', hangin', crushin', and driftin' harkening back to Rosie and her "cracklin' crossed wires" on *Devils & Dust*. (As Browne jokes, "Springsteen has rarely meet a letter-G he couldn't drop.")[13]

"Radio Nowhere," the single released in advance of the album, betrayed little of what was to come on the rest of the album. Though hard-driving and ultimately catchy, the song progresses little from its opening guitar chords, which called to mind for some the hit "867-5309 Jenny" by Tommy Tutone. (When people start comparing any new Springsteen tune to a quasi-novelty song from the 1980s, there doesn't seem to be much hope.) In "Radio Nowhere" we find a desperate driver much like the one in "State Trooper" on *Nebraska*. "It's an end-of-the-world scenario—he's seeing the apocalypse," Springsteen explained.[14] "All communications are down: 'Trying to find my way home/All I heard was a drone bouncing off a satellite/Crushing the last lone American night.' That's my business, that's what it's all about—trying to connect to you." It's eerie, this end-of-the-world scenario—we can almost picture the driver racing by the "lunar landscape" from "Open All Night"—but it's also a quaint sort of apocalypse, the notion that someone would spend the last day on earth scanning the FM band. One has to admit that in the days of emo, iPods, thug-hop, and *American Idol* test-tube babies, the lyrical allusion to Elvis's "Mystery Train" seems anachronistic by two generations or so, way more so than Springsteen's retro-Crystals stage did in 1975. "Does anyone care about rock 'n' roll anymore?" the man who was once its future seems to be asking. (One could imagine Pearl Jam covering it onstage, juxtaposed with "Spin the Black Circle," their ode to seven-inch vinyl.)

With the cover image of the somber-looking singer hinting that the title wasn't an artistic boast, the title song made it plain that we were dealing with, as Browne wrote, a more "sinister" type of magic.[15] "I never sit down to make a 'political' record or a 'not political' record," Springsteen told Dave Marsh for a segment on Amazon.com. "But I think if you're tapping into basically who you are and what you're thinking, those things have to come through in what you're creating." Citing his desire to not "burden" the record with a heavy-handed message, he described the first part of the record as saying, "it's a little more in the subtext, and then the record reveals itself in the last three or four songs, where the subtext rises to the surface . . . that's when the subtext become text."[16]

In that light, "Your Own Worst Enemy" may not be explicitly about war, but in both sound and story it seems to occupy a space somewhere between two of the "post-9/11" songs on *The Rising*, "Nothing Man" and "You're Missing." It's a song of the before and after, contrasting a past in which the "you" addressed felt secure and self-assured with a present plagued by guilt and doubt. The fingerprints were "Left clumsily at the scene," and the once high-flying flag has "drifted into the sky." Who the "you" is, is never clear, just as the songs on *The Rising* didn't need to be about 9/11 widows to convey emotional truths of a relationship left in ruins.

"Livin' in the Future" likewise contemplates the end of a relationship, the news of which comes via a letter "blown' in on an ill wind," and the bigger picture of the singer awakening to "gunpowder" gray skies on Election Day (an easily made connection to the 2004 reelection of Bush the Lesser) link the personal and the political. It's one of the more impenetrable songs on the album: it's a story of endings and lost faith, told to the strangely reassuring, "Glory Days"–sounding chorus of "We're livin' in the future and none of this has happened yet." In the end, it's a song that leaves a sense of enduring in the face of whatever may come, a vow to fight the future, the hope that maybe, baby, the gypsy lied.

A promised future also figures in "You'll Be Coming Down," the musical and lyrical antecedent to "Lucky Town." It's a joyful curse of comeuppance, a warning to a pretty-faced former lover that her luck will run out. She's on top of the world now, her head "spinnin' in diamonds and clouds," but as soon as she loses her looks she'll be kicked out of lucky town and come crashing down like the proverbial drunk on a barroom floor. Balancing out the bitterness is "I'll Work For Your Love," a pledge of devotion made to an angelic bartender. The song is wrought (perhaps overwrought) with religious metaphors: the sun forms a halo around her head, her lips are Jesus' crown of thorns, her tears "fill the rosary," the "pages of Revelation" seen in her blue eyes. (Telling a woman that you see the Four Horsemen of the Apocalypse in her gaze might not be the most effective pickup line.) In the singer's erotic ecstasy, he vows to study the bones in Theresa's back as she turns to dust off a glass—an act he compares to the Stations of the Cross—and in his eyes the rays of the low-hanging sun transform the smoke in the barroom into the "mist" of the Garden of Eden.

The trope of Girl as Saving Grace is nothing new in Springsteen's songs, and it's at the heart of "Girls in Their Summer Clothes," which itself is the album's pop centerpiece. Shaking off an ex-lover who "cut me like a knife," the singer quickly propositions the next beautiful girl who walks by him, asking/telling her, "maybe you could save my life." If the title of the album was any allusion to the magic of pop music, it's this song of romantic regeneration where that old-time magic is best captured. It's an instant Springsteen classic—with its overdubbed vocals, layered orchestrations, and ringing glockenspiel, it's tempting to say that "Girls" sounds like an outtake from the *Born to Run* sessions, except it's more uplifting than any of that album's doomed romanticism. One gets the feeling that *this* is the type of song that he was trying to write all those years ago—a pop masterpiece harkening back to the classic tunes that used to play up and down the boardwalk during summers past. (Reviewers heard the influence of the West Coast 1960s sound of the Byrds and the Beach Boys on "Girls" and "You'll Be Coming Down.") Springsteen himself said, "It's The Byrds, The Beach Boys, a California album,"[17] and it's on this perfect pop song that he most closely nailed that. In short, it's a better song than a fifty-eight-year-old should be allowed to write. "I wanted one thing on the record that was the perfect pop universe," Springsteen told A. O. Scott.[18]

The images in "Girls" are delivered almost like the lines of imagism poetry or haiku: the shining streetlights on Blessing Avenue, the procession of lovers walking two by two, the spinning of bicycle spokes, the chiming of the bank clock, the neon sign at Frankie's Diner, the flickering fluorescent lights over Pop's Grill—and, of course, the girls in their summer clothes who pass him by. "It's the longing, the unrequited longing for that perfect world," he continued. "Pop is funny. It's a tease. It's an important one, but it's a tease, and therein resides its beauty and its joke."[19] The phrases paint a collective picture that's brilliant in its simplicity and universal accessibility. Though even here we seem to visit past songs—the same breeze crossing the porch that once made Mary's dress wave, the claim of "I still got my feet" that recalls the days of dancing in the dark—the sound here is too fresh to be mere nostalgia. It's moments like these, scattered throughout *Magic*, that create the album's dramatic tension—points at which past and future collide, contrast, and conflate.

Those who saw *Magic* as a return to romance missed the angry and bitter lines strewn throughout the record: the unanswered plea for signs of life on "Radio Nowhere"; the "dirty sun" and "ship Liberty" that "sailed away on a bloody red horizon" in "Livin' in the Future"; the flag that once "flew so high" in "Your Own Worst Enemy"; the soldier in "Gypsy Biker" on whose blood the "speculators made their money"; "Magic"'s dead bodies in the trees; the blood drawn in "Last to Die."

The palming of a coin, the card up the sleeve, the rabbit in the hat, Harry Houdini—these images from the title song all take on sinister meanings against the eerie backdrop of the violin, upright bass, and Chamberlin keyboard. "I got a shiny saw blade/All I need's a volunteer," Springsteen sings in a restrained delivery, and one need not even complete the metaphor of the saw blade to the tools of death or the volunteer from the audience to volunteer servicemen to get the real meaning here. Nor did Springsteen really need to say on the tour's stop in Washington, DC, "Hey, this is where it happens! This is the City of Magic!"[20] And with the line "Trust none of what you hear/And less of what you see," one need not look too hard to see it as a shot at an administration that was able to convince the American people of the existence of WMDs in Iraq without displaying any evidence—and which was reelected even after this deception was revealed. The magic here is the magic of illusion and the art of deception as practiced in Spin City.

"Last to Die," with its allusion to John Kerry's question to Congress in April 1971 ("How do you ask a man to be the last man to die for a mistake?") draws the inevitable comparison between Vietnam and Iraq. A couple flees with their kids from an unnamed, almost metaphysical evil, driving on to Truth or Consequences, a town in New Mexico whose name points none too subtle at the hazards of a nation falling for political sleight of hand. As they drive past a downtown store window, televisions broadcast a news report of war dead ("Faces of the dead at five" that "Petition the drivers as we pass by.") In her review, Linden said, "Bruce, I love you—but unless you're giving directions, no more highways."[21] But throughout the album he *does* seem to be giving directions to an apocalyptic landscape that, with its dead bodies and raging environment, often has more to do with Cormac McCarthy's *The Road* than the highway promised to Mary on "Thunder Road." This *Magic* world has red mornings, rolling thunder, a cinnamon sky gone candy-apple green, clouds the color of gunpowder, a dirty sun, a hanging sun, crumbling cities, images that invoke the dust of ages.

The family in "Gypsy Biker" receives home the dead body of a biker-turned-soldier, and as the town is divided over the war, the singer remembers having argued with his "brother" (whether literal or figurative) about which side was right and which wrong: "You asked me that question, I didn't get it right." As a final ceremonial act, the singer's family brings the fallen man's motorcycle out to the foothills and sets it on fire—a metallic cremation. "Now all that remains/Is my love for you brother," muses the singer as the white lines of the road remind him of the lines of cocaine he does, perhaps to fill the void.

"Devil's Arcade" is the most haunting song on the album and one of Springsteen's most haunting, period—and one of his most enigmatic, leaving Internet message-board posters to debate its meaning. A wash of synthesizer and the sway of a cello introduce the thoughts of a wounded or dying soldier's lover. This first stanza has a weird phallic juxtaposition of his gun and the night she helped him "get it in." The next recounts his getting wounded in an explosion of metal and plastic, leaving him in a blue-walled hospital ward, a nameless "sea" where he "lie[s] adrift." The final one seems to shift to the wounded soldier's thoughts as he yearns for someone to whisper promises of a "tomorrow" for him, the chance to return to a "house on a quiet street, a home for the brave." The song's end is consumed in heat: the soldier's thoughts stay on the beating of his lover's heart, and smoldering passion morphs into the life-and-death tension of some mysterious, demonic game. While he was interviewing Springsteen for *Rolling Stone*, Levy pointed out a progression from the album's opening search for "rhythm" and "anybody alive" to the "beat of the heart" on this last song on the album. "That's what 'Devil's Arcade' answers in the end. There *is* somebody alive, and at the end it's the beat of the heart, that's what ends the record. That's somebody's rhythm," Springsteen said, explaining something that had been present only in his subconscious while working on *Magic*. "That's something that's happening, but you don't know it's happening."[22]

In "Devil's Arcade," reviewer Robert Gillis saw a musical familiarity here with Gordon Lightfoot's "The Wreck of the Edmund Fitzgerald," and although I don't quite see it, I love the comment because parts of *Magic* are so melodic in a mode of the best hits from 1970s AM radio. If segments of the album were Springsteen's love letter to his old songs, or to old songs in general, "Long Walk Home" is perhaps the most personal inclusion. "It's sort of the summational song of the album," said Jon Landau. "I think it's one of Bruce's great masterpieces."[23] The reviewer-turned-manager has long since waived his objectivity toward anything Springsteen, but the song has an undeniable sense of looking back: the visit home, the faces of strangers, the father speaking on the meaning of place and right and wrong, the boarded-up windows of a city in ruins. "Most of my records . . . they're struggles against alienation, and so that character comes back to town and feels very estranged because the place has changed," Springsteen explained. "I've set up in a couple of different instances, they're idyllic small towns, and then I like to mess with them a little bit and use them as a setting for the way times have changed."[24]

"That's one of my favorite songs that he's done in a long time," O'Brien said. "It's mournful, but also hopeful. It has very introspective verses and then he opens up lyrically as the song progresses."[25] Joyce Millman writes, "On 'Long Walk Home,' Springsteen turns the map around, so that he's coming home out of the darkness—'in the distance I could see the town where I was born.' He's out of the car and walking, just like Woody Guthrie in 'This Land Is Your Land,' but as he enters the heart of town, he sees that something has gone very wrong. The diner is shuttered, the VA hall is abandoned, the townspeople are 'rank strangers.' Once upon a time, his father proudly told him, this town— which is, of course, America itself—was a 'great place to be born,' and the flag flying over the courthouse 'meant certain things are set in stone/ Who we are, what we'll do/ And what we won't.' "[26]

After two full-length dress rehearsals at the Asbury Park Convention Hall and a third at the Continental Airlines Arena in September, the *Magic* tour "officially" touched off at the Hartford Civic Center on October 2. The setlist for the opener was: "Radio Nowhere," "The Ties That Bind," "Lonesome Day," "Gypsy Biker," "Magic," the three-song centerpiece of "Reason to Believe"/"Night"/"She's the One," "Livin' in the Future," "The Promised Land," "Town Called Heartbreak" (a Patti Scialfa song), "Darkness on the Edge of Town," "Darlington County," "Devil's Arcade," "The Rising," "Last to Die," "Long Walk Home" and "Badlands," with an encore of "Girls in Their Summer Clothes," "Thundercrack," "Born to Run," "Waitin' on a Sunny Day" and "American Land." As the tour progressed, the band revisited old favorites along the way, and the question from night to night was which classic Springsteen would call for: "Backstreets," "Racing in the Street," "Growin' Up," "Spirit in the Night," "Incident on 57th Street," or twofers like "Meeting Across the River" into "Jungleland" or "4th of July, Asbury Park" into "The E Street Shuffle." This last pairing on November 19 allowed Danny Federici to shine on accordian and keyboard solos. It had just been announced that Federici would not be accompanying the band on its European dates, as he had to focus on treatments for melanoma. During the final bows, Springsteen went over to Federici, put his arm around him, and brought him to center stage so that the founding E Street member could take a curtain call.

With legendary status comes the price of getting old, and the *Magic* album and tour has been marked by the passing of two Springsteen friends who dated back to the Upstage Club in Asbury Park during the late 1960s.

Terry McGovern, a friend of Springsteen since their Asbury Park days, passed away in April 2007. McGovern had gone to work for Springsteen on the *Tunnel of Love* Express Tour and, over the years, was a jack-of-all-trades in the Springsteen camp: road manager, personal assistant, trusted friend. Springsteen wrote and recorded "Terry's Song," a hidden track at the end of *Magic* that honors his fallen friend "gone into that dark ether."

Then, on April 17, 2008, Federici succumbed to the skin cancer he had been battling for three years. A key figure in the signature "Springsteen sound" over the years, from the accordion on "4th of July, Asbury Park" to the organ solo on "Hungry Heart" to the electronic glockenspiel, Federici had performed one last time with Bruce and the band during segments of the March 20 show in Indianapolis. Delivering the eulogy at the funeral, Springsteen remembered, "Before we went on I asked him what he wanted to play and he said, 'Sandy.' He wanted to strap on the accordion and revisit the boardwalk of our youth during the summer nights when we'd walk along the boards with all the time in the world." Springsteen then recalled the shore legend of the Middletown riot during which Federici earned his nickname. "So today, making another one of his mysterious exits, we say farewell to Danny, 'Phantom' Dan, Federici."[27]

And then, at the time of this writing, Marie Castello—"Madam Marie" from "4th of July, Asbury Park"—passed away at the age of 93. The song had immortalized the woman who had told fortunes in her Temple of Knowledge on the Asbury Park boardwalk since the 1930s. "Well the cops finally busted Madam Marie for tellin' fortunes better than they do," Springsteen had sang to Sandy back in 1973. ("That was just the Boss," maintains Jim Bruno, Asbury Park's deputy mayor. "She was never arrested. But Springsteen turned her into an icon.") In the spring, Castello had told the *Asbury Park Press*, "He always comes by to say hello....He knows where he came from."[28] After her passing, Springsteen posted a remembrance of younger days, sitting across from her booth on the boardwalk and watching as she "led the day trippers into the small back room where she would unlock a few of the mysteries of their future."[29]

On the 2007–08 tour, setlists often included two of the new songs, "Livin' in the Future" and "Long Walk Home," followed respectively by two classic *Darkness* tracks, "The Promised Land" and "Badlands," followed by "Long Walk Home." Celebrating the 30th anniversary of *Darkness* in June 2008, essayist Joyce Millman described the album as "A Map of the Future" for Springsteen's vision of America. "Bruce Springsteen drew a map and wrote 'here be dragons' on it ... The 'darkness' haunts this album like a living, often fire-breathing, presence." But juxtaposed with the *Magic* tracks, those classic anthems become statements of reaffirmation. She observes that the harmonica intro to "The Promised Land" sound like "cleansing rain" after the bleak vision in "Livin'" while the "I believe in a promised land" statement "never sounded so cathartic"; likewise, the "fervent declaration" of "I wanna spit in the face of these badlands" sung live after "Long Walk Home" delivers a "rejection of the moral wasteland of the Bush years, a refusal to remain a community under siege."[30]

For a benefit concert at the 80-year-old Count Basie Theatre in Red Bank on May 7, Springsteen and the E Street Band paid tribute to the album with a dream setlist: the entire *Darkness* album played live and in sequence—followed with the entire *Born to Run* album, plus encores of "So Young and in Love," "Kitty's Back," "Rosalita" and "Raise Your Hand." Hipster concert purists might argue that track-for-track album performances rob live shows of their intrinsic "What will they play next?" suspense, but still ... *Darkness* and *Born to Run*! On hand for the event, noted Bruce fan Brian Williams raved in his blog, "It's never been done, and won't be done again. It was heaven. Those of us who were present for it knew it at the time—there were shared looks of amazement among complete strangers last night. In all our years together—we'd never seen or heard anything like it."[31]

Springsteen indeed seems to be having a romance with his older material, even as he keeps churning out new material that sounds fresh in these days of downloadable music and satellite radio. A February 2008 online feature from *USA Today* listed the rotation that could be found on Springsteen's iPod, and it showed an eclectic mix largely given to populist-roots music though scattered across the musical spectrum. The artists most represented were Roger McGuinn/The Byrds and Bob Dylan, while the roster ranged from Jimmie Rodgers's "My Blue Eyed Jane," Woody Guthrie's "Hard Travelin'" and Hank Williams's "Lost Highway" to Paul Robeson's "Joe Hill," Mahalia Jackson's "God's Gonna Separate the Wheat from the Tares," Sam Cooke's "Touch the Hem of His Garment," and Jimmy Cliff's "Sufferin' in the Land" to Leonard Cohen's "Everybody Knows," Van Morrison's "Sweet Thing," and Victoria Williams's "Summer of Drugs." There were self-references courtesy of Robert Mitchum's "Ballad of Thunder Road," Sleater-Kinney's cover of "The Promised Land," wife Patti Scialfa's "Valerie," as well as tunes from newer acts like Jay Farrar, Jeff Tweedy, Beck, Bright Eyes, Neko Case, and Nas.

It's a new world, the one confronted by singer-songwriter Springsteen as he faces the approach of his 60th birthday. He's neither burned out nor faded away; instead, he simply endures as the leading American voice in his craft, one who still believes in the transformative magic of popular music.

✶ Discography ✶

STUDIO ALBUMS

Greetings from Asbury Park, N.J. Released January 5, 1973, produced by Mike Appel and Jim Cretecos, engineered by Louis Lahav, recorded at 914 Sound Studios, Blauvelt, New York. Tracks: "Blinded by the Light," "Growin' Up," "Mary Queen of Arkansas," "Does This Bus Stop at 82nd Street?," "Lost in the Flood," "The Angel," "For You," "Spirit in the Night," "It's Hard to Be a Saint in the City."

The Wild, the Innocent & the E Street Shuffle. Released November 5, 1973, produced by Mike Appel and Jim Cretecos, engineered by Louis Lahav, recorded at 914 Sound Studios, Blauvelt, New York. Tracks: "The E Street Shuffle," "4th of July, Asbury Park (Sandy)," "Kitty's Back," "Wild Billy's Circus Story," "Incident on 57th Street," "Rosalita (Come Out Tonight)," "New York City Serenade."

Born to Run. Released September 1, 1975, produced by Bruce Springsteen, Jon Landau, and Mike Appel, engineered and mixed by Jimmy Iovine, recorded at Record Plant in New York, NY; "Born to Run" produced by Bruce Springsteen and Mike Appel, engineered by Louis Lahav, recorded at 914 Sound Studios in Blauvelt, New York. Tracks: "Thunder Road," "Tenth Avenue

Freeze-Out," "Night," "Backstreets," "Born to Run," "She's the One," "Meeting Across the River," "Jungleland." (Note: In November 1975, a *Born to Run:
30th Anniversary Edition* three-disc box set was released with a remastered
version of the album along with a documentary DVD, *Wings for Wheels: The
Making of Born to Run,* and a concert DVD, *Hammersmith Odeon, London '75.*)

Darkness on the Edge of Town. Released June 6, 1978, produced by Jon Landau
and Bruce Springsteen with assistance from Steve Van Zandt, recorded by
Jimmy Iovine, mixed by Charles Plotkin and Jimmy Iovine, recorded at the
Record Plant in New York City. Tracks: "Badlands," "Adam Raised a Cain,"
"Something in the Night," "Candy's Room," "Racing in the Street," "The
Promised Land," "Factory," "Streets of Fire," "Prove It All Night," "Darkness
on the Edge of Town."

The River [double LP]. Released October 17, 1980, produced by Bruce Spring-
steen, Jon Landau, Steve Van Zandt, recorded by Neil Dorfsman at The
Power Station in New York City, mixed by Chuck Plotkin and Toby Scott.
Tracks: "The Ties That Bind," "Sherry Darling," "Jackson Cage," "Two Hearts,"
"Independence Day," "Hungry Heart," "Out in the Street," "Crush on You,"
"You Can Look (But You Better Not Touch)," "I Wanna Marry You," "The
River," "Point Blank," "Cadillac Ranch," "I'm a Rocker," "Fade Away," "Stolen
Car," "Ramrod," "The Price You Pay," "Drive All Night," "Wreck on the High-
way."

Nebraska. Released October 4, 1982, recorded by Mike Batlan in New Jersey,
mastered by Dennis King. Tracks: "Nebraska," "Atlantic City," "Mansion on
the Hill," "Johnny 99," "Highway Patrolman," "State Trooper," "Used Cars,"
"Open All Night," "My Father's House," "Reason to Believe."

Born in the U.S.A. Released June 4, 1984, produced by Bruce Springsteen, Jon
Landau, Chuck Plotkin, Steve Van Zandt, recorded by Toby Scott at the
Power Station and The Hit Factory in New York City, mixed by Bob Clear-
mountain at the Power Station. Tracks: "Born in the U.S.A.," "Cover Me,"
"Darlington County," "Working on the Highway," "Downbound Train," "I'm
on Fire," "No Surrender," "Bobby Jean," "I'm Goin' Down," "Glory Days,"
"Dancing in the Dark," "My Hometown."

Tunnel of Love. Released October 6, 1987, produced by Bruce Springsteen, Jon
Landau, Chuck Plotkin, recorded and engineered by Toby Scott in New
Jersey, mixed by Bob Clearmountain; "One Step Up" recorded at A&M Stu-
dios, Los Angeles; additional recording at The Hit Factory, New York City;
Kren Studio, Los Angeles; and A&M Studios, Los Angeles. Tracks: "Ain't Got

You," "Tougher Than the Rest," "All That Heaven Will Allow," "Spare Parts,"
"Cautious Man," "Walk Like a Man," "Tunnel of Love," "Two Faces," "Brilliant
Disguise," "One Step Up," "When You're Alone," "Valentine's Day."

Human Touch. Released March 31, 1992, produced by Bruce Springsteen,
Chuck Plotkin, Roy Bittan, engineered by Toby Scott, mixed by Bob Clear-
mountain, additional recording at Soundworks West, Oceanway Studios,
Westlake, and the Record Plant, New York City. Tracks: "Human Touch,"
"Soul Driver," "57 Channels (And Nothin' On)," "Cross My Heart," "Gloria's
Eyes," "With Every Wish," "Roll of the Dice," "Real World," "All of Nothin' At
All," "Man's Job," "I Wish I Were Blind," "The Long Goodbye," "Real Man,"
"Pony Boy."

Lucky Town. Released March 31, 1992, produced by Bruce Springsteen with Jon
Landau and Chuck Plotkin, additional production by Roy Bittan, recorded
by Toby Scott at Thrill Hill Recording, mixed by Bob Clearmountain.
Tracks: "Better Days," "Lucky Town," "Local Hero," "If I Should Fall Behind,"
"Leap of Faith," "The Big Muddy," "Living Proof," "Book of Dreams," "Souls
of the Departed," "My Beautiful Reward."

The Ghost of Tom Joad. Released November 21, 1995, produced by Bruce Spring-
steen and Chuck Plotkin, recorded and mixed by Toby Scott at Thrill Hill
Recording Studios. Tracks: "The Ghost of Tom Joad," "Straight Time," "High-
way 29," "Youngstown," "Sinaloa Cowboys," "The Line," "Balboa Party," "Dry
Lightning," "The New Timer," "Across the Border," "Galveston Bay," "My Best
Was Never Good Enough."

Blood Brothers [five-track EP]. VHS/CD package released in 1996, produced by
Bruce Springsteen, Jon Landau, and Chuck Plotkin, recorded and mixed by
Toby Scott at The Hit Factory; "Murder Incorporated" mixed by Bob Clear-
mountain; "Secret Garden" mixed by David Kahne and Michael Brauer;
"Murder Incorporated" recorded at Tramps, New York City. Tracks: "Blood
Brothers (Alternate version)," "High Hopes," "Murder Incorporated" (live
from Tramps), "Secret Garden" (with strings), "Without You."

The Rising. Released July 30, 2002, produced and mixed by Brendan O'Brien,
recorded by Nick Didia, recorded and mixed at Southern Tracks Recording
Studios in Atlanta; "Let's Be Friends (Skin to Skin)" recorded by Toby Scott at
Thrill Hill Studios in New Jersey; additional recording at The Sound Kitchen
Recording Studios, Franklin, Tennessee, and Henson Recording Studios,
Hollywood. Tracks: "Lonesome Day," "Into the Fire," "Waitin' on a Sunny Day,"
"Nothing Man," "Countin' on a Miracle," "Empty Sky," "Worlds Apart," "Let's

Be Friends (Skin to Skin)," "Further On (Up the Road)," "The Fuse," "Mary's Place," "You're Missing," "The Rising," "Paradise," "My City of Ruins."

Devils & Dust. Released April 26, 2005, produced and mixed by Brendan O'Brien; "All the Way Home" and "Long Time Comin'" produced by Brendan O'Brien, Bruce Springsteen, and Chuck Plotkin; "Black Cowboys," "Jesus Was an Only Son" and "Matamoros Banks" mixed by Toby Scott; recorded by Toby Scott and Nick Didia at Thrill Hill Recording in Los Angeles and New Jersey, additional recording at Southern Tracks Recording, Atlanta, and Masterphonics in Nashville. Tracks: "Devils & Dust," "All the Way Home," "Reno," "Long Time Comin'," "Black Cowboys," "Maria's Bed," "Silver Palomino," "Jesus Was an Only Son," "Leah," "The Hitter," "All I'm Thinkin' About," "Matamoros Banks."

We Shall Overcome: The Seeger Sessions. Released April 25, 2006, produced by Bruce Springsteen, recorded by Toby Scott at Thrill Hill Recording Studios and Boxwood Studios in New Jersey, mixed by Bob Clearmountain. Tracks: "Old Dan Tucker," "Jesse James," "Mrs. McGrath," "O Mary Don't You Weep," "John Henry," "Erie Canal," "Jacob's Ladder," "My Oklahoma Home," "Eyes on the Prize," "Shenandoah," "Pay Me My Money Down," "We Shall Overcome," "Froggie Went A Courtin'."

Magic. Released September 25, 2007, produced by Brendan O'Brien, recorded at the Southern Tracks Recording Studio in Atlanta, March–May 2007. Tracks: "Radio Nowhere," "You'll Be Comin' Down," "Livin' in the Future," "Your Own Worst Enemy," "Gypsy Biker," "Girls in Their Summer Clothes," "I'll Work for Your Love," "Magic," "Last to Die," "Long Walk Home," "Devil's Arcade," "Terry's Song" (hidden track).

COMPILATIONS

Greatest Hits, released February 28, 1995. Tracks: "Born to Run," "Thunder Road," "Badlands," "The River," "Hungry Heart," "Atlantic City," "Dancing in the Dark," "Born in the U.S.A.," "My Hometown," "Glory Days," "Brilliant Disguise," "Human Touch," "Better Days," "Streets of Philadelphia," "Secret Garden," "Murder Incorporated," "Blood Brothers," "This Hard Land."

Tracks [four-disc box set], released November 10, 1998. Tracks: "Mary Queen of Arkansas," "It's Hard to Be a Saint in the City," "Growin' Up," "Does This Bus

Stop at 82nd Street?," "Bishop Danced," "Santa Ana," "Seaside Bar Song," "Zero and Blind Terry," "Linda Let Me Be the One," "Thundercrack," "Rendezvous," "Give the Girl a Kiss," "Iceman," "Bring on the Night," "So Young and In Love," "Hearts of Stone," "Don't Look Back," "Restless Nights," "A Good Man Is Hard to Find" (Pittsburgh), "Roulette," "Dollhouse," "Where the Bands Are," "Loose Ends," "Living on the Edge of the World," "Wages of Sin," "Take 'Em As They Come," "Be True," "Ricky Wants a Man of Her Own," "I Wanna Be With You," "Mary Lou," "Stolen Car," "Born in the U.S.A.," "Johnny Bye-Bye," "Shut Out the Light," "Cynthia," "My Love Will Not Let You Down," "This Hard Land," "Frankie," "TV Movie," "Stand on It," "Lion's Den," "Car Wash," "Rockaway the Days," "Brothers Under the Bridge" ('83), "Man at the Top," "Pink Cadillac," "Two for the Road," "Janey Don't You Love Heart," "When You Need Me," "The Wish," "The Honeymooners," "Lucky Man," "Leavin' Train," "Seven Angels," "Gave It a Name," "Sad Eyes," "My Lover Man," "Over the Rise," "When the Lights Go Out," "Loose Change," "Trouble in Paradise," "Happy," "Part Man, Part Monkey," "Goin' Cali," "Back in Your Arms," "Brothers Under the Bridge."

18 Tracks, released April 13, 1999. Tracks: "Growin' Up," "Seaside Bar Song," "Rendezvous," "Hearts of Stone," "Where the Bands Are," "Loose Ends," "I Wanna Be with You," "Born in the U.S.A.," "My Love Will Not Let You Down," "Lion's Den," "Pink Cadillac," "Janey Don't You Love Heart," "Sad Eyes," "Part Man, Part Monkey," "Trouble River," "Brothers Under the Bridge," "The Fever," "The Promise."

The Essential Bruce Springsteen [three-disc set], released November 11, 2003. Tracks: "Blinded by the Light," "For You," "Spirit in the Night," "4th of July, Asbury Park (Sandy)," "Rosalita (Come Out Tonight)," "Thunder Road," "Born to Run," "Jungleland," "Badlands," "Darkness on the Edge of Town," "The Promised Land," "The River," "Hungry Heart," "Nebraska," "Atlantic City," "Born in the U.S.A.," "Glory Days," "Dancing in the Dark," "Tunnel of Love," "Brilliant Disguise," "Human Touch," "Living Proof," "Lucky Town," "Streets of Philadelphia," "The Ghost of Tom Joad," "The Rising," "Mary's Place," "Lonesome Day," "American Skin (41 Shots)" (live), "Land of Hope and Dreams" (live), "From Small Things (Big Things One Day Come)," "The Big Payback," "Held Up Without a Gun" (live), "Trapped" (live), "None But the Brave," "Missing," "Lift Me Up," "Viva Las Vegas," "County Fair," "Code of Silence" (live), "Dead Man Walkin'," "Countin' on a Miracle" (acoustic).

LIVE RECORDINGS

Live/1975–85 [five-LP or three-disc boxed set]. Released November 10, 1986, produced by Bruce Springsteen, Jon Landau, Chuck Plotkin, engineered by Toby Scott, mixed by Bob Clearmountain; recorded at various concert venues throughout the United States. Tracks: "Thunder Road," "Adam Raised a Cain," "Spirit in the Night," "4th of July, Asbury Park (Sandy)," "Paradise by the 'C,'" "Fire," "Growin' Up," "It's Hard to Be a Saint in the City," "Backstreets," "Rosalita (Come Out Tonight)," "Raise Your Hand," "Hungry Heart," "Two Hearts," "Cadillac Ranch," "You Can Look (But You Better Not Touch)," "Independence Day," "Badlands," "Because the Night," "Candy's Room," "Darkness on the Edge of Town," "Racing in the Street," "This Land Is Your Land," "Nebraska," "Johnny 99," "Reason to Believe," "Born in the U.S.A.," "Seeds," "The River," "War," "Darlington County," "Working on the Highway," "The Promised Land," "Cover Me," "I'm on Fire," "Bobby Jean," "My Hometown," "Born to Run," "No Surrender," "Tenth Avenue Freeze-Out," "Jersey Girl."

In Concert: MTV Plugged. Released in the United States August 26, 1997, produced by Bruce Springsteen and Jon Landau, engineered by Toby Scott, mixed by Bob Clearmountain. Tracks: "Red Headed Woman," "Better Days," "Atlantic City," "Darkness on the Edge of Town," "Man's Job," "Human Touch," "Lucky Town," "I Wish I Were Blind," "Thunder Road," "Light of Day," "If I Should Fall Behind," "Living Proof," "My Beautiful Reward."

Chimes of Freedom [EP]. Released August 1998, recorded on tour in the United States and Sweden, March-July 1988. Tracks: "Tougher Than the Rest," "Be True," "Chimes of Freedom," "Born to Run."

Live in New York City [two-disc set]. Released April 3, 2001, produced by Bruce Springsteen and Chuck Plotkin, recorded by Toby Scott at Madison Square Garden. Tracks: "My Love Will Not Let You Down," "Prove It All Night," "Two Hearts," "Atlantic City," "Mansion on the Hill," "The River," "Youngstown," "Murder Incorporated," "Badlands," "Out in the Street," "Born to Run," "Tenth Avenue Freeze-Out," "Land of Hope and Dreams," "American Skin (41 Shots)," "Lost in the Flood," "Born in the U.S.A.," "Don't Look Back," "Jungleland," "Ramrod," "If I Should Fall Behind."

Hammersmith Odeon, London '75 [two-disc set]. Released February 28, 2006, recorded by Dave Fromberg at Hammersmith Odeon, London, produced and edited by Thom Zimny, mixed by Bob Clearmountain. Tracks: "Thunder Road," "Tenth Avenue Freeze-Out," "Spirit in the Night," "Lost in the

Flood," "She's the One," "Born to Run," "The E Street Shuffle," "It's Hard to Be a Saint in the City," "Backstreets," "Kitty's Back," "Jungleland," "Rosalita (Come Out Tonight)," "4th of July, Asbury Park (Sandy)," "Detroit Medley," "For You," "Quarter to Three."

Live in Dublin. Released June 5, 2007, produced by George Travis and Thom Zimny, edited by Thom Zimny, mixed by John Cooper, recorded in Dublin, Ireland, in November 2006. Tracks: "Atlantic City," "Old Dan Tucker," "Eyes on the Prize," "Jesse James," "Further On (Up the Road)," "O Mary Don't You Weep," "Erie Canal," "If I Should Fall Behind," "My Oklahoma Home," "Highway Patrolman," "Mrs. McGrath," "How Can a Poor Man Stand Such Times and Live?," "Jacob's Ladder," "Long Time Comin'," "Open All Night," "Pay Me My Money Down," "Growin' Up," "When the Saints Go Marching In," "This Little Light of Mine," "American Land," "Blinded by the Light," "Love of the Common People," "We Shall Overcome."

Magic Tour Highlights [EP]. Digitally released on July 15, 2008, recorded by John Cooper, mixed by Bob Clearmountain, mastered by John Ludwig, recorded March and April on the 2008 America tour. Tracks: "Always a Friend," (with Alejandro Escovedo), "The Ghost of Tom Joad," (with Tom Morello), "Turn! Turn! Turn!" (with Roger McGuinn), "4th of July, Asbury Park (Sandy)."

∗ Notes ∗

INTRODUCTION

1. Timothy White, "A Man Out of Time Beats the Clock," *Musician* Issue 60 (October 1983), 52.

2. Jimmy Guterman, *Runaway American Dream* (New York: Da Capo Press, 2005), v.

3. Lester Bangs, "Hot Rod Rumble in the Promised Land," *Creem* (November 1975), home.theboots.net/theboots/articles/bangs_btr_review.html (accessed April 2006).

4. Bob Geldolf, quoted in Eric Alterman, *It Ain't No Sin to Be Glad You're Alive: The Promise of Bruce Springsteen* (Boston: Back Bay, 2001), 63.

5. Jack Kerouac, *The Portable Jack Kerouac,* edited by Ann Charters, *On the Road* (New York: Penguin, 1996), 144.

6. Jerry Gilbert, "Bruce Springsteen: It's Hard to be a Saint in the City," *ZigZag* (August 1974), home.theboots.net/theboots/articles/bangs_btr_review.html (accessed 2006).

7. *Bruce Springsteen: VH1 Storytellers* (DVD), Columbia Music Video, directed by Dave Diomedi (2005).

CHAPTER 1

1. Jim Cullen, *Born in the U.S.A: Bruce Springsteen and the American Tradition* (Middletown, CT: Wesleyan University Press, 2005), 9.

2. Eric Alterman, *It Ain't No Sin to Be Glad You're Alive: The Promise of Bruce Springsteen* (Boston: Back Bay, 2001), 14.

3. Kevin Coyne, quoted in June Skinner Sawyers, ed., *Racing in the Street: A Bruce Springsteen Reader* (New York: Penguin, 2004), 368–69.

4. Dave Marsh, *Bruce Springsteen: Two Hearts: The Definitive Biography, 1972–2003* (New York: Routledge, 2004), 25.

5. Christopher Sandford, *Springsteen: Point Blank* (New York: Da Capo Press, 1999), 20.

6. Ibid., 17.

7. Ibid., 20.

8. Quoted, in Marianne Meyer, *Bruce Springsteen* (New York: Ballantine Books), 17.

9. Marsh, 27.

10. Ibid., 28.

11. Alterman, 19–20; Sandford, 29.

12. Gary Graff, ed., *The Ties That Bind: Bruce Springsteen A to E to Z* (Canton, MI: Visible Ink Press, 2005), 311–12.

13. Ibid., 141–42.

14. *Brucebase,* www.brucebase.org (accessed April 2006).

15. Ibid.

16. Marsh, 40.

17. Ibid., 30.

18. Ibid., 32.

19. Charles Cross et al., *Backstreets: Springsteen; The Man and His Music* (New York: Harmony, 1989), 168.

20. Marsh, 33.

21. Marc Eliot, *Down Thunder Road: The Making of Bruce Springsteen* (New York: Simon & Schuster, 1992), 32.

22. Marsh, 40.

23. Daniel Wolff, *4th of July, Asbury Park: A History of the Promised Land* (New York: Bloomsbury, 2005), 3.

24. Ibid., 149.

25. Ibid., 160.

26. Ibid., 174–75.

27. Ibid., 176.

28. Ibid., 175.

29. Ibid.

30. Ibid., 194.

31. Ibid.

32. Marsh, 47.

33. Clare Marie Celano, "Musicians' Best Friends to Be Honored in Freehold," *News Transcript,* April 17, 2002 http://newstranscript.gmnews.com/News/2002/0417/Front_Page/003.html (accessed September 2006).

34. Bruce Springsteen, *Songs* (New York: Avon, 1998), 3.

35. Marsh, 41.

36. Sandford, 45.

37. Cross et al., 168.

38. Wolff, 177–78.

39. Cross et al., 168.

40. Ibid.,171.

41. Sylvie Simons, "Soul on Ice," *Mojo* (April 1995), www.rocksbackpages.com/article .html?ArticleID=5402 (accessed September 2006).

42. Graff, 84.

43. Eliot, 54–55.

44. Fred Goodman, *The Mansion on the Hill: Dylan, Young, Geffen, Springsteen, and the Head-On Collision of Rock and Commerce* (New York: Vintage, 1997), 256.

45. Ibid., 257.

46. Ibid.

47. Ibid., 263.

48. John Hammond, quoted in *MTV Rockumentary*, directed by Pete Demas, broadcast on MTV in November 1992.

49. Mike Appel, quoted in Dunstan Prial, *The Producer: John Hammond and the Soul of American Music* (New York: Farrar Straus & Giroux, 2006), 271.

50. Dunstan Prial, 274.

51. Goodman, 263.

52. *MTV Rockumentary.*

53. Dunstan Prial, 271.

54. Springsteen, 6.

55. Graff, 172.

56. Dunstan Prial, 275.

57. Springsteen, 5.

58. Marsh, 58.

59. *MTV Rockumentary.*

60. Goodman, 266.

61. Lester Bangs, quoted in Meyer, 44.

62. Peter Knobbler, quoted in Sawyers, 36.

63. Bob Crane, *A Place to Stand: A Guide to Bruce Springsteen's Sense of Place* (Silver Springs, MD: Palace Books, 2002), 2–3.

64. Marsh, 59.

65. Steve Simels, quoted in Alterman, 45.

CHAPTER 2

1. Bruce Springsteen, *Songs* (New York: Avon, 1998), 23.

2. June Skinner Sawyers, ed., *Racing in the Street: A Bruce Springsteen Reader* (New York: Penguin, 2004), 40–41.

3. Dave Marsh, *Bruce Springsteen: Two Hearts: The Definitive Biography, 1972–2003* (New York: Routledge, 2004), 77.

4. Jimmy Guterman, *Runaway American Dream: Listening to Bruce Springsteen* (New York: Da Capo Press, 2005), 62.

5. Ibid., 62.

6. Ibid., 61.

7. Springsteen, 25–26.

8. Fred Goodman, *The Mansion on the Hill: Dylan, Young, Geffen, Springsteen, and the Head-On Collision of Rock and Commerce* (New York: Vintage, 1997), 224.

9. Guterman, 65.

10. Ibid., 66.

11. Springsteen, 25.

12. Ibid.

13. Ariel Swartley, quoted in Sawyer, 81.

14. Springsteen, 25.

15. Ibid., 26.

16. Ibid.

17. Ibid., 72.

18. Ibid., 76.

19. Marsh, 91.

20. Ibid., 95.

21. Springsteen, 26.

22. Ibid.

23. Swartley, quoted in Sawyer, 81.

24. Guterman, 77.

25. Janet Maslin, quoted in Marc Eliot, *Down Thunder Road: The Making of Bruce Springsteen* (New York: Simon & Schuster, 1992), 101.

26. Ken Emerson, quoted in Eliot, 100.

27. Jon Landau, quoted in Marsh, 112–13, and Goodman, 225.

28. Marsh, 85.

29. Ibid., 98.

30. Guterman, 63.

31. Charles Cross et al., *Backstreets—Springsteen: The Man and His Music* (New York: Harmony, 1989), 174.

32. Gary Graff, ed., *The Ties That Bind: Bruce Springsteen A to E to Z* (Canton, MI: Visible Ink Press, 2005), 244.

33. *MTV Rockumentary,* directed by Pete Demas, broadcast on MTV in November 1992.

34. Landau, quoted in Goodman, 227.

CHAPTER 3

1. Dave Marsh, *Bruce Springsteen: Two Hearts: The Definitive Biography, 1972–2003* (New York: Routledge, 2004), 72.
2. Marc Eliot, *Down Thunder Road: The Making of Bruce Springsteen* (New York: Simon & Schuster, 1992), 116.
3. *Wings for Wheels* (DVD), directed by Thom Zimny, *Born to Run: 30th Anniversary Edition* (box set), Columbia Records, 2005.
4. Ashley Kahn, "Springsteen Looks Back on 'Born to Run,'" *The Wall Street Journal Online* (November 10, 2005), online.wsj.com (accessed November 2005).
5. Brian Hiatt, "Bruce Gets 'Born' Again," *RollingStone.com* (November 11, 2005), http://www.rollingstone.com/news/story/8789518/bruce_gets_born_again (accessed September 2006).
6. Bruce Springsteen, *Songs* (New York: Avon, 1998), 43.
7. Ibid., 44.
8. Hiatt.
9. Springsteen, 44.
10. "The 100 Best Singles of the Last 25 Years," *Rolling Stone* 534 (September 8, 1988), 74.
11. *Wings for Wheels.*
12. Hiatt.
13. Christopher Sandford, *Springsteen: Point Blank* (New York: Da Capo Press, 1999), 89.
14. Gary Graff, ed., *The Ties That Bind: Bruce Springsteen A to E to Z* (Canton, MI: Visible Ink Press, 2005), 208–9.
15. Nick Hasted, "The Runaway American Dreamer," *Uncut* (November 2005), 74.
16. Marsh, 121.
17. Marianne Meyer, *Bruce Springsteen* (New York: Ballantine Books), 33.
18. *Wings for Wheels.*
19. June Skinner Sawyers (ed.), *Racing in the Street: A Bruce Springsteen Reader* (New York: Penguin, 2004), 46.
20. Springsteen, 44
21. Marsh, 132.
22. Jon Bream, "Springsteen: The Man & His Fans," *Star Tribune* (May 10, 2005), http://www.startribune.com/stories/457/5393956.html (accessed May 2005).
23. *Wings for Wheels.*
24. Hasted, 76.
25. *Wings for Wheels.*
26. John Rockwell, *Rolling Stone,* 197 (October 9, 1975).
27. *Wings for Wheels.*
28. Fred Goodman, *The Mansion on the Hill: Dylan, Young, Geffen, Springsteen, and the Head-On Collision of Rock and Commerce* (New York: Vintage, 1997), 279.
29. *Wings for Wheels.*

30. Robert Hilburn, *Springsteen* (New York: Scribner, 1985), 67.

31. Graff, 47–48.

32. Hilburn, 67.

33. Quoted in Marsh, 134.

34. Robert Duncan, quoted in Eric Alterman, *It Ain't No Sin to Be Glad You're Alive: The Promise of Bruce Springsteen* (Boston: Back Bay, 2001), 63.

35. *Wings for Wheels.*

36. Kahn.

37. Marsh, 137.

38. Marsh, 151.

39. Hiatt.

40. David Fricke, "Live! Twenty Concerts That Changed Rock & Roll," *Rolling Stone* 501 (June 4, 1987), 89–90.

41. Ibid.

42. Ibid.

43. Ibid.

44. Springsteen, 47.

45. Lester Bangs, quoted in Sawyers, 76.

46. Marsh, 142.

47. Hiatt.

48. *Wings for Wheels.*

49. Hiatt.

50. Hilburn, 68.

51. Henry Edwards, *The New York Times* (October 5, 1975).

52. Maureen Orth, et al., quoted in Sawyers, 53–63.

53. Jay Cocks, quoted in Sawyers, 64–73.

54. Bangs, quoted in Sawyers, 75–77.

55. Alterman, 176.

56. Simon Frith, "Casing the Promised Land: Bruce Springsteen at Hammersmith Odeon," *Creem,* 1975, www.rocksbackpages.com/article.html?ArticleID=362 (accessed September 2006).

CHAPTER 4

1. Marc Eliot, *Down Thunder Road: The Making of Bruce Springsteen* (New York: Simon & Schuster, 1992), 199, 218.

2. Ibid., 218.

3. Ibid., 222.

4. Robert Hilburn, *Springsteen* (New York: Scribner, 1985), 92.

5. Gary Graff, ed., *The Ties That Bind: Bruce Springsteen A to E to Z* (Canton, MI: Visible Ink Press, 2005), 344.

6. Dave Marsh, *Bruce Springsteen: Two Hearts: The Definitive Biography, 1972–2003* (New York: Routledge, 2004), 163.

7. Bruce Springsteen, *Songs* (New York: Avon, 1998), 66.

8. June Skinner Sawyers, ed., *Racing in the Street: A Bruce Springsteen Reader* (New York: Penguin, 2004), 308.

9. Springsteen, 65–66.

10. Marsh, 98.

11. Lester Bangs and Greil Marcus, quoted in Eric Alterman, *It Ain't No Sin to Be Glad You're Alive: The Promise of Bruce Springsteen* (Boston: Back Bay, 2001), 108.

12. Graff, 106.

13. Dave Marsh, "Bruce Springsteen Raises Cain," *Rolling Stone* (August 24, 1978), http://www.rollingstone.com/news/story/5933433/bruce_springsteen_raises_cain (accessed September 2006).

14. Hilburn, 121.

15. Ibid., 117.

16. Charles Cross et al., *Backstreets: Springsteen: The Man and His Music* (New York: Harmony, 1989), 154.

17. Graff, 107.

18. Hilburn, 118.

19. Springsteen, 66.

20. Alterman, 100.

21. Hilburn, 121.

22. Daniel Wolff, *4th of July, Asbury Park: A History of the Promised Land* (New York: Bloomsbury, 2005), 216.

23. Ibid.

24. Jimmy Guterman, *Runaway American Dream: Listening to Bruce Springsteen* (New York: Da Capo Press, 2005) 108.

25. Hilburn, 121.

26. *Bruce Springsteen: VH1 Storytellers* (DVD), Columbia Music Video, 2005, directed by Dave Diomedi (2005).

27. Marsh, 194–95.

28. Ibid., 186–87.

29. Alterman, 102.

30. Graff, 107.

31. Quoted in Christopher Sandford, *Springsteen: Point Blank* (New York: Da Capo Press, 1999), 155.

32. "The Top 100: The Best Albums of the Last Twenty Years," *Rolling Stone* 507 (August 27, 1987), 102.

33. Sandford, 155.

34. Eliot, 230.

35. *MTV Rockumentary: Bruce Springsteen,* directed by Pete Demas (November 1992).

36. Graff, 105–6.

37. *MTV Rockumentary.*

38. *VH1 Legends: Bruce Springsteen,* broadcast on VH1 in 1999.

39. Marsh, "Bruce Springsteen Raises Cain."

40. Graff, 265.

41. Cross, quoted in Sawyers, 179.

42. Eliot, 247.

43. McLeese, quoted in Sawyers, 100.

44. Stephen Metcalf, "Faux Americana: Why I Still Love Bruce Springsteen," *Slate* (May 2, 2005), http://www.slate.com/id/2117845/ (accessed September 2006).

45. Fred Goodman, *The Mansion on the Hill: Dylan, Young, Geffen, Springsteen, and the Head-On Collision of Rock and Commerce* (New York: Vintage, 1997), 300.

46. Springsteen, 69.

47. Goodman, 300–301.

48. Marsh, "Bruce Springsteen Raises Cain."

CHAPTER 5

1. Kit Rachlis, quoted in Dave Marsh, *Bruce Springsteen: Two Hearts: The Definitive Biography, 1972–2003* (New York: Routledge, 2004), 218.

2. Marsh, 220.

3. Ibid., 229.

4. Ibid., 281.

5. Jim Cullen, *Born in the U.S.A: Bruce Springsteen and the American Tradition* (Middletown, CT: Wesleyan University Press, 2005), 15.

6. Marsh, 299.

7. Ibid., 301.

8. Marc Eliot, *Down Thunder Road: The Making of Bruce Springsteen* (New York: Simon & Schuster, 1992), 232.

9. Bruce Springsteen, *Songs* (New York: Avon, 1998), 66.

10. Marsh, 339.

11. Joel Bernstein, quoted in Christopher Sandford, *Springsteen: Point Blank* (New York: Da Capo Press, 1999), 168–69.

12. Sandford, 166.

13. Ibid., 168.

14. Gary Graff, ed., *The Ties That Bind: Bruce Springsteen A to E to Z* (Canton, MI: Visible Ink Press, 2005), 303.

15. Marsh, 221.

16. Bruce Springsteen, *Songs* (New York: Avon, 1998), 98.

17. Sandford, 160.

18. Robert Hilburn, *Springsteen* (New York: Scribner, 1985), 228–29.

19. Springsteen, 97–98.

20. Jimmy Guterman, *Runaway American Dream: Listening to Bruce Springsteen* (New York: Da Capo Press, 2005), 115–16.
21. Don McLeese, quoted in June Skinner Sawyers, ed., *Racing in the Street: A Bruce Springsteen Reader* (New York: Penguin, 2004), 101.
22. Springsteen, 97.
23. Sandford, 167.
24. Graff, 303.
25. Marsh, 230–31.
26. Ibid., 229.
27. Ibid., 234–35.
28. Quoted in Marianne Meyer, *Bruce Springsteen* (New York: Ballantine Books, 1984), 117–18.
29. Ira Robbins, "Bruce Springsteen: The River," *Trouser Press* (January 1981), www.rocks backpages.com/article.html?ArticleID=1176 (accessed September 2006).
30. Frances Lass, quoted in Sandford, 181.
31. Geoffrey Himes, *Born in the U.S.A.* (New York: Continuum, 2005), 48.
32. David Hinckley, "Night that City Stopped Cold," *New York Daily News Online* (December 6, 2005), www.nydailynews.com/news/crime_file/story/371401p-315985c .html (accessed September 2006).
33. Marsh, 276.

CHAPTER 6

1. Bruce Springsteen, *Songs* (New York: Avon, 1998), 135.
2. Ibid., 138–39.
3. Ibid., 138.
4. Ibid., 165.
5. Stephen Metcalf, "Faux Americana: Why I Still Love Bruce Springsteen," *Slate* (May 2, 2005), http://www.slate.com/id/2117845/ (accessed September 2006).
6. Geoffrey Himes, *Born in the U.S.A.* (New York: Continuum, 2005), 62–63.
7. June Skinner Sawyers, ed., *Racing in the Street: A Bruce Springsteen Reader* (New York: Penguin, 2004), 307.
8. Himes, 63.
9. Springsteen, 136.
10. Flannery O'Connor, *A Good Man Is Hard to Find, and Other Stories* (San Diego: Harvest, n.d.), 52.
11. Ibid., 191.
12. Ibid., 28–29.
13. Himes, 61.
14. Springsteen, 138.
15. Bryan K. Garman, *A Race of Singers: Whitman's Working-Class Hero from Guthrie to Springsteen* (Chapel Hill: University of North Carolina Press, 2000), 209.

16. Springsteen, 136.
17. Christopher Sandford, *Springsteen: Point Blank* (New York: Da Capo Press, 1999), 198.
18. Springsteen, 138.
19. Garman, 205.
20. Jim Cullen, *Born in the U.S.A: Bruce Springsteen and the American Tradition* (Middletown, CT: Wesleyan University Press, 2005), 21.
21. Ibid.
22. Ibid., 20.
23. Bob Crane, *A Place to Stand: A Guide to Bruce Springsteen's Sense of Place* (Silver Springs, MD: Palace Books, 2002), 2.
24. Sandford, 198.
25. Robert Coles, *Bruce Springsteen's America: The People Listening, a Poet Singing* (New York: Random House, 2004), 117–18.
26. Ibid., 123.
27. Dave Marsh, *Bruce Springsteen: Two Hearts: The Definitive Biography, 1972–2003* (New York: Routledge, 2004) 378.
28. Marsh, 379–80.

CHAPTER 7

1. Quoted in June Skinner Sawyers, ed., *Racing in the Street: A Bruce Springsteen Reader* (New York: Penguin, 2004), 307.
2. Elizabeth Kunreuther, Center for Documentary Studies, Duke University, www-cds.aas.duke.edu/exhibits/past/frank.html (accessed April 2006).
3. Peter Marshall, "Robert Frank—The Americans and After," *About.com,* http://photography.about.com/library/weekly/aa071000c.htm (accessed September 2006).
4. Geoffrey Himes, *Born in the U.S.A.* (New York: Continuum, 2005) 23.
5. Himes, 31.
6. Bruce Springsteen, *Songs* (New York: Avon, 1998), 165.
7. Dave Marsh, *Bruce Springsteen: Two Hearts: The Definitive Biography, 1972–2003* (New York: Routledge, 2004), 354.
8. Flynn McLean, "The Lost Masters: Introduction," *TheBoots.Net,* home.theboots.net/theboots/lostmasters/default.html (accessed April 2006).
9. Jimmy Guterman, *Runaway American Dream: Listening to Bruce Springsteen* (New York: Da Capo Press, 2005), 151–52.
10. Debby Bull, quoted in Parke Puterbaugh, ed., *Bruce Springsteen, the Rolling Stone File: The Ultimate Compendium of Interviews, Articles, Facts and Opinions from the Files of Rolling Stone* (New York: Hyperion, 1996), 144.
11. Himes, 49.
12. Marsh, 427.
13. Springsteen, 166.

14. Marsh, 400.
15. Fred Goodman, *The Mansion on the Hill: Dylan, Young, Geffen, Springsteen, and the Head-On Collision of Rock and Commerce* (New York: Vintage, 1997), 335.
16. Springsteen, 167.
17. Himes, 101–2.
18. Marsh, 409.
19. Ibid., 410.
20. Mason, 190.
21. Bull, quoted in Puterbaugh, 142.
22. Larry David Smith, *Bob Dylan, Bruce Springsteen, and American Song* (Westport, CT: Praeger, 2002), 138.
23. Marsh, 486–87.
24. Ibid, 479.
25. George Will, quoted in Sawyers, 107–9.
26. Bryan K. Garman, *A Race of Singers: Whitman's Working-Class Hero from Guthrie to Springsteen* (Chapel Hill: University of North Carolina Press), 216.
27. Ibid., 217.
28. Ibid., 219.
29. Ibid., 212.
30. Ibid., 213.
31. Springsteen, 167.

CHAPTER 8

1. Lester Bangs, *Mainlines, Blood Feasts, and Bad Taste: A Lester Bangs Reader*, ed. John Morthland (New York: Anchor, 2003), 353–54.
2. Dave Marsh, *Bruce Springsteen: Two Hearts: The Definitive Biography, 1972–2003* (New York: Routledge, 2004), 651.
3. James Henke, "Bruce Springsteen: The Rolling Stone Interview," *Rolling Stone* (August 6, 1992), http://www.rollingstone.com/news/story/5933539/human_touch.
4. Christopher Sandford, *Springsteen: Point Blank* (New York: Da Capo Press, 1999), 277.
5. Bruce Springsteen, *Songs* (New York: Avon, 1998), 189.
6. Springsteen, 190.
7. Bryan K. Garman, *A Race of Singers: Whitman's Working-Class Hero from Guthrie to Springsteen* (Chapel Hill: University of North Carolina Press, 2000), 231.
8. Springsteen, 191.
9. Jimmy Guterman, *Runaway American Dream: Listening to Bruce Springsteen* (New York: Da Capo Press, 2005), 171.
10. Springsteen, 191.
11. Guterman, 175.

CHAPTER 9

1. Robert Penn Warren, *All the King's Men* (San Diego: Harvest, 1996), 270.
2. Christopher Sandford, *Springsteen: Point Blank* (New York: Da Capo Press, 1999), 304.
3. Eric Alterman, *It Ain't No Sin to Be Glad You're Alive: The Promise of Bruce Springsteen* (Boston: Back Bay, 2001), 202.
4. Ibid.
5. James Henke, "Bruce Springsteen: The Rolling Stone Interview," *Rolling Stone* (August 6, 1992), http://www.rollingstone.com/news/story/5933539/human_touch.
6. Jimmy Guterman, *Runaway American Dream: Listening to Bruce Springsteen* (New York: Da Capo Press, 2005), 185.
7. Parke Puterbaugh, ed., *Bruce Springsteen, the Rolling Stone File: The Ultimate Compendium of Interviews, Articles, Facts and Opinions from the Files of Rolling Stone* (New York: Hyperion, 1996), 304.
8. Bruce Springsteen, *Songs* (New York: Avon, 1998), 216.
9. Puterbaugh, 327–28.
10. Ibid.
11. Ibid.
12. Springsteen, 218.
13. Guterman, 182.
14. Alterman, 219.
15. Springsteen, 219.

CHAPTER 10

1. Bruce Springsteen, *Songs* (New York: Avon, 1998), 274.
2. Ibid., 274.
3. Christopher Sandford, *Springsteen: Point Blank* (New York: Da Capo Press, 1999), 369.
4. Springsteen, 276.
5. Jimmy Guterman, *Runaway American Dream: Listening to Bruce Springsteen* (New York: Da Capo Press, 2005), 207.
6. Springsteen, 276.
7. Tom Moon, quoted in Larry David Smith, *Bob Dylan, Bruce Springsteen, and American Song* (Westport, CT: Praeger, 2002), 189.
8. Springsteen, 205–6.
9. Quoted in Smith, 189.
10. Springsteen, 278.

CHAPTER 11

1. Gary Graff, ed., *The Ties That Bind: Bruce Springsteen A to E to Z* (Canton, MI: Visible Ink Press, 2005), 6.
2. Ibid., 298.
3. Ibid., 299.
4. Mark Godfrey, "Bruce Springsteen: A Review of His Album 'The Rising,'" *cluas.com* (2002), http://www.cluas.com/Music/albums/bruce-springsteen.htm (accessed April 2006).
5. Graff, 368–69.
6. Quoted in Graff, 298.
7. A. O. Scott, quoted in June Skinner Sawyers, ed., *Racing in the Street: A Bruce Springsteen Reader* (New York: Penguin, 2004), 362.
8. Tom Laskin, "*The Rising*" (review). *Isthmus: The Daily Page*, www.thedailypage.com/going-out/music/cdreviews/managedit.php?intcdrevid = 323 (accessed April 2006).
9. *Bruce Springsteen: VH1 Storytellers* (DVD), Columbia Music Video, directed by Dave Diomedi (2005).
10. *Backstreets.com*, www.backstreets.com/setlists2003R.html (accessed September 2006).

CHAPTER 12

1. Renée Montagne, "Springsteen Goes Soul Searching with 'Devils,'" *Morning Edition*, April 26, 2005, National Public Radio, www.npr.org/templates/story/story.php?storyId=4616189 (accessed September 2006).
2. Christopher Phillips, "The Devil's in the Details," *Backstreets* 83/84 (Winter 2005/2006), 51.
3. Jon Pareles, "Bruce Almighty," *The New York Times*, April 24, 2005.
4. Christopher Phillips, "The Devil's in the Details," *Backstreets* 83/84 (Winter 2005/2006), 54.
5. Ibid.; Pareles.
6. Jesse Young with Chris Flynn and Joe Kunecki, "The Devil's Workshop," *Backstreets* 83/84 (Winter 2005/2006), 94.
7. Nick Hornby, "A Fan's Eye View," *The Observer* (July 17, 2005), http://observer.guardian.co.uk/omm/story/0,13887,1527571,00.html (accessed September 2006).
8. Will Hermes, "Born to Strum," *The New York Times* (April 16, 2006), www.dlackey.org/weblog/docs/Born%20to%20Strum%20-%20New%20York%20Times.html (accessed September 2006); Neil Strauss, "Springsteen Hears Voices," *Rolling Stone* (April 21, 2006), http://www.rollingstone.com/news/story/9961901/springsteen_hears_voices (accessed September 2006).

9. Sean Sennett, "Now Hear This, Says the Boss," *The Courier Mail* (July 1, 2006), the couriermail.news.com.au.

10. David Hinckley, "The Next Chapter," *New York Daily News* (April 25, 2006), www .nydailynews.com/front/story/411023p-347616c.html (accessed September 2006).

11. Dave Marsh with Matt Orel, liner notes to *We Shall Overcome: The Seeger Sessions* (CD), Columbia, 2006.

12. Sennett.

13. Hermes, "Born to Strum."

14. "Bruce Springsteen Escapes from the Box," Associated Press (April 25, 2006), http://www.cnn.com.

15. Hinckley, "The Next Chapter."

16. Edna Gundersen, " 'Seeger Sessions' Sends a Message," *USA Today* (June 6, 2006), www.usatoday.com.

AFTERWORD

1. Eric Alterman, *It Ain't No Sin to Be Glad You're Alive: The Promise of Bruce Springsteen* (Boston: Back Bay, 2001), 78.

2. Reviews quoted in Gary Graff, *The Ties That Bind: Springsteen A to E to Z* (Canton, MI: Visible Ink Press, 2005), 179–80.

3. Simon Frith, "Casing the Promised Land: Bruce Springsteen at Hammersmith Odeon," *Creem*, 1975, www.rocksbackpages.com/article.html?ArticleID=362 (accessed September 2006).

UPDATE: THAT OLD-TIME MAGIC

1. Harry Browne, "Sinister Magic," *Counterpunch* (September 25, 2007).

2. Thom Jurek, *Live in Dublin* (review), *AllMusic*.

3. www.SpringsteenLyrics.com

4. Joe Levy, "Bruce Springsteen: The Rolling Stone Interview," *Rolling Stone* (November 15, 2007), 54.

5. Andy Greene, "More on New Bruce Springsteen Album: Producer Brendan O'Brien Reveals All," *Rolling Stone*, rollingstone.com, August 17, 2007.

6. Joe Levy, "Bruce Springsteen: The Rolling Stone Interview," Rolling Stone (November 15, 2007).

7. Dave Marsh, *Two Hearts*, 251.

8. Dave Fricke, *Magic* (review), *Rolling Stone* (October 18, 2007).

9. Hugo Lindgren, "Bruce Almighty," *New York* (September 30, 2007).

10. Amy Linden, "The Treading," *The Village Voice* (September 25, 2007).

11. Fricke.

12. *Sputnik Music*, www.sputnikmusic.com.

13. Browne.
14. Levy.
15. Browne.
16. "Bruce Springsteen—Making of *Magic*," Amazon.com
17. Robert Gillis, "Review: Bruce Springsteen, MAGIC,"*Boston City Paper*, www.robertxgillis .com.
18. A. O. Scott, "In Love with Pop, Uneasy with the World," *The New York Times*, nytimes .co (September 30, 2007).
19. Scott.
20. Gillis.
21. Linden.
22. "Bruce Springsteen—Making of *Magic*," Amazon.com
23. Greene.
24. "Bruce Springsteen—Making of *Magic*," Amazon.com.
25. Greene.
26. Joyce Millman, "A Map of the Future: *Darkness on the Edge of Town* at 30," Asbury Park Public Library: The Bruce Springsteen Special Collection (Web site).
27. Bruce Springsteen, brucespringsteen.net.
28. "Boardwalk Fortune Teller Madam Marie Dies," *Asbury Park Press*, www.app.com/ apps/pbcs.dll/article?AID=/20080701/NEWS/80701031
29. brucespringsteen.net.
30. Millman.
31. Brian Williams, "Springsteen and Obama," *The Daily Nightly*.

✳ Bibliography ✳

BOOKS

Alterman, Eric. *It Ain't No Sin to Be Glad You're Alive: The Promise of Bruce Springsteen.* Boston: Back Bay, 2001.

Bangs, Lester. *Mainlines, Blood Feasts, and Bad Taste: A Lester Bangs Reader.* Edited by John Morthland. New York: Anchor 2003.

Coles, Robert. *Bruce Springsteen's America: The People Listening, A Poet Singing.* New York: Random House, 2004.

Crane, Bob. *A Place to Stand: A Guide to Bruce Springsteen's Sense of Place.* Silver Springs, MD: Palace Books, 2002.

Cross, Charles, et al. *Backstreets: Springsteen: The Man and His Music.* New York: Harmony, 1989.

Cullen, Jim. *Born in the U.S.A.: Bruce Springsteen and the American Tradition.* Middletown, CT: Wesleyan University Press, 2005.

Eliot, Marc. *Down Thunder Road: The Making of Bruce Springsteen.* New York: Simon & Schuster, 1992.

Garman, Bryan K. *A Race of Singers: Whitman's Working-Class Hero from Guthrie to Springsteen.* Chapel Hill: University of North Carolina Press, 2000.

Goodman, Fred. *The Mansion on the Hill: Dylan, Young, Geffen, Springsteen, and the Head-On Collision of Rock and Commerce.* New York: Vintage Books, 1997.

Graff, Gary, ed. *The Ties That Bind: Bruce Springsteen A to E to Z.* Canton, MI: Visible Ink Press, 2005.

Guterman, Jimmy. *Runaway American Dream: Listening to Bruce Springsteen*. New York: Da Capo Press, 2005.

Hilburn, Robert. *Springsteen*. New York: Scribner, 1985.

Himes, Geoffrey. *Born in the U.S.A.* (33 1/3 series). New York: Continuum, 2005.

Jones, Tennessee. *Deliver Me from Nowhere*. Brooklyn: Soft Skull, 2005.

Kaye, Jessica, and Richard J. Brewer, eds. *Meeting Across the River: Stories Inspired by the Haunting Bruce Springsteen Song*. New York: Bloomsbury, 2005.

Kovic, Ron. *Born on the Fourth of July*. New York: Akashic, 2005.

Marcus, Greil. *Mystery Train: Images of American in Rock 'n' Roll Music*. New York: E. P. Dutton, 1975.

Marsh, Dave. *Bruce Springsteen: Two Hearts: The Definitive Biography, 1972–2003*. New York: Routledge, 2004.

Meyer, Marianne. *Bruce Springsteen*. New York: Ballantine Books, 1984.

Prial, Dunstan. *The Producer: John Hammond and the Soul of American Music*. New York: Farrar Straus & Giroux, 2006.

Puterbaugh, Parke, ed. *Bruce Springsteen, the Rolling Stone File: The Ultimate Compendium of Interviews, Articles, Facts and Opinions from the Files of Rolling Stone*. New York: Hyperion, 1996.

Sandford, Christopher. *Springsteen: Point Blank*. New York: Da Capo Press, 1999.

Sawyers, June Skinner, ed. *Racing in the Street: A Bruce Springsteen Reader*. New York: Penguin, 2004.

Smith, Larry David. *Bob Dylan, Bruce Springsteen, and American Song*. Westport, CT: Praeger, 2002.

Springsteen, Bruce. *Songs*. New York: Avon, 1998.

Wolff, Daniel. *4th of July, Asbury Park: A History of the Promised Land*. New York: Bloomsbury, 2005.

ARTICLES

Associated Press. "Bruce Springsteen Escapes from the Box." *CNN.com*. April 25, 2006.

Bangs, Lester. "Hot Rod Rumble in the Promised Land." *CREEM*. November 1975.

Bream, Jon. "Springsteen: The Man & His Fans." *Star Tribune Online*. May 10, 2005. www.startribune.com/stories/457/5393956.html. Accessed May 2005.

Browne, Harry. "Sinister Magic." *Counterpunch*. September 25, 2007. http://www.counterpunch.org/browne09252007.html. Accessed June 1, 2008.

"Bruce Springsteen—Making of *Magic*." Amazon.com. http://www.amazon.com/gp/mpd/permalink/m32YDKOJ1YALPE:m2H211MVWUONMK. Accessed June 1, 2008.

Celano, Clare Marie. "Musicians' Best Friends to Be Honored in Freehold." *News Transcript*. April 17, 2002. newstranscript.gmnews.com/News/2002/0417/Front_Page/003.html. Accessed September 2006.

Fricke, David. "Live! Twenty Concerts that Changed Rock & Roll." *Rolling Stone*, 501. June 4, 1987.

Fricke, David. *Magic* (review). *Rolling Stone*. October 18, 2007. http://www.rollingstone .com/reviews/album/16587992/review/16682049/magic. Accessed June 1, 2008.

Frith, Simon. "Casing the Promised Land: Bruce Springsteen at Hammersmith Odeon." *Creem*. 1975. www.rocksbackpages.com/article.html?ArticleID=362. Accessed September 2006.

Gilbert, Jerry. "Bruce Springsteen." *Sounds*. March 16, 1974. www.rocksbackpages.com/ article.html?ArticleID=3152. Accessed 2006.

Gilbert, Jerry. "Bruce Springsteen: It's Hard to be a Saint in the City," *ZigZag*. August 1974. www.rocksbackpages.com/article.html?ArticleID=411. Accessed September 2006.

Gillis, Robert. "Review: Bruce Springsteen, MAGIC." *Boston City Paper*. http://www .robertxgillis.com/2007/11/album-review-bruce-springsteen-magic.html. Accessed June 1, 2008.

Godfrey, Mark. "Bruce Springsteen: A Review of His Album 'The Rising.'" *cluas.com*. 2002. www.cluas.com/Music/albums/bruce-springsteen.htm. Accessed September 2006.

Goldberg, Michael. "Bruce Springsteen's Non-Event: He may be on the cover of *Time* again, but *The Rising* sure ain't *Born to Run*." *Neumu*. August 2002. www.rocksback pages.com/article.html?ArticleID=3047. Accessed September 2006.

Greene, Andy. "More on New Bruce Springsteen Album: Producer Brendan O'Brien Reveals All." *Rolling Stone*. August 17, 2007. http://www.rollingstone.com/rockdaily/ index.php/2007/08/17/more-on-new-bruce-springsteen-album-producer-bren-dan-obrien-reveals-all/. Accessed June 1, 2008.

Hasted, Nick. "The Runaway American Dreamer." *Uncut*. November 2005.

Henke, James. "Bruce Springsteen: The Rolling Stone Interview." *Rolling Stone*. August 6, 1992. www.rollingstone.com/news/story/5933539/human_touch. Accessed September 2006.

Hermes, Will. "Born to Strum." *The New York Times*. April 16, 2006. www.dlackey.org/ weblog/docs/Born%20to%20Strum%20-%20New%20York%20Times.html. Accessed September 2006.

Hiatt, Brian. "Bruce Gets 'Born' Again." *Rolling Stone.com*. November 11, 2005. www .rollingstone.com/news/story/8789518/bruce_gets_born_again. Accessed September 2006.

Hinckley, David. "Night that City Stopped Cold." *New York Daily News* (nydaily news.com). December 6, 2005. www.nydailynews.com/news/crime_file/story/ 371401p-315985c.html. Accessed September 2006.

———. "The Next Chapter." *New York Daily News*. April 25, 2006. www.nydailynews .com/front/story/411023p-347616c.html. Accessed September 2006.

Hornby, Nick. "A Fan's Eye View." *The Observer*. July 17, 2005. observer.guardian.co.uk/ omm/story/0,13887,1527571,00.html. Accessed September 2006.

Jurek, Thom. *Live in Dublin* (review). *AllMusic*. http://www.allmusic.com/cg/amg.dll?p= amg&sql=10:3vftxz85ldhe⬜T1. Accessed June 1, 2008.

Kahn, Ashley. "Springsteen Looks Back on 'Born to Run.'" *The Wall Street Journal*. November 10, 2005. online.wsj.com. Accessed November 2005.

Laskin, Tom. "*The Rising*" (review). *Isthmus: The Daily Page*. 2002. www.thedailypage.com/ going-out/music/cdreviews/managedit.php?intcdrevid=323. Accessed April 2006.

Levy, Joe. "Bruce Springsteen: The Rolling Stone Interview." *Rolling Stone*. November 15, 2007. http://www.rollingstone.com/artists/brucespringsteen/articles/story/ 16941890/bruce_springsteen_the_rolling_stone_interview. Accessed June 1, 2008.

Linden, Amy. "The Treading." *The Village Voice*. September 25, 2007. http://www .villagevoice.com/music/0740,linden,77950,22.html. Accessed June 1, 2008.

Lindgren, Hugo. "Bruce Almighty." *New York*. September 30, 2007. http://nymag.com/ arts/popmusic/reviews/38317/. Accessed June 1, 2008.

Magic (review). Sputnik Music. www.sputnikmusic.com/review_13711. Accessed June 1, 2008.

Marsh, Dave. "Springsteen Raises Cain." *Rolling Stone*. August 24, 1978. www.rolling stone.com/news/story/5933433/bruce_springsteen_raises_cain. Accessed September 2006.

McLean, Flynn. "The Lost Masters: Introduction." *TheBoots.Net*. home.theboots.net/ theboots/lostmasters/default.html. Accessed April 2006.

Millman, Joyce. "A Map of the Future: 'Darkness on the Edge of Town' at 30." Asbury Park Public Library: The Bruce Springsteen Special Collection (Web site). http:// www.asburyparklibrary.org/BSSC/BSSC_Darkness30.htm. Accessed June 1, 2008.

Metcalf, Stephen. "Faux Americana: Why I Still Love Bruce Springsteen." *Slate*. May 2, 2005. www.slate.com/id/2117845/. Accessed September 2006.

Montagne, Renée. "Springsteen Goes Soul Searching with 'Devils.'" *Morning Edition*. National Public Radio. April 26, 2005. www.npr.org/templates/story/story.php ?storyId=4616189. Accessed September 2006.

Pareles, Jon. "Bruce Almighty." *The New York Times*. April 24, 2005. www.nytimes.com/ 2005/04/24/arts/music/24pare.html?ex=1271995200&en=6e6d04c36feb776e &ei=5088&partner=rssnyt&emc=rss. Accessed September 2006.

Phillips, Christopher. "The Devil's in the Details." *Backstreets*. 83/84 (Winter 2005/ 2006).

Robbins, Ira. Review of *The River*. "Bruce Springsteen: *The River*." *Trouser Press*. January 1981. www.rocksbackpages.com/article.html?ArticleID=1176. Accessed September 2006.

Rockwell, John. *Rolling Stone*. 197, October 9, 1975.

Scoppa, Bud. "Bruce Springsteen: At the Roxy, Los Angeles." *Phonograph Record*. November 1975. www.rocksbackpages.com/article.html?ArticleID=3907. Accessed September 2006.

Scott, A. O. "In Love with Pop, Uneasy with the World." *The New York Times*. September

30, 2007. http://www.nytimes.com/2007/09/30/arts/music/30scot.html?_r=1& oref=slogin. Accessed June 1, 2008.

Simons, Sylvie. "Soul on Ice." *Mojo*. April 1995. www.rocksbackpages.com/article.html ?ArticleID=5402. Accessed September 2006.

Springsteen, Bruce, as told to Cal Fussman. "It Happened in New Jersey." *Esquire*. 144(2), August 1, 2005.

Strauss, Neil. "Springsteen Hears Voices." *Rolling Stone*. April 21, 2006. www.rollingstone .com/news/story/9961901/springsteen_hears_voices, April 21, 2006. Accessed September 2006.

Tarlach, Gemma. "For Springsteen, Somber 'Rising.'" *Milwaukee Journal Sentinel*. July 29, 2002. www.jsonline.com/story/index.aspx?id=62523. Accessed September 2006.

"The Top 100: The Best Albums of the Last Twenty Years." *Rolling Stone,* 507. August 27, 1987.

"The 100 Best Singles of the Last 25 Years." *Rolling Stone,* 534, September 8, 1988.

Turner, Steve. "Was Bob Dylan the Previous Bruce Springsteen?" *New Musical Express*. October 6, 1973.

Williams, Brian. "Springsteen and Obama." *The Daily Nightly*. http://dailynightly.msnbc .msn.com/archive/2008/05/08/998238.aspx. Accessed June 1, 2008.

Young, Jesse, with Chris Flynn and Joe Kunecki. "The Devil's Workshop." *Backstreets,* 83/84 (Winter 2005/2006).

DOCUMENTARIES

Demas, Pete, dir. *MTV Rockumentary: Bruce Springsteen*. MTV broadcast. November 1992.

VH1 Legends: Bruce Springsteen. VH1 broadcast. July 1999.

Zimny, Thom, dir. *Wings for Wheels: The Making of Born to Run* (DVD). *Born to Run: 30th Anniversary Edition* (box set). Columbia Records. 2005.

WEB SITES

Backstreets.com—The Boss Website, www.backstreets.com.

TheBoots.Net—The Bruce Springsteen Web Connection, home.theboots.net/the boots/.

Bruce Springsteen CD "Brucelegs" Discography, www.mv.com/ipusers/richbreton/ brucelegs.htm.

Brucebase, www.brucebase.org.

Greasy Lake—The Ultimate Bruce Springsteen Tribute Page, *www.greasylake.org*.

Bruce Springsteen Database—The Killing Floor, *www.brucespringsteen.it*.

∗ Index ∗